Missouri & Me
A Poker Odyssey

By Glen Garrod

Published by Glen Garrod
Printed in the United States of America
1st printing, 2024

This is a work of non-fiction. Some names have been changed to protect
the character's identity, while others have not. Some locations have
been changed. Some stories and dialogue have been embellished at
the author's discretion. The stories told on these pages are authentic as
experienced and best recalled by the author, related to him by others or
garnered by research.

Category (Adult)
Genre (Creative Non-Fiction/Memoir/Short Stories)

ISBN: 979-8-218-46722-7
Library of Congress Control Number: 2024914200

Website: missouriandme.com

Praise for
Missouri & Me, A Poker Odyssey

Buckle up!

You are about to step into a lost era of professional poker. Where personal freedom was the common denominator, the driving force that drove these long ago gunslingers of poker.

Glen Garrod has captured "old school" poker to perfection and the colorful characters that inhabited that insular world. Those were players who risked it all at the poker tables on a regular basis and lived life to the fullest while doing so.

This fun-filled, rollicking, revealing, real life collection of stories, will give readers the feeling of being at the table and its environs with the players.

The stories center around Glen's long friendship with Missouri Dave, the best no-limit poker player I ever played with.

And I've played with many of the best there is.

I am proud to call both Missouri Dave and Glen Garrod my friends, along with many of the other poker players in this entertaining look back in time.

You're going to love it...

Dave Olson, longtime professional poker player

I traveled the roads for 57 years playing Hold'em poker. In my travels I encountered the duo of Hippie Glen and Missouri Dave. If you were to win Glen's chips you better bring your lunch for he was a tough nut to crack. My first encounter with Dave was in Lake Tahoe in the early 70's. We faced off 'heads- up' and before I could get my luggage to the room he had my bankroll in his pocket.

Not only them being good poker players they were fine individuals of the utmost character and integrity. I am proud to call both of them friends.

Carl McKelvey, professional poker player and one of the last of the Texas road gamblers

Dedicated
to two dear friends
and the most amazing women
Professor Eve Imagine
mentor, editor and the inspiration
that kept me going
and
Kathy Dotson
master graphic artist
whose talent and perseverance
brought fruition

grateful til dead

Table of Contents

Introduction

In the world of poker, being broke comes in different forms. You can get broke in a poker game by losing the money you have invested in the game yet there's still money in your pocket, at home or in the bank or in a sock in your drawer or buried in a coffee can in the back yard. Then there's broke-broke when your pockets are empty, the bank, the socks and the coffee cans are empty as well, but the bills are paid and you still have enough money to eat, drink and be merry. Finally, there is flat broke.

Foreword

Poker Stories

It was just before the millennium, and poker by way of the television, had just become a phenomenon. It had begun to permeate TV screens around the world; it had entered people's homes. And that day for all who were watching, a player had just caught a miracle card to 'draw out' on his opponent and knock him out of a major tournament. The winner's personal cheering section rose in unison, hooting and hollering, high fives for their man who had just made a bad play, put his money in jeopardy as a twenty-one to one underdog, gotten extremely lucky, won the huge pot and eliminated his unlucky opponent. Rochambeau and scissors had just broken rock. It was all a very strange spectacle, a loud twisted celebration of luck over science in the game of poker. But it wasn't always that way.

Poker used to be different. For better or worse the game has changed. Poker, a sport for some, a way and means of life for others, was almost never played with wild fanfare. There were no celebrations when the loser lost his money; there was an occasional expletive, a few good-byes, a tip of the cap, an exit in quiet dignity.

Poker games were populated with colorful characters with names like Austen Squatty, Bones Berland, The Owl, The Wizard, Tree Top Jack Straus, Monterey Jack (who when he beat you, used to tell you your hand was a piece of cheese), Snowplow Larry, Skyhawk, 'Pots and Pans' and The Junkyard Dog. Some had a distinctive presence with signature attire: Top Hat Ken in his tuxedo and top hat, Amarillo Slim with his rattlesnake hatband, the Oregon Beaver with his coonskin cap, Barbed Wire from Montana in his 'High-top native American cowboy hat' that sat on top of a huge mound of kinky hair. You would play with Cajuns from Louisiana whose accents were so thick you'd require an interpreter, the very best players from New York City, Texans who'd spit their chew into coke bottles, the hustlers from everywhere, the cowboys, the grinders, the romantics, the rounders, the road gamblers and all the great legends and folk heroes of the game. These one-of-a-kind, rugged individuals have been replaced by guys that look like clean-cut college students, who dress like accountants, and played Texas Hold'em with the precision of scientists who have mastered the game. To me, it seemed the very essence of the world of poker had changed.

For forty-five years I had played with the old guard of poker players. I was immersed in a game where one's fortune could change with the turn of a card.

I was also immersed in a culture that valued honor and integrity; however, charlatans and thieves lurked in the shadows.

These are my stories.

CHAPTER 1

THE BEGINNINGS

For Old Time's Sake

The logical explanation was that he was seeing double, but logic had grabbed its hat and left the cabin. Dean Drake's first card, face up, in a variation of seven card stud, appeared to be the King of Clubs. He began manically blinking as he tried to refocus, for his second face up card also appeared to be the identical King of Clubs. He stared at the kings and they smiled and stared back. The game, already barely moving along, came to a complete halt. We all looked at Dean; to me his face was contorting. His throbbing lips moved like those of a feeding fish as he tried to form the words to articulate his confusion. However, speech had abandoned him and all he could do was point, mumble and throb.

North Lake Tahoe in 1970. What was supposed to be a poker game was crawling along at a snail's pace in my cabin at the historic Granlibakken ski resort.

In the bigger picture, I had just begun to get my feet wet playing six-card stud at The North Shore Club in Crystal Bay, Nevada. The game was a low stakes-limit poker game in a small two-table poker room in what was predominantly a local's casino. Besides the usual assortment of casino games, the casino had a jumpin' good bar with live music and occasionally star headliners like Jerry Jeff Walker and Hoyt Axton. Arlo Guthrie once graced the stage in the showroom behind the bar. The North Shore Club would often morph into a raging party. I loved the atmosphere of that casino. I liked the poker dealers, I liked the people that ran the poker-room and I liked that I was learning a new game. That particular night, however, I would be hosting my own poker game in my very private mountain residence.

The seeds for my poker game were planted at the University of California at Davis when I stumbled upon a garage sale and a beautiful green felt poker table grabbed my attention. For a mere $100, that table became mine. In a heartbeat I had a poker game in the fraternity house several nights a week. Two months later I was financially able to quit my University research job. Upon graduation, three fraternity brothers and I lit out for a summer in South Lake Tahoe. At the end of that summer the brothers left but I remained to manage the Christiana Inn, a small year-round mountain lodge with a busy bar and restaurant. Fast forward two years and I found myself the general manager of The Four Seasons at Lake Tahoe, a large resort hotel, conference center and ski area on Tahoe's North Shore. Occasionally I would invite my old poker buddies from UC Davis to stay as my guests at the resort and we'd have a poker game in my cabin. However, there was a problem. The games had gotten too big as some of the guys were losing way too much money and I was the beneficiary. I felt a moral obligation to stop hosting those games.

I had informed my college poker pals how I felt about our poker games and that I was not going to be having them anymore. Because these guys loved venturing to Tahoe and taking advantage of the complimentary amenities I provided: drinks in our bar, gourmet meals in the restaurant and very posh rooms in the lodge, the suggestion was made that we have one more game with much smaller stakes just for old time's sake. I agreed to host one last game.

When I was at school in Davis I had a fraternity brother who spent a summer in Arizona living with indigenous people in Navajo Nation. He became a member of The Native American Church and eagerly participated in sacred peyote ceremonies. Peyote, derived from the peyote cactus with flowering buttons that are highly hallucinogenic, is used in spiritual ceremony in Navajo Nation, but when the brother brought a U-Haul trailer full of peyote buttons back to Davis they tended to be used more recreationally. Several trips to Arizona were made while I was in college and a sweat lodge with peyote tea became a thing. It was the sixties and in our circle, there was often some peyote around.

The day of the poker game I met a couple of very friendly ladies at our lodge who were up for a weekend of skiing. I told them of the poker game at my cabin and invited them to drop by. They seemed to like the idea.

The night of the poker game, seven of us gathered at my cabin. Now, here's the wildcard: one of the guys had brought up a load of powdered peyote that he put into gelatin capsules. All of us ingested some. Plenty some!

We cracked open some beers, talked some story, had a few chuckles and decided to start the game.

It was when we started buying chips that I noticed people were becoming very quiet and quite deliberate in their movements. The simple process of exchanging money for poker chips turned extremely slow and arduous. Without a word spoken, it was clear the peyote was kicking in. Eventually, we cut for the deal and Dennis Stark dealt the first hand. Each hand tended to have long pauses between each player's turn to act. Everyone was completely lost in his own head. Small comments that probably weren't funny evoked hysterical laughter.

Richie Bee, in his pillbox hat, wore a tie-dyed t-shirt with a red tie-dyed heart surrounded by swirling greens, yellows and blues. Visually, Rich had begun to look like the Jack of Hearts.

When Randy Weber, whose verbal acuity had massively diminished, asked Bob Tetz, "Are you still writing music?" It sounded to me like he was asking, "Is Will a writhing moose?" Although I had absolutely no idea who Will was, it seemed a perfectly legitimate question; yet, the question brought a flood of tears caused by the wave of contagious belly laughter that passed amongst all the players. All the players, that is, except the Jack of Hearts whose blissful grin suggested he was lost in and enjoying his own private thoughts.

It was Bob's turn to deal, and he shuffled the cards and shuffled again and again and again. People were staring, completely transfixed on his hands. Finally, in an exceedingly slow, deep voice, Joe West said, "Bob, you should deal now." When cards were dealt, they appeared to me like huge spinning red dragonflies floating from dealer to player. No one else seemed to notice! Each of us was insanely high as we attempted to play poker in the carnival house of magic and wavy mirrors. A record played on the stereo, loud enough so the dark knots on the vibrant, shiny knotty pine walls of my cabin started to expand and contract, shimmering to the sounds of the Beatles and *Sgt. Peppers Lonely Hearts Club Band*. The walls pulsed and poker players' heads began to bob to the beat of the music. *With A Little Help From My Friends* started to play. Our bodies began to sway.

The game slowed another notch. Colors were acute. The ridges of the plastic chips felt curious.

As the game plodded along it was apparent that some unusually big poker hands were being made. There were multiple full houses and even a couple of four-of-a-kinds. We were probably 6 or 7 hands into the game when Dean Drake had his confusing mental collapse when showing his two, face up, identical Kings of Clubs. After lots of staring and head scratching, the music was turned off and we rather miraculously came to the realization that we had been playing poker with a Pinochle deck. A Pinochle deck has only 48 cards, there are no cards lower than a nine and two each of nines through aces of all four suits; in other words, the deck had eight aces and eight Kings, and so on down to nines. Fact: a Pinochle deck is not conducive to playing poker.

We stopped the game, managed to give everyone back the money they started with and began again with a regular 52-card deck of cards.

There was a knock on the door. I got up, opened the door and standing there were the two ladies I had invited over. I barely managed to eke out something semi-coherent like "welcome" or "come in" and I sat back down. They took seats behind two players. No one said a word as the poker game proceeded to inch slowly along. Stoned players and stone silence. Finally, one of the new guests said, "Well, how about some introductions?"

After a short pause, and, almost like it had been rehearsed, seven poker players all simultaneously stood up, introduced themselves to each other; "Howdy, I'm Dennis Stark,"

"Hello, pleased to meet you."

Players shook hands all around, sat back down in unison and fell into a comatose silence. The front door closed, two chairs sat empty; the ladies had evaporated into the night.

I have looked back at that night for years and I consider it to have been both one of the most hilarious things I've ever been part of as well as one of the rudest. If only I could apologize.

The Guamanians

I grew up in southern California. When I was about ten years old and it was my mom and dad's turn to host the monthly poker party, I was allowed to stay up late and watch as my parents and their friends played poker. I sat behind one of my parents totally glued to the action. I was fascinated by a card game where people bet actual money on their hands. I was amazed at the large assortment of card games they played – games like Seven Card Stud High-Low Split, Spit in the Ocean, Pass the Trash, Baseball, No Peaky, Seven Stud Low Hole Card Wild, and High-Low Roll'em. I watched and I learned.

Poker became our family card game. As a thirteen-year-old I would occasionally play for small change next door at my oldest sister's house with her and her friends. My mother was a cocktail waitress and she used to keep the change she brought home from her tips in a big change jar. She brought that jar to my sister's poker games. The jar played. In 1961 I entered high school and I considered myself a pretty fair poker player.

I met Manual Mesa in my gym class. Manual was born in Guam but came to America as a child. We became friends mostly through playing football and basketball. As friends, we ended up doing a lot of teenage stuff together. I got to know his family; I liked them and they liked me. One day, out of the blue, Manual asked me if I ever played poker and, when I said yes, a whole new world was about to open up to me.

I was sixteen at the time. I had been working since I was thirteen; first, as a paperboy and then as cheap labor in a small family-run plastics shop. Manual and I both managed to get jobs at McDonald's; I left the plastic shop. The day I turned sixteen I had my own car, which I bought and paid for before I had my driver's license. It was a 1953 Studebaker that looked like a sleek, white bullet on wheels. My dad taught me to drive and I immediately passed the driving test and now with my license, I was off and rolling. Because I always had a job I was able to help my

mother with a few of the bills and I always had a few bucks in my pocket. When Manual asked if I would be interested in playing in his family's
poker game I was so stoked I could barely contain myself.

Manual had a big family; he had several brothers who had wives
and children. The extended family was made up of everyone's aunts and
uncles and cousins and old friends from Guam who had settled in the same
neighborhoods. They were very tightly connected and they loved to eat,
drink, party and gamble. The first and third Friday of every month they
would gather at Mr. and Mrs. Butler's house for a poker party that would
last through the weekend. It was some serious poker and some serious
partying and I had been extended an invitation. I was one of the few white
people there and, to my knowledge, the only one not married into the family. I was deeply honored.

I also come from a big family. Seven of us kids grew up in our
house. My grandmother and an uncle lived next door. There were lots
of dogs and cats and birds and even a monkey, along with our pals, constantly running around and through our house, creating family style chaos
much of the time. But, that was nothing at all like what went on at Mr. and
Mrs. Butler's house a couple weekends each month.

The Butler's house was a modest three-bedroom house with a
fenced-in backyard in a neighborhood of the suburbs of Torrance, California. The Butler's poker game started about 6:00pm, giving all the working
people time to clean up and come over. There was a cooler filled with beer
and sodas just outside the kitchen door. There were the makings for cocktails on the kitchen counter. I was introduced to the people I did not know,
which was nearly everyone. Because I was Manual's good friend, I was
extended a warm welcome.

A blanket was spread over the dining room table. The maximum of
seven players took their seats and bought chips. The chips were white, red
and blue standard plastic chips worth a nickel, dime and a quarter respec-
tively. We played twenty-five cent limit. I bought in for twenty dollars.
The game was dealer's choice and the games to choose from were similar
to those I played in family games at our home in Lomita. I was introduced

to the game Two or Twenty-Two, which was a popular choice that night. The game started and all was calm and orderly. That was not to last.

Soon, women starting showing up and all were bearing food. Bowls of dips accompanied by chips magically appeared, green salads and potato salad were placed on the counter dividing the kitchen and the poker game; smoking hot ribs covered in sauce started to filter in from the backyard barbeque, baked chickens began to be disassembled and a seemingly endless flow of down home delights were laid out for all to fill their plates. The massive amount of food being brought in was staggering until I realized that this was a poker game that would last until the last dog died more than 48 hours later on Sunday night. Players would come and go and new ones would show up and wait for a seat. With the women came children and lots of them. The noise level would rise but Manual and I sat with five grown men, all of us oblivious to the growing frenzy around us.

More people arrived, people hugging and welcoming and sharing stories with each other in this large and growing gathering of Guamanians. They talked about graduations and marriages and newborn babies. They laughed and enjoyed being in the presence of family. The record player was turned on and the music had the place bouncing. Manual's cousin, Bobby, passed the deck and another hand was dealt. Chips were flowing around the table and a few were stopping with me. The barbeque and the kitchen continued spilling out food. Everyone ate including the poker players but the game never missed a beat. More people came. At some point the music was turned down so the ladies could hear the caller for the Bingo game. It was ten cents a card Bingo and some of the women loaded up with four or five cards. The living room was so full of Bingo players, weaving one's way to the bathroom was quite an adventure.

There was always a wait for the bathroom and kids were jetting in and out and all around. Manual told me to go outside and check out the garage. In there I found the majority of the kids and they were pitching pennies up against a big sheet of plywood. They were playing for keeps. I was impressed by the sheer volume of gambling going on in and around that house. Moreover, I was quite overwhelmed by the level of hospitality I had been shown. Nearly everyone stopped and introduced themselves to me. This was the first time I had ever actually played poker for stakes this high and I was winning.

At about 11:30 or so I needed to take my leave, as I had to work in the morning. I thanked everyone in the game and, of course, Mr. and Mrs. Butler for their kind hospitality. Manual walked to my car with me and I could not thank him enough. He assured me I would be welcomed back.

I had won about fifteen dollars and I had a great time doing it. My every-other Friday nights would change. Throughout high school I played at the Butler's house whenever I had that Friday night open. I think I probably averaged winning about twenty-five dollars each session. To put that into perspective I was working at McDonald's for a dollar an hour.

Playing with the Guamanians I learned so much about poker. I began to understand some of the many nuances of the game. I realized the value of patience. I was able to use my skills at mathematics in determining when to fold a hand or when to carry on. I learned to read my opponents. I became adept at playing each player differently. I knew who would fold and, thus, who could be bluffed; and I learned who would not fold, and, thus, I would never try to bluff Mr. Butler. I began to understand the clues that told me who had a high hand and who had a low hand. I learned how to build big pots. Because the competition was not at an exceptionally high level I found I could put all that I was learning to use and that allowed me to consistently do well in the game. I continued to learn.

To say the least, I was deeply touched to be surrounded and accepted by that large, generous and caring extended family.

My First Poker Tournament

While I was still the hard-working general manager of The Four Seasons at Lake Tahoe, I had become a frequent visitor to Tahoe's casino poker rooms.

One day I encountered a brand-new pick-up truck on display at the entrance to the Sahara Tahoe poker room. A big poster board sign announced: The Sahara Tahoe First Annual Six Card Stud Tournament. I was excited. It was the early 1970s and that would be the first poker tournament I ever entered.

In the game of Six-Card Stud, each player starts with two cards down and one card up. Then there is a betting round, which is followed by three more cards up with a betting round after each card. Players make the best five card hand using five of their six cards. The format for this Sahara Tahoe tournament was totally different from tournaments today. At that tournament, each player would check-in at the tournament desk and buy chips from $20 to as much as one wanted. The play took place in live games*, with subsequent buy-ins* and cash-outs recorded. Players started and quit when they wanted. Each day the betting limits would go up. Starting at noon on the first day, the limits were $2/4; the limits went up progressively each day so by the fourth day the limits were $8/16. On the fifth day, the top eight money winners would square off at the final table. Those eight players at the final table would play for exactly eight hours and, when the bell rang, the biggest winner would win a brand-new pick-up truck. A board would be updated daily with the current standing of all the participants.

This tournament was a really big deal to me. It was the first time I had played against the best players from the lake. Those players usually played in the Hold'em game, but I knew nothing about Hold'em. I did, however, know very well how to play Six-Card Stud.

*go to Glossary of Terms for meaning

Starting the fourth day I found myself in 15th place on the leader board amongst the 60 to 70 players who began the tournament. I bought in for $200, which was the most I had ever bought into a poker game. I lost my $200 and bought in for another $200. I was dead set on not buying in again, as I would have a mountain to climb getting back into contention. It was just after I made my second $200 buy-in when I was dealt a seven face up; I looked down at my two hole cards and found two more sevens. A wired three of a kind was the single best starting hand in Six-Card Stud and I was holding three wired sevens.

With just three cards, I was absolutely positive I had the best hand. On the inside, my heart started racing, yet, on the outside I appeared calm. I was determined not to allow my excitement betray me. I put on my best, unemotional poker face. From the betting it was obvious that three other players also either had big hands or they had decided to start gambling. Four of us put the maximum number of bets and raises allowed on the first three betting streets. A crowd had gathered along the railing around our table. The pot became huge, weighing between seven and eight hundred dollars and winning it would propel me well back into the tournament mix. The crowd grew. Playing that hand against Tahoe's best in that tournament, at that very moment, I experienced about five minutes of poker excitement bounding between dread and euphoria. Dread that my hand might get beat and euphoria that I was on the verge of winning a really big pot. I had never before experienced that level of emotional intensity in a poker game.

From the next three cards I was dealt, I did not catch a fourth seven. I never made another pair to give me a full house. My hand never improved. I only had the three sevens I started with.

With all the cards out, I bet my last $16. I was called by all three of the remaining players. It was time for the showdown. The large crowd fell silent. I turned over my three sevens. The next two players tossed their hands into the muck.*

There was only one player to beat. That player had been trying to make a flush with his first four cards being diamonds. He did not catch the fifth diamond he needed to make the flush, as his last two cards were black. However, both were black eights and it just so happened, one of his down cards was the eight of diamonds! Three eights beat my three sevens. That player took down what, to that point, was the biggest pot of the tournament.

I was devastated. I was broke. The tournament was over for me. The last thing I did before walking away was to take those three sevens and rip them in half. I put those three half-sevens in my wallet as a remembrance of my first poker tournament.

The next evening, a poker dealer named Sonny Murray drove off in his brand-new pick-up truck.

The First Time Around: Playing for a Living

In 1971, a new journey began. Since I graduated from University, I had begun to foster two dreams simultaneously; the first was to travel to Europe and the second was to try to make a living playing poker. Though I had what most people my age would have considered the perfect job in the most idyllic of places, I decided to chase my dreams. So, I gave notice and left my job at The Four Seasons at Lake Tahoe.

With two friends, I contracted to drive and deliver a car across the states to Boston. We flew to London, parted company in Amsterdam and I hitchhiked to Spain. Four months later, following an eye-opening trip to Morocco and a whirlwind romance, I returned to America with an English lady named Karen Clare who would one day become my wife.

The time had come and I was about to earn my living playing poker.

In South Lake Tahoe I rented a small one-bedroom cabin for $200 a month. I had an unemployment check coming every other week in the amount of $130. I had a starting bankroll of $500. I was beaming with confidence and raring to go. I planned to play $2 and $4 limit Six-Card Stud at the Sahara Tahoe. I knew I played far better than most stud players. However, a big win in that game was about $100. I had some better days, but not many. I soon found that not having an adequate bankroll was a major handicap. I also found that living expenses would quickly devour my less than grand winnings from playing in a game so small.

I was a couple months into my bold career change and I found myself waiting anxiously for each unemployment check. When the check came, Karen and I would buy groceries and I would set aside $40 for my next buy-in. A loss of that $40 buy-in would be devastating. It would create a dilemma: buy more groceries or buy-in a poker game again! I did have a back-up plan in the form of a credit card. When poker did not go well life was somewhat bleak. On the upside, I had a new romance and I became really good at crossword puzzles. We always budgeted enough money to buy pot. I found myself getting stoned and watching daytime

TV a lot. Life was not exactly how I had pictured it, nor was it what I had told Karen to expect.

After six months we found ourselves in a most desperate situation. For the very first time in my life I was flat broke. My credit card was maxed out at $600. Karen was ill. Our dog needed a vet. The rent was due the next day. My car was in need of repair and I needed to repair it in a raging blizzard. And, we were out of pot. Playing poker for a living: Act 1 was over.

My friend Joe West had invited us to move into his spare bedroom in Davis. All I had to do was fix the car that night and pack up. For lack of an alternator bracket I used bailing wire and some wild creativity. I finished at midnight in a huge snowstorm. We were off to Davis.

We stayed with Joe for a spell and then went from Davis to San Francisco where I took a bartending job. I hated everything about living in the city. We did not fare well at all. I got laid off. We spent the rent money on a ticket to England for Karen. I returned to Joe's spare bedroom in Davis. I found a landscaping job and after two months I earned enough money to join Karen in England. I bought a one-way ticket to London and my life was looking up again. In fact, the next year and a half was to become a most amazing and transformational chapter in my life.

Though her family was from Manchester, Karen had lived for years in Oxford. There Karen had found a free place to live. She took a restaurant job. I worked with a demolition crew tearing down old buildings. In five months we had saved enough money to head to the continent and begin traveling.

Joe West had made plans to travel with us and he joined us in Oxford.

In Amsterdam, we bought a VW Van. We traveled to Mojocar on the Mediterranean Sea in southern Spain where Karen and I first met. There we connected with Karen's old Oxford mates, Helen Wild and Julian Peto. We rented two small houses on the beach and two more dear friends from California, Art Read and Carole Hayes, joined us.

One day at morning coffee a small group of us, the only people on the patio, sat at our table next to the sea when an old American gentleman happened by. A conversation ensued and we were treated to a story when, digging deep, he told of traveling through Spain many years ago with his dear old friend Ernest Hemingway. By the time he finished tears were streaming down his face. Tears can be contagious.

Mojocar was special and most days were glorious. We swam in the sea, found beaches where the only footprints were our own, were embraced by the community of ex-pats, ate tapas in the Spanish bars and dined in small bistros. Some mornings we would move our kitchen table on to the beach outside our front door and play bridge for hours by the sea. One day Karen and I were alone on a remote beach. We heard a song. We looked up and high on a ridge above us we saw an old Moorish-looking woman, all in black, attached by a rope to her donkey, singing out to the ocean. We discovered a gypsy village fifteen kilometers inland and joined a raging party of locals in a bar filled with Flamenco guitars and beautiful, dancing gypsy ladies. Life was beautiful there.

Then things shifted. An English friend from Oxford turned up after smuggling a half a kilo of hash from Morocco to Spain. In Generalissimo Franco's fascist Spain the penalty for procession of pot or hash was seven years plus a day in a Spanish prison. The house on the beach Karen and I rented was formerly the headquarters for the local Guardia Civil. Because they were in the habit of being there, often there would be lots of heavily armed pseudo military police hanging out around our house. And, because we were almost always stoned on smuggled hash, the level of fear and paranoia reached almost unimaginable heights. It is hard to describe the feeling of walking home late at night, to be greeted by several Guardia Civil with loaded weaponry sitting on your veranda, wishing to engage in conversation in Spanish, when you are not fluent at the best of times and you are stoned out of your head, all the while thinking of seven years and a day in a Franco prison. To say it was a frightening, friggin' nightmare would be a gross understatement. After six months living in paradise, life had suddenly become too intense.

The five of us decided to pack up and go to Morocco.

With mixed feelings we departed Mojocar and ventured east across southern Spain. In Tarifa we put our van on a ferry and crossed the Mediterranean to Morocco. From Tangier we headed south to Marrakesh and Casablanca. We explored those amazing cities with their winding Medinas. We turned east. I remember lying under the stars one night in the Atlas Mountains and reflecting on both my attempt at playing poker full-time and the incredible education I was getting by living, working and traveling abroad. The sense of freedom and adventure was truly life altering and yet I knew, deep down, poker still loomed large in my future.

We traveled through Algeria and onto Tunisia, took a ferry to Sicily and another to the boot of Italy. In Rome Joe West split from us to go to Greece. Our friends Art and Carole bought bicycles and began to cycle to the UK. Karen and I drove the VW north to Holland. We arrived in Amsterdam with very little money and a VW van in need of repair. A fellow traveler helped us with some repairs. We had to sell the van to pay for the ferry tickets back to England. We stood outside the American Express office for three days, holding a handmade sign, trying to sell our van. The price posted on the sign kept getting crossed out and lowered each day. The weekend came and the American Express office was closed until Monday. We bought bread, cheese and sardines to eat over the week-end. We had $15 left. Unfortunately, we got a parking ticket, which we had to pay on the spot. That left us with $7. We bought two liters of gas and calculated how far out of the city we could go to be able to spend the weekend in the countryside.

We left the city and drove a few miles. We found a spot under some trees and parked. In the middle of the night, mosquitos attacked us so viciously that, in the pitch dark, I frantically drove to a spot not far off and parked. In the morning we woke to the sound of rain and traffic and discovered we were parked in the middle of a roundabout on a busy Dutch highway.

It rained all weekend. We played lots of cards in the middle of that roundabout. On Sunday an ice-cream truck parked nearby. We spent our very last $4 in the whole world on ice cream cones. We were once again flat broke with not a dollar or a Dutch gilder to our names.

Monday came and we arrived in Amsterdam on petrol fumes.

As we stood outside the American Express Office with our cardboard for-sale sign, our price dropped about every thirty minutes. In desperation we sold our van that had taken us on a trip south to North Africa and back and had been our home for so long for 90 Pounds Sterling or about $150. We were just able to pay for our passage on the ferry back to England.

We were home free, again flat-ass broke, yet enormously richer for having had the experience of about eight months of travel and adventure. All that felt way better than struggling at low limit Six-Card Stud, working crossword puzzles, staying stoned and watching daytime TV.

I went to work for Karen's father in his steel fabrication business. Karen and I returned to America in December of 1973.

Tahoe Four Seasons

Karen and I landed in Los Angeles and arrived at my mom's house in Lomita just in time for Christmas with my family. I had no plans or good ideas. We'd spent what little money we had on airfare. I decided to call M. Hughes Miller, my friend and former employer at The Four Seasons at Lake Tahoe, I told him I was back in the states and asked if he had anything for me in the way of work. While I was away things had changed. The Four Seasons at Lake Tahoe had incorporated and been rebranded as The Tahoe Four Seasons. Condominiums and a new 60-unit lodge had been built to raise the rental capacity to 250 rooms. Once again I became the general manager of the larger and much shinier resort and conference center. It was good to be back in Lake Tahoe.

Again I took up playing poker in the casinos of South Lake Tahoe and at The North Shore Club in Crystal Bay. I also started playing a little Texas Hold'em.

Although the hotel and conference center were on a major uptick, the condominium sales side of the project was a complicated disaster. Just under two years after I returned, the lending bank foreclosed and I was out of a job.

There was, however, a good ending to this story. I had saved some money and I was able to buy a modest house in Kings Beach, a vibrant little town on the north shore of Lake Tahoe. The house sat high on a hill. In addition to remodeling the entire house, I cut out a section of the roof, built our bed into the dormer I had added and suddenly we had a view of the lake from the upstairs bedroom.

There was some additional good news: I had been offered a space to open a poker room in North Lake Tahoe.

The Fanny Bridge Inn

Water from Lake Tahoe can only exit from Tahoe City. There, when the water level rises above the lake's natural rim, water from the lake contacts a dam with gates that open and close to maintain the seasonally desired water level. On the outflowing side of the dam, there is a pool where abundant rainbow trout congregate; many are huge. The highway which goes all the way around the lake has a bridge that passes over the pool and during the summer months the bridge is constantly packed with tourists, bent over the railing, their butts pointed up in the air, observing the trout; thus the name Fanny Bridge. A stone's throw away from the myriad of skyward butts sat a deli/bar/restaurant called The Fanny Bridge Inn.

In late 1975, my friend Dave Mercer was the owner and operator of The Fanny Bridge Inn and he had just offered me a space in the bar to operate a poker- room. I was all in. As soon as the county granted me a license, people started playing poker in Tahoe City in the new one-table card room in town.

The card room looked like something out of a John Steinbeck novel. It was in the liquor storage room that sat between the very busy deli and the very busy bar. There were glass-paned doors that led in and out to both places; however, three of the four walls were piled to various heights with boxes of liquor and one could only enter and exit through the bar. Players used the liquor boxes to store their jackets, backpacks, ashtrays and beers. The game was a trip. There were some regular players as well as a bunch of local Tahoe characters coming and going. There was usually live music in the bar and a party in progress just out-side our door. At times we would take a short break, en masse, to smoke a joint or snort some cocaine. Every night was fun-night.

The game was Jacks Back to Low*, a variation of Five Card Draw*, and I charged every player $4 each half hour to play. I split the collection money with Dave Mercer and I played in the game, consis-tently beating it. It was 1975 and I was making good money, about $500 a week, working four nights each week doing what I loved. I still occasionally played poker in the Nevada casinos.

It was that year, running a draw poker game at the Fanny Bridge Inn, that I began actually studying the game of Texas Hold'em. The game was being played daily at the Sahara Tahoe. A pal had obtained a copy of *Hold'em Poker* by David Sklansky. It was our bible and we kept it hidden from our competitors. This was so unlike the modern era, where people can learn to play through a constant flow of information. In 1975, our book contained valuable information; we guarded it so we would have an edge over the competition.

After my year of running a poker game in the liquor storage room, Dave Mercer sold The Fanny Bridge Inn and the poker-room was history. When I reflected on that night, a few short years back and so far away in the Atlas Mountains of Morocco, I came to the conclusion that the time had come to follow my dream. I decided to continue with poker in Nevada and to try again at playing for a living. By this time, I had a firm grasp of Sklanky's book and had been having some success with Texas Hold'em. So, with my total assets being a newly remodeled house with a view of the lake, two month's mortgage paid in advance, enough money in the bank to pay my bills, a VW Bug with a full tank of gas, a ton of confidence and a playing bankroll of $50, I was off to South Lake Tahoe for my second attempt at becoming a professional poker player.

I never looked back.

CHAPTER 2

FLYER

Searching for Paul Fellner

Back at Davis when I was running my poker game at the Kappa Sigma fraternity house there was talk of two legendary poker players from the fraternity who graduated in the late fifties. Some of the old timers had either known or heard about them. They were Tony and Paul Fellner, also known as the Fellner brothers. In January of 1968 it so happened that three of my fraternity brothers and I were planning to go to Squaw Valley for the big annual festival and ski event, The Winter Carnival. I didn't ski at the time but I loved the idea of a big party. I was told that I should try to connect with one of the infamous Fellner brothers named Paul. It happened that, just prior to the 1964 Winter Olympics in Squaw Valley, the Fellner brothers had opened a bar with a poker-room in the valley called the Bear Pen. We were told that Paul managed The Bear Pen and played poker there.

We arrived in Squaw, checked into our rooms at the Squaw Valley Inn and headed straight over to the Bear Pen. Paul was not in. Nor was he ever in when I wandered over to The Bear Pen during weekend. The Winter Carnival was a great time and I left having never met Paul Fellner.

Fast forward to 1970 when I was the GM of The Four Seasons at Lake Tahoe. During the previous year, working as a bartender, I had become a quite proficient player of a dice game played in bars called Liar's Dice. In fact, I would eagerly accept any and all challengers at any time to put their money up against mine. One night I was out drinking with a friend, and on our way home we stopped at a local bar and restaurant called the Chicken House. We bellied up to the bar, ordered two beers and I asked the bartender if he shook for drinks? ("Shaking" for drinks was a local custom that meant you would play the best two out of three hands of bar-dice and you would either pay double or get the drinks for free.) The bartender responded: "let's shake." I chose Liar's Dice. We shook. I lost. I paid $5, double, for the beers. Now I had exactly $50 left in my pocket, a decent amount of money in 1970. There was a gentleman sitting at the bar next to where I was standing. He very casually asked if I liked to play Liar's Dice? I answered in the affirmative and the game was on. We settled on playing for $5 a hand. I was broke in less than 20 minutes. I was in shock. This was not supposed to happen.

As I stood up to leave, I held out my hand and said: "I'm Glen Garrod. You, my friend, play good."

He, in turn, shook my hand and said: "Pleased to meet you. My name is Paul Fellner, but people call me Flyer"

I responded: "Honest to God! I've been looking for you for quite some time."

Thus, I proceeded to tell him my story. That night marked the beginning of a very long friendship.

Old School Poker

Frank Sinatra owned the Cal Neva Lodge from 1960 to 1968. By 1968, gone were the days of the infamous *Rat Pack*: Frank Sinatra, Sammy Davis Junior, Peter Lawford, Dean Martin and Joey Bishop. And also gone were the many Hollywood celebrities who partied in the limelight of North Lake Tahoe. By 1970 the casinos in Crystal Bay, Nevada had become old and tired. That was when, with great flare and spectacle, the King's Castle opened in nearby Incline Village. Though it had the slick feel of a Las Vegas establishment, a welcome sense of new vitality permeated the thin north Tahoe air.

Prior to my departure from The Tahoe Four Season, I discovered a huge Pot-Limit* Dealers Choice game being spread weekly at The Kings Castle. The game was far too big for me as the players sat with thousands in chips and piles of one hundred dollar bills in front of them. The games played were many of the same games I had grown up with back home playing with the Guamanians as well as with my fraternity brothers in Davis. Scanning the table, I saw a familiar face; it was Flyer playing in the game. Because of the amount of money involved, the game was featured as a casino attraction with lots of folks watching from the rail*. With so much money going into the pots, the game produced high drama. For a while, I too watched the game from the rail.

*****

When playing Texas Hold'em, the format for each hand is always the same: each player is dealt two cards, there's a flop, two additional cards, four betting rounds and then a showdown. There is so much thought and strategy involved in the game of Hold'em, yet the procedure is the same hand after hand.

In 'Dealer's Choice,' there are many games to choose from and the format for each game is different. To this day I fully believe the many old-school games played mostly in people's homes, are the most intelligent, creative and imaginative games of poker ever played. I would not have a clue where to find these games being played in a public card room today. Most games are 'high-low split declare.'* When the betting is over, players use chips to 'declare' which way they are going: high, low or both ways (see appendix, High Low Declare Games). The strategies for each game can differ. At times you might try to keep players in the hand to get value for a big hand. At other times you might try to force those who are playing for the same half of a pot as yourself to drop out in order to ensure you win your half uncontested. At other times you may just want to build a bigger pot and win it. You must be able to read your opponents and their cards to determine whether they are going high or low or possibly both ways. Clues are dropped along the way. Conversely, you try to hide your intentions. You disguise your hand. Knowing when to stay with a hand and when to bail is crucial. Seeing what likely betting action lies ahead can lend clarity to a hand and can allow you to leverage situations. The nuances of the games can be complex. The various forms of the games differ enough to affect strategies and at the end of each hand is the declaring. Can declaring opposite from your opponents, bail you out of a bad situation? If you go both ways are you certain enough that no opponent can beat or tie you one way, causing you to lose all of a huge pot? In short, with all the intricacies, complexities, the clues and deceptions, there are no poker games quite like 'high-low split declare games.'

Watching from the rail that night at The Kings Castle, I studied the players. I took in the hands they turned over and how they were played. I had never before seen poker, much less the games I had cut my teeth on, played at this level. I quickly realized that Flyer was the dominant player. I dreamed of having the money to play in that game one day. Before that dream came true, the game abruptly ended.

It was shortly after I took the leap and began playing poker for a living that the Dealer's Choice game was re-invented as a $10/20 limit game played at the North Shore Club in Crystal Bay. The club was a quarter mile from my new home. I was the first person to arrive on the night of the game. My bankroll had grown enough so I was financially comfortable in taking a seat. Flyer was in the game and he and I began to become more acquainted. The first time I played I won $2,500. That was by far my biggest win ever in a poker game. I was ecstatic. I celebrated with a few cold beers.

The next day, the financial aid officer at UC Davis contacted me about being in arrears on my student loan. With one night's winnings equal to my total unpaid debt I immediately paid it off.

Flyer had begun serving as a mentor to me. Within two years, I became a top-limit Hold'em player in the Reno/Tahoe area, moving up to playing $15/30 and $30/60. Mostly, however, I looked forward to and thrived on the weekly Dealer's Choice game at the North Shore Club. It was old school poker at its finest.

My favorite games at the time were High Low Roll'em Declare with an Exchange and Five Card Stud High-Low Declare with an Exchange.

Flyer

Besides being a hugely talented poker player, Flyer had the sharpest wit of anyone I ever played with. To this day any player who has ever known him can tell more than one hilarious Flyer story.

Flyer told me the story of getting in some minor trouble in Spain in his youth. He was sentenced to thirty days in a Spanish jail. Even back then, Flyer wasn't just a poker player, he was an excellent card player in all games where gambling was involved. The game of Gin was no exception.

Every morning in the Spanish jail, the prisoners lined up to shower. The line passed the Gin game in which the jail's Commandant played with a fellow jailer. The line moved rather slowly and one morning as Flyer approached the game he could see the Commandant's hand. The Commandant had Gin but because of the manner in which his cards were arranged, the Commandant didn't know it. Flyer reached over the Commandant's shoulder and moved a couple of cards in his hand so that the Commandant could see he had Gin. After that Flyer never again had to line up for a shower. He became a regular in the Gin game and showered at his leisure.

I began playing regularly with Flyer in the Dealer's Choice game at the North Shore Club. Flyer was an extremely accomplished player and I was just beginning my career. We became friends and I benefitted from his mentoring.

On an early trip to The World Series of Poker in Las Vegas, Flyer invited me to sit behind him in a big No-Limit game. I had played some No-Limit Hold'em but had never seen a game of this size before. Besides Flyer, some real heavyweights of poker were in the game including Sam Petrillo, Dickie Carson, Bobby Baldwin and the convicted drug kingpin Jimmy Chagra. Mr. Chagra was soon due to enter prison and with many millions of dollars he could not use behind bars, he was livening up the biggest poker games in Las Vegas. The sheer volume of poker chips and one hundred dollar bills circulating around the table in that game was astonishing. I had never seen anything like it before and Flyer was getting his fair share of it. That night Flyer's persona grew in my eyes.

In 1980 Amarillo Slim produced his second annual Super Bowl of Poker. This was a poker tournament second only to the World Series of Poker. It was held at the Sahara Reno. The world of poker, especially in 1980, tended to be dominated by Texans. Many of the older and more traditional Texans were cowboys and definitely had a more macho attitude than most northern Californians. Flyer, on the other hand, was movie star handsome; he hunted, he fished, he skied; he was a three-sport athlete, an extraordinary golfer and a gourmet cook. He was certainly manly but was also a little eccentric. So, when Flyer arrived directly from a vacation in Hawaii wearing a kaftan, all eyes were upon him. Many mistakenly believed Flyer was wearing a loose, unbelted, Hawaiian dress called a muumuu. However, to most Texans, in his colorful, full-length, long sleeved, flowing, traditional Persian garment, Flyer was a man about to play poker in a dress!

Flyer checked into his room, headed directly to the poker room in his kaftan and started playing in the largest No-Limit Hold'em game going. Early that first evening a crowd of people four-deep circled the table where Flyer was playing. There was well over $100,000 in a pot and Flyer was in it.

Late in the evening, Flyer was an $80,000 winner in the No-Limit Hold'em game and the players decided to change the game to a $500/1,000 Limit Hold'em game. This was a gigantic limit game. The blinds were $250 and $500. This meant the first two betting rounds were in increments of $500 and the second two betting rounds were in increments of $1,000. This was surely one of the largest limit games of all time, or as Flyer described it to me: "It's the game of the century and I want to be a part of it!" And a part of it he was, a big part of it!

Flyer was from the part of the country where Limit Hold'em was the main game. He was a dominant player. Most of his opponents were elite No-Limit players. Flyer was, quite likely, the best of the lot playing limit poker. Only there was a major bump in Flyer's road: Flyer's opponents slept and Flyer did not. Except for an occasional cat-nap, Flyer played straight through, never actually going to bed for the entire tournament, just short of a week, all the while still wearing his kaftan. Other players rested and returned in shifts as Flyer played on. Sometime during that sleepless haze, perhaps day three or day whenever, Flyer began losing badly, so he sent for more money from home.

In the middle of this epic Limit Hold'em session he took a break long enough to play in and win the Seven Card Stud Hi-lo Split tournament for a $25,000 first place prize. Then he hopped back into the huge game that wouldn't end. When the smoke cleared and the curtain came down, Flyer was devastated. He began the tournament with $90,000 in his pocket and he had another $40,000 that he had sent for from home, in reserve. He was initially an $80,000 winner when they changed games and when it was over he had lost everything, including the $25,000 tournament prize money. On top of that he owed about $40,000 he had borrowed in the game. That constituted a loss in the Limit Hold'em of $275,000 1980 dollars! I'm guessing the only liquid assets he had after the game was the $1,000 I had borrowed from him.

To this day I will, from time to time, run into an old Texan who, after I tell him I was from Lake Tahoe, will ask, "Say, do you know that old boy from Tahoe who used to play in a dress?"

The Last Eight in the State of Nevada

It was the morning after a long night in a $30/60 Limit Hold'em game at the Sahara Reno. Because of the late hour, I had decided to take a room and get some sleep before leaving. In the morning I packed my bag and was ready to head back to Lake Tahoe. I walked by the poker room and I saw the game was still going. Only three players had persevered through the night: Flyer, Seattle Slew and Laughing Al. There were mountains of chips in front of each and they were playing the game at lightening speed. I stopped to a watch a few hands. It appeared to me like it was a contest to see who could make the last raise; extremely large pots were built fast. Flyer and Laughing Al were premier short-handed players and had played some legendary heads-up matches. Slew was a top player from the Pacific Northwest. He had relocated to Reno and became a regular in Reno's biggest games. Besides being a fine gentleman, he too was no slouch in a short handed poker game and could hold his own with the best of players.

After a few hands, I witnessed a hand that left a lasting impression on me. There was a bet and the maximum number of raises before the flop. All three took the flop:

Flyer: **J/7**   Al: **A♦/8♦**   Slew: **8/7**

Flop: **J♦...8...7♦**

Flyer had two pair: Jacks and sevens. Al had a pair of eights and the nut flush draw. Slew had two lower pair: eights and sevens. There was the bet and the maximum five raises. On fourth street* came a 7:

4th Street: **7**

The Board: **J♦...8...7♦......7**

Flyer had a full house: 7's full of Jacks. Al had: 8's and 7's and the nut flush* draw. Slew had a smaller full house: 7's full of 8's. They again went the maximum bet and five raises.

On the river, the very last eight was placed on the board. Of the forty-two cards remaining in the deck, that eight was absolutely, positively the only card in the entire deck that Flyer could lose with:

Flyer

Laughing Al

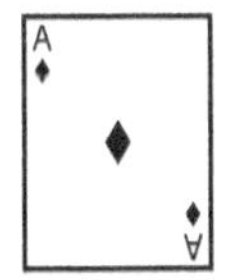 

Seattle Slew

Board

That eight gave both Al and Slew a tie, each with 8's full of 7's, full houses higher than Flyer's. Again, the maximum bet and five raises. Though the pot was massive, Flyer threw his full house away after losing only two additional bets.

Now here's the part I will never forget, a most imaginative and hilarious scene, a direct result of the ultimate 'bad beat.'*

Flyer, processing what had just happened to him, jumped to his feet and shouted, "That's it! That's it! That was the last eight in the entire state of Nevada…NO! NO!…no there was one other eight… that eight was sitting in a truck stop in Wells…Wells, Nevada…that eight was sitting there in that truck stop in Wells, Nevada eating chili and chicken gumbo." And Flyer stormed off through the casino, totally crazed, his arms flailing wildly in the air, shouting, "CHILI AND CHICKEN GUMBO…CHILI AND CHICKEN GUMBO" over and over and over.

CHAPTER 3

MISSOURI DAVE

Blind Luck and an Encounter
with Missouri Dave

Texas Hold'em had intrigued me since I first saw it being played. One afternoon in the early seventies I traveled to South Lake Tahoe, entered The Sahara Tahoe, intending to play Six Card Stud, saw an open seat in the Hold'em game in progress and I took it. I was pretty much clueless about the nuances of Texas Hold'em.

The game had two $5 blinds* in front of the rotating button; it was $5 to enter the pot and there were $5 betting increments on each betting street.

I had played less than an hour when a new player, who all of the locals seemed to know and acknowledge, took a seat in the game. The player looked somewhat familiar but I really couldn't recall where I had seen him. He bought in for $500.

He was sitting in a middle position relative to the dealer button.* He put up $10 of his own money for the player next to the second $5 blind and said, "I'm straddling* for him;" in sequence he put up his own money, straddled for $20, then $40 for the next two players and finally he straddled $80 for himself. The blinds were now $5-5-10-20-40-80. To put it into perspective, there was $160 total, in blinds posted before the cards were dealt and $150 of it paid by one guy.

It now became $80 to enter the pot in a $5 limit game. Four other players were in the pot and when it was this crazy new guy's turn, he raised an additional $5 in the dark, meaning he had not looked at his hand. The other players called. The pot stood in excess of $400.

I do not at all recall what the remaining hands were or what the board* looked like when it was over. I do remember that the new guy bet or raised at every opportunity and never even peeked at his two cards. When the dust settled, the remaining hands were shown down* and this crazy new guy turned over the winning hand. He won, as they say, a pig of a pot, or more appropriately: the crazy new guy won a huge pot by blind luck! He then grabbed a couple of racks and cashed out. He said good-bye to everyone and left the card room.

Four players were stunned at how much money they had lost in one hand in such a small game to a guy who never looked at his cards! All were left shaking their heads at what had just taken place.

As for me, I never paid the $80 to see the flop so I lost nothing. I sat there in disbelief at what I had just witnessed. I asked a player next to me, "Who the hell was that?"

He replied, "That was Missouri Dave." He went on to describe him as a local legend, a poker player who played in the biggest games in Tahoe, when he was around, and also played in Hawaii, where he lived much of the time. I had never seen anything quite like what had just transpired.

Little did I know at the time, Missouri Dave and I would one day form a friendship that would last a lifetime.

Getting to Know Missouri Dave

I had begun to make the transition from Limit Hold'em to No-Limit Hold'em by way of Pot-Limit* Hold'em. There is a world of difference between limit games and no-limit games, much like the difference between checkers and chess. Pot-limit lies much closer to no-limit. Each game has its nuances and a player who plays one well does not necessarily translate to playing the others well. At this point in time I was a top limit player and was just beginning to play some pot-limit.

At times, Flyer would mentor me. Flyer was an accomplished player and had played in the few large no-limit games around Lake Tahoe as well as some even bigger games in Las Vegas. There was a $5/10 Pot-limit Hold'em game getting started in South Tahoe. As the poker community in Lake Tahoe was small and fairly well connected, Flyer and I heard about the game and claimed a seat the first night it was spread. Other than Flyer, there was one player who stood head and shoulders above the others. He was called Missouri Dave. Our paths had crossed though we had never spoken. I certainly remembered him and I was positive he did not remember me.

During the night, Missouri Dave and I engaged in some conversation and I could tell right away that he was a hugely unique human being and every bit the large persona I had borne witness to some years earlier. We both played until the game was over. He asked if I'd like a beer, so we went to the bar. We spent several hours there. We came to realize that we both shared a strong respect for the game of poker. The longer we talked, the more we drank. We realized that we both placed the highest value on honesty and integrity, that our word was our bond.

That night at the bar, I shared with Dave some of my stories and, in turn, I was treated to a few really remarkable stories of his; stories that were testament to the extraordinary life Missouri Dave had lived right up to that moment. He was in his mid-thirties and four years my senior. His stories were of having his pockets filled with cash one day, finding them empty the next, only to rebound again. He lived as a free spirit and never let the size of his bankroll distract from the quality of his life. I would come to know he lived and played poker with a ton of heart. That night I felt like I was in special company.

As night became morning I needed to head back to north Tahoe. Before we parted company, I told him I had one more story myself. Earlier in the evening I had connected the old dots from six or seven years prior and realized when it was that I first sat in a poker game with him. I told him of a Six-Card Stud Poker tournament I had been in some years ago. I expressed to him that it was a big deal to me at the time. I recalled that I had played a really big pot that was crucial to my survival in the tournament. I remembered having three wired sevens to start the hand and I told him of the three eights that he made to beat me and send me packing. I explained to him how I ripped those sevens in half and had carried them in my wallet since that day. I opened my wallet and asked if he would autograph them for me. He obliged. Until I lost my wallet some thirty years later, I carried with me three half-sevens, each individually signed: "Suck on it turkey, Mo Dave."

That night was the beginning of our partnership that would take us many times across the country playing poker at a very high level while maintaining a well-deserved reputation as good men, as men whose word was their bond. Men whose integrity was never in question, who could borrow money and would pay it back when they said they would. As men who would never cheat, collude, short a pot or hang out with those who would. It was important to us to be on a level with the most honorable of poker players.

Although Dave now lives in Thailand, our relationship remains solid. That bond has been one of the highlights of my life.

Missouri Dave

When they made Missouri Dave, as the saying goes, they broke the mold. I doubt there has ever been a human being quite like him or, perhaps, will ever be again.

Dave's story began in Moberly, Missouri. Olevia, his single mother, raised him and his sister and two brothers. She owned and operated a hair salon and raised all her children to be honest, have integrity and work hard. Dave scored high on those first two qualities, but found himself allergic to work. He grew up fiercely independent. He learned to shoot pool as a teenager. Underage, he hung out at Hickman's Tavern and beat much older players out of their cash. He went by the name of Pork Chop then, and folks in Moberly knew Pork Chop. He started playing poker and found he was good at it. Pork Chop started organizing and running his own poker game when he was seventeen. Between pool and poker, Pork Chop, while still in high school—which he excelled in—always had a flashy car and a pocket full of dough.

He was admitted to the University of Missouri in Columbia. The first order of business was to find a poker game, which he did. The game was beatable but the guys who ran it were raking* way too much money from the game. That prompted Pork Chop and another player from the game to team up and start their own game. His new partner was called Cornbread. They not only had a poker game but they built their own craps table and ran a dice game as well.

According to Dave, Cornbread was a powerful, charismatic Missourian, a legendary football player and a College All-American from the University of Missouri. He was only 5'11" but weighed 260 lbs. He was quick and powerful. He could chase down most of the opposition quarterbacks or wrap-up anyone carrying the football. After he graduated from the university, Cornbread opened The Italian Village, the biggest bar and restaurant on the campus. Amongst his many attributes, Cornbread was a world-class consumer of large quantities of food. His eating contests were imbedded in local mythology.

Dave told of the time when someone came to Columbia to challenge Cornbread to a massive chow-down. Cornbread agreed to take the challenge but told the fella he would lay down the ground rules. First, they would each put up a $1,000 for the winner. Second, they would eat in Cornbread's restaurant and the loser would pay for the food. Plates of food would be prepared with equal portions and brought from the kitchen. Third, they would take a twenty-minute break every four hours. When the challenger heard the 'every four hours thing' he excused himself and quietly slid out the back door. The Italian Village was a hub for students, alumnae and those in the know. Although they sounded like a menu at a country barbecue, Cornbread and Pork Chop became cultural icons of the alternative community in Columbia.

The poker game and craps game were run out of Cornbread's family farm. Both began with a flourish. The poker game was dealer's choice. An old road gambler found his way into the game. He brought with him a game new to the Missouri players called Texas Hold'em. He educated Pork Chop in the nuances of the game. Before Texas Hold'em was widely played in Las Vegas, Pork Chop had become an exceptional player in Columbia and a better player than the old road gambler who taught him the game.

In the early 1960's and prior to reaching the legal drinking age, Pork Chop was producing concerts around Columbia. He would pay the bands the proceeds from ticket sales and he made his money selling keg beer by the cup. Between beating the poker game, collecting his share of the rake, his winnings from the craps games he and Cornbread banked, and the beer sales from concerts he produced, Pork Chop did not lack for funds in college.

He was cruising through school when he made the critical mistake of letting his student deferment lapse. He was drafted into the army and promptly sent to Vietnam.

As Dave tells it, the transport plane landed in a hot war-zone in Vietnam. When Dave exited the plane, the shear power of the humidity nearly overwhelmed him. Transport planes were flying in and out, and fighter jets flew high overhead. In the distance, he could hear mortar shells exploding. Soldiers scurried about, and still the humidity was relentless; wet, sticky and unbearable. Amid the chaos, with his company lined up, his sergeant shouted, "Does anyone here know how to use a typewriter?" When no one responded, the company was ordered to prepare to board transport helicopters.

As Dave lined up with three days' supply of food, water and ammunition on his back in a ninety-pound rucksack, he began grasping the reality of his situation. He started thinking about the typing class he took in high school. The proverbial light bulb lit in his head and with a sense of urgency he managed to locate his sergeant. He said, "Sir, that thing you said about typing, well I want you to know I'm one shit-hot typing son of a bitch." He was excused from the line he had been standing in and taken to the Company Commander and his new job. Of those who boarded those transport helicopters that first day in Vietnam nearly half lost their life within weeks.

As time passed Dave hunted and pecked on that typewriter as fast as humanly possible. He handled all the Commander's forms, memos and correspondence. He assumed the role of the company historian. Dave became known as the Remington Raider. At some point through his proximity to the commander, Dave was able to requisition beer and bags of ice by the pallet. He became a purveyor of ice-cold cases of beer. Icy cold beer made the poker games he ran much more inviting in the high humidity. He introduced more than a few soldiers to the game of Texas Hold'em. Unfortunately, Dave did end up seeing his share of combat when his company was sent to the A Shau Valley, an entry point into South Vietnam for North Vietnamese soldiers and supplies along the Ho Chi Minh trail. The fighting there was fierce.

Dave returned home from Vietnam in one piece and not mentally scarred like so many of the American veterans of that war. He picked up in Missouri right where he left off. Pork Chop traveled between Columbia and St. Louis, earning the reputation as a top poker player and a highly competitive pool player.

After a while he migrated to Lake Tahoe. The first time he got on the list for a seat in a poker game at the Sahara Tahoe Casino, there were already several 'Daves' on the list so he said, "Put me down as Missouri Dave." The name stuck and Pork Chop became a name from the past. From Lake Tahoe, Missouri Dave moved to Hawaii. He managed to create a great life living off and on between the Hawaiian Islands and the mountains of the Sierra Nevada. He spent years beating poker games between Reno, Tahoe, Las Vegas and Honolulu.

Besides being an accomplished poker player, he was a character so outlandish as to cause heads to shake by all who came to know him. He was fiercely competitive yet as generous as a human could be. He had a total disregard for money or possessions. He lived for today. He always picked up the dinner check. He knew the price of his hand against yours, but never knew the price of the bottle of wine he just ordered. Neither his honesty nor his integrity was ever questioned. He knew how to enjoy life. People would point him out and say, "That is Missouri Dave." He was one of my mentors and my partner in our many adventures together. He's a rogue. And he loved his mother.

Missouri once found a small leather bag in a hotel corridor at the Cajun Cup, a poker tournament in New Orleans. He didn't open it because he did not want to allow himself to be tempted. He turned it into the hotel front desk and left only his name. Many years later, in a poker game, someone mentioned his name. A gentleman in the game asked: "Are you really Missouri Dave?" He acknowledged that he was. The gentleman told of his lost bag that was returned to him in New Orleans. He asked Dave if he knew what was in it. Dave said he did not. The gentleman told him the bag contained $45,000 in cash. He thanked Dave and said he'd like to buy him a drink. Dave was not at all fazed about the $45,000. He was, though, bothered that the guy never bought him that drink. That is the kind of guy Dave was.

Sometimes when heavily drinking, Missouri Dave billed himself as: "a fucker, a fighter, and a wild horse rider, 160 pounds of rompin' stompin' shit." Some of his oldest friends referred to him the 'Tasmanian Devil.'

When my wife and I split up in the early eighties, I had been living in my Volkswagen van all around Lake Tahoe. On one particular night when I was planning on staying with Dave and his sweetheart, Mindy, I showed up at the Sahara Tahoe and the buzz around the card room was Dave had gotten in a big-money game of pool and had won a ton of dough from a local named John Jergens.

It happened that Missouri Dave and John Jergens had dinner and drinks together at The Bella Union in South Lake Tahoe. They left and headed up the street to the Sahara Tahoe. John was an heir to a family fortune and lived on an extremely generous monthly stipend. He was a notorious gambler at blackjack, craps, sports and whatever else he could bet on. Once they were in the casino, John headed to the blackjack table, while Dave sat in a poker game. At some point, John came to Dave and borrowed $1,000 to continue playing blackjack. He lost the money and suggested that Dave go with him to his house so he could pay him the $1,000 he borrowed.

Driving east on Highway 50 they stopped at Sam's, a local Nevada bar. They ordered beers and John asked Dave to let him try to get even on the loan by playing a game of *Nine Ball* on the pool table. Dave agreed to play but, as he was a more gifted player, he would spot John the 7-ball and the 9-ball. The game is played by potting the balls in order, one through nine, and whoever pots the 9-ball wins regardless of how many balls each player pots. Getting spotted the 7-ball and the 9-ball meant John was allowed to remove the 7-ball when it was his shot at it, he then could win by knocking in the 8-ball as he was given the 9-ball in the spot.

When Dave told me the story, he said they played the first game for $500. Dave won so they played the second game for $1,000. Dave won. At some point John changed the game to *Chicago*, which is played by putting three balls on the table and the player who pots his three balls in the fewest shots wins. John kept doubling the stakes and they progressively played for larger amounts of money. Soon they were playing for $10,000 a game. They were both pretty wasted when they left Sam's and went up the hill to John's house. They poured drinks and John called a Nevada cathouse where he had credit. He arranged for three or four prostitutes to be taxied to the house. After being up all night playing blackjack, poker and pool while drinking through it all, they still managed to party with the ladies. When Dave left John's house he had a huge hangover and an I.O.U from John for $306,000.

After Dave and Mindy split up, Dave and I rented a house together on the south shore. Four months later, when Karen vacated our home in north Tahoe, Dave and I moved there. Over the years Dave's fortunes grew and shrank. There were nights when Dave would be in a poker game and I would get a phone call from a concerned friend telling me Dave was playing fast and furious and without regard to the amounts of money he was putting in the pot as his chips became more and more alcohol propelled. Dave would often play a hand without even looking at his cards. "Glen," the caller would say, "maybe you should come talk some sense into Dave." I tried more than a few times. It never worked. Dave would often say, "The only thing better than drinking and gambling is drinking and gambling and winning." Ultimately, I gave up and would just hope for the best for him.

Sometimes Dave would come home with his pocket bulging with cash and sometimes he would come home empty. He always woke up with a fresh attitude and never complained about a loss. Dave always contended that he was the exact same person with or without money.

There did come a time when Dave got a firm handle on the drinking and gambling. That was when he started accumulating all the money, hanging onto it and elevating his game to new heights. He did continue to drink, but he waited until the game was over. There were more than a few times when he'd find money stashed away that he did not remember. He once found fifteen $1,000 poker chips from the Reno Peppermill Casino in a small cardboard box in his bedroom. He found $20,000 in the pocket of a jacket he seldom wore. Once he was leaving The Big Game quite drunk after celebrating a big win, his backpack stuffed with $10,000 bundles of cash. The zipper to his backpack was halfway down and he was dropping the bundles as he walked to the casino cashiers. It was just like Hansel and Gretel with the breadcrumbs. Fortunately, our friend Dave Olson was following close behind picking up the breadcrumbs.

CHAPTER 4

RENO/TAHOE

Reno/Tahoe

The arched sign reading *The Biggest Little City in the World*, still spans Virginia Street in downtown Reno, Nevada. This high desert metropolis sits at an elevation of 4,500 feet in the northern half of the state. Settlers first flocked to Nevada for gold and silver mining. In 1931, gambling was legalized and in the thirties people began coming to the Silver State for quick marriages and quick divorces. When I began frequenting Reno, the historic downtown felt small and inviting. You could get a casino breakfast for forty-nine cents and, just as in Lake Tahoe, I saw many legendary greats perform in the casino lounges for the price of the two-drink minimum. Musicians like Count Basie, B.B. King, Waylon Jennings and a long list of distinguished entertainers graced the small stages of Reno lounges. The late 1970's build-up of new casinos outside of the city center led to Reno's tremendous growth and the eventual erosion of the downtown charm as people once knew it. The biggest little city wasn't so little anymore.

About 50 miles over the mountain from Reno, sits Lake Tahoe, known as the Jewel of the Sierra Nevada. Mark Twain said of Lake Tahoe, *"The water is clearer than air, and the air is the air angels breathe."*

I hold an image in my heart from my many winters in Lake Tahoe. It comes after days and nights of a wild intense snowstorm. I would wake to the shine of fresh, white, deep snow piled in large drifts with a huge number of pines and firs, limbs pinned tight to the trees with the weight of heavy frozen snow. In the morning stillness the trees rise in the form of giant white cones, lit by sunlight, pointed up to the clearest deep blue sky on earth; pristine, mesmerizing, beautiful.

In 1968, on the day I graduated from University, I headed straight to the lake for only the summer; yet, life in Tahoe was so magical, many like myself found it difficult to leave and I remained for 26 years. Lake Tahoe was affordable then for families and working people. As time rolled on, that gradually changed. Many long-time residents who rented, lost their homes as they were converted to vacation rentals. Workers were left with few places to live. Like all of California, home prices rose astronomically and regular folks were priced out of the market. In 2020, Pandemic refugees from big cities flooded into Tahoe; many remained and telecommuted. The four once distinct tourist seasons had melded into just one. It had become extremely busy and crowded all year long. An old friend spoke about a recent summer and said of a once quiet locals beach, "You couldn't see the sand for the beach towels." Greed, the Pandemic and the extreme disparity of wealth had an effect on Lake Tahoe. While the incredible beauty of Lake Tahoe remained mostly unchanged, the energy has been drastically altered.

I was most fortunate to have played so much of my poker in Reno and Lake Tahoe.

The Quinella

The word was out. Cole Dickson was playing poker in Reno and the game was on fire.

It was 1978 and I was playing mostly limit poker those days. The biggest and best Texas Hold'em games were either at The Sahara Tahoe or the newly opened MGM Grand in Reno. The game I had just heard of was a $30/60 game that had been going for two days, non-stop, with an evolving cast of players at The Grand. The game was built around Cole Dickson. Cole was a big money pool player. He was one of the premier Nine Ball players in the country and had been since he was a teenager back some nine or ten years ago. He lived in Carson City but would go on the road shooting pool around the states. Usually when he returned he'd have a big bag full of money. He loved to drink and gamble and put that money in action and I was on my way to Reno to try and get some of it.

It was the second day of the poker game when I sat down. Amongst those of us playing was David Sklansky. David was the author of the definitive book on Texas Hold'em called *Hold'em Poker*. David's ex and their son lived in Kings Beach where I lived. Often, when he was in town visiting his child, he would join our Dealer's Choice game. As well as being an excellent poker player, David was an accomplished mathematician and the authority on the mathematics of poker. He also had a keen eye for a bargain.

David Sklansky took a break and went to the Sports Book to check on a bet. When he returned he said he found a bet that was too good to be true.

This was the year that a horse called Affirmed won the Triple Crown. There was another horse that year named Alydar. These two horses had a storied rivalry and were many notches above all the other thoroughbreds in America. In horse racing there is a bet called a Quinella. To win the Quinella the bettor picks two horses to come in first and second place in any order.

The bet David found that was too good to be true was essentially a gigantic error on the part of the MGM Grand Sports Book. They had a "futures" bet meaning the bet was a fixed price and not a variable bet base on track betting. The fixed price on Affirmed and Alydar, the two absolute best horses in the land, coming in first and second was, as memory serves me, about two or three to one. Now here's the kicker: there were only four horses in the race. David had come to cash out of the poker game so he could bet every dime he had on the race.

In the next instance the poker game was put on hold as each player followed David's lead. Every chip in the game was cashed in and every cent each of us could muster was taken to the Sports Book and bet on that Quinella. We had to wait about an hour for the race to be run and to collect our winnings before the poker game could resume. Each player now had several times the money they had before. The game that was on fire just became quite a bit hotter.

A Welcome Gift from the Poker Gods!

Karen and I had recently separated. While she was living in our house, I was living in my VW van or staying with various friends. It was an early Saturday evening in the summer of 1981. On this particular night I was staying in the Tahoe Keys with Missouri Dave and his girlfriend Mindy. I was flat broke. I borrowed $500 from Dave and headed for the Sahara Tahoe.

I got a seat in a $15/30 Limit Hold'em game. It was mostly locals with only two or three out-of-town players; one of whom had a very large target on his back. That dude was loud and talkative and was looking for someone who would converse with him. He was also looking for someone to drink with. I was his guy. I started beating the game pretty good and beating my new drinking buddy really good. The more he drank, the louder he got, the more I was winning and the more irritated with me he became. Eventually he challenged me to play him heads-up and for bigger stakes, which absolutely thrilled me but did not seem to please the other players. I was the target of some extremely foul looks.

He wanted to play **his** game: 5 Card Stud. We played $5 ante and the low card was forced to open the pot for $25 and then bets were in $25 increments on the first two streets, and $50 bets the second two streets. There was no limit on the number of raises. We agreed to buy in for $2,000 each. That presented a small problem. I was winning $1,300 in the $15/30 game and only had $1,800. A player from Washington jumped at the chance to get 10% of my action for $200. Problem solved.

Now we had both been drinking, he more than me, so to protect the casino and me from any accusations of wrong-doing, Larry Saunders, the card room manager, dealt and the game was filmed. My opponent had just sold a bar in Wisconsin and was retired. He was on his way to Mexico and said he had several hundred thousand dollars in a safety deposit box at the Sahara. We began playing and right away I knew two things: first, he had no chance of winning and, second, I needed to get him to slow down his drinking. After he lost his first $2,000 he wanted to raise the stakes to $50/100. I agreed and he bought in $4,000 more. Then he bought $5,000 more. When he started to get up to go to his box again I did what I felt was right. I told him I would love to keep playing but he was getting too drunk for me to continue and feel good with myself. I offered to continue the game the next day at noon if he wanted. He said he wanted to play more now but I stood my ground. We agreed to play Sunday.

That night, after tips and the house drop, I beat the stud game for $10,600. I cut Steve out his initial $200 investment plus $1,060 for his 10% share of the win. Counting the $1,300 I won in the Hold'em game plus $9,540 I netted in Stud, I had won $10,840 on the night. I was no longer broke.

The guy never showed up on Sunday.

Buena suerte y adios amigo.

Laughing Al and the Curse

Laughing Al had moved from Las Vegas to Reno in the latter half of the 70s. He was an outstanding Limit Hold'em player, a very good No-Limit Hold'em player and had been playing for a living for quite a long time. Al marched to the beat of his own drum. He had longish salt-and-pepper hair, a full unkempt gray beard and wild bushy eyebrows that looked like two overgrown gray caterpillars were camping above his constantly smiling eyes. He usually wore dark slacks from another era, and an old and tattered winter sports coat that appeared as if it came from a long-ago thrift store's close-out sale. With a Rasputin-like aura and with his ever-present fedora he looked like a cross between a gypsy and a mad professor. His perpetual grin and his frequent low tonal chuckle earned him the handle of Laughing Al. When Laughing Al played poker he smoked incessantly and always had his sweetheart either by his side or playing Low-Limit Stud nearby. Laughing Al was a most formidable opponent.

*****

Two things must be discussed to make this story easy to understand.

First when two players in a No-Limit or Pot-limit Texas Hold'em game have all their money in the pot, (providing there are no other players still with money left in the hand), with one or two additional cards yet to come, they might want to stop the dealer from continuing to deal while they discuss *doing some business.* This is more of an old-school approach and does not occur often in the modern game. Doing business entails determining the chances of each player winning the hand before the final one or two cards are dealt and then dividing the pot in an agreed-upon manner relative to each player's odds of winning the pot.

Second is the concept of *holding over* someone. This is when one player beats the same player an absolute inordinate amount of times.

If Joe Blow has the best hand against Bob Knob before all the cards are dealt out, Joe Blow always holds on and wins when the cards are dealt out. On the other hand, if Bob Knob has the best hand before all the cards are dealt out, Joe Blow always draws out and ends up winning when the hand is completed. When this happens over and over, Joe Blow is said to *hold over* Bob Knob.

*****

Now, here's the story.

Since Laughing Al always played in the biggest games in Reno and Tahoe we were bound to be in the same games quite often. Since we both liked to play heads-up or in short-handed games, we got to know each other's style of play fairly well. For the first several years we played each other about even. Then suddenly everything changed acutely. Perhaps the poker gods took a liking to Al and I fell into their bad books. Or, perhaps Al, who I believed practiced witchcraft, put a spell on me and he began to *hold over* me like no human should be able to do.

For a full year, no matter what, when or where, Al won the pot and I lost it. I tried *playing around* him; that is, I purposely avoided playing pots with him. That was hard as we played in the same games so often. Losing to Al so consistently was unnerving. It affected my confidence; my swagger diminished when I was around him. We both were absolutely and totally aware of this phenomenon. It was downright spooky. And, it cost me a lot of money.

It was 1980 and I was playing at The Sahara Tahoe one night in a relatively big Pot-Limit Hold'em game with $5/10 blinds. Missouri Dave was playing, as well as Flyer, a few other locals and, of course, Laughing Al.

After playing for an hour or so, a hand came down like this: Al raised the pot with **two black Queens**; I re-raised with the **King of Hearts** and the **King of Clubs**; Al called. The flop was: **2♥...7♥...10**.

56

Al bet, I raised and Al called. 4th street brought the **3 of hearts**.

Al checked, I moved all-in. Al called. The pot weighed **$2600**. Although I had good credit, the money I had just shoved into the pot was all the money I had on me and pretty much all the money I had in the world. Besides, I owed Al $500 from a prior game.

"Hold the deck," I said to the dealer. "Al, let's *do some business.*"

Me

Laughing Al

Board

Al needed a Queen to win, but it couldn't be the Queen of hearts because, although that would have given him three Queens, it would have given me a heart flush. This meant he could catch only one card in the deck that would beat me, that card being the Queen of diamonds.

"I don't see much business we can do," Al said.

We both were totally aware of the freakish curse, that, for a year, Al *held over* me, so I was just not going to let that last card come off the deck.

With only one out of forty-four cards to win with, Al's equity in the pot was $59 ($2,600 divided by 44). Thus, to be fair and precise, Al would take $59 and I would take $2,541 and we would go onto the next hand. But there was no way Al was going to take just $59. So, I made the outlandish offer that he could take $200 and I would take $2,400 and we'd be done with it.

"No thanks," Al said, laughing.

"Wait, how about $300?" I said.

"No," he said, no longer laughing.

Missouri Dave chimed in, "Glen, are you nuts?"

"He must be," observed Flyer.

"OK, Al $400?"

Again, Al declined my offer. Dave asked what the hell was going on. Flyer broke out laughing. As a rule, I am not at all a superstitious player; I rely on, amongst other things, mathematics and a firm grasp of probability. I had never ever in my life made such a ridiculous proposition and I have not done so since that night. Yet, way down very deep in my soul I knew I could not let the final card come off the deck.

At this point, my feelings about Al being a witch were validated, and I knew for certain witchcraft was involved, for no reasonable player would have turned down my offer of $200 much less the subsequent offers of $300 and $400. It absolutely defied probability, logic and reason. I was starting to shake with the intensity and the absurdity of the situation; I'm sure it showed in my voice. My friends already thought I'd lost my marbles and their feelings were verified when I made, what possibly may have been, my final offer.

"Al, look, this is all the money I have. I will give you $500 and I will take the $2,100. I will also pay you the $500 I owe you."

Perhaps Al feared he would be exposed, beyond any doubt, that he was a witch. Who really knows, but I will always remember what Laughing Al, the man who had brutally *held over* me for a year said. "Well, OK, but I don't like it!" We then divided the pot accordingly.

"So let's see that last card," Flyer told the dealer.

"No, don't deal the card, I do not want to see it," I responded.

"Then shut your eyes. Dealer, turn off the card," Dave said.

The dealer turned up the last card. There it was, as big and as bad as any card that had ever been laid on a poker table: the QUEEN OF FRIGGIN' DIAMONDS.

In unison, the players at the table, as well as the fairly large crowd that had formed around the negotiation, erupted in loud vociferous incredulity. No one could believe it, that is, no one except myself and 'the definitely not Laughing Al.' People would talk about that moment for months to come. People must have thought of me being anywhere from psychic to insane.

The room calmed down and players returned to their seats and their business of checking, betting, calling and raising. Flyer made a comment, something to the effect that if Al had not taken my ridiculous offer, they would have found my head stuffed in a pickle jar sitting on a shelf in the poker room.

"Years from now," Flyer said, "a person would walk into this very poker room and ask, "What's with the head in the pickle jar?" Always the response would be, "Oh, that's Glen Garrod, a player from many years ago, after he saw a certain Queen of Diamonds.'"

I looked at Laughing Al and stated, "It's over Al." And it was. Al stopped *holding over* me from that night on.

The Lady from Macau

Maybe her name was Shawna or maybe it wasn't. Shawna was tall and thin with dishwater blonde hair. She was naturally calm and non-verbose. She had a forlorn look in her eyes and was very pleasing to the eyes of most others. But Shawna had a talent that elevated her above so many; she was a card counter in the game of Blackjack. Shawna was no ordinary card counting Blackjack player; no, it was said that she possessed similar abilities as those exhibited by Dustin Hoffman's character in the film *Rainman* and that Shawna could even track two games next to each other simultaneously.

Here is how most of Shawna's story was told to me. Shawna was part of a very successful 'card counting Blackjack team' that had been playing in gambling hotspots all over the world. They had winnings that totaled over two million dollars. As the team was running out of places to play, they chose to move to Southeast Asia. When in Indonesia, they encountered a gentleman reported to be a relative of the Royal family; he wanted in on their action. There was a chance for Shawna and the team to get in on a percentage of ownership in an Indonesian casino in exchange for cash and a piece of their team's action. It turned out to be a ruse. Shawna and her partners lost hundreds of thousands of dollars; moreover, Shawna was arrested for illegal gambling activities and spent three unimaginable months confined in an Indonesian prison with utterly inhumane conditions. Shawna emerged, quite likely, as a somewhat damaged human being.

Shawna and the team reassembled in Macau. They were playing in various casinos on a nightly basis. The key was not to get caught counting cards and become barred from playing not just from one, but all of the casinos in Macau. So, when the team leader said it was time to go, each member of the team needed to pull up immediately, cash out and hit the door. On one particular night, when the team leader gave the signal, everyone followed procedure and packed it in. Everyone that is except Shawna. There was no telling what was going on in Shawna's head at that moment? Perhaps she was on a huge roll and couldn't tear herself away from the table. Maybe she just decided to go rogue. Maybe she was fed up and wanted out. Or, just maybe, the horrible experience of an Indonesian prison had something to do with her actions. Who knows? Regardless of her reasons, that was the last time she played Blackjack for the team. She was paid off for her share of what remained of their accumulated winnings and unceremoniously told to piss off! Shawna stayed in Macau for another week, continuing to play Blackjack, counting cards and adding to her winnings. When she stepped onto her flight back to the United States her net worth was $250,000.

Shawna was free as a bird. She didn't really have a home base, nor did she have much family. She chose Las Vegas as her point of entry; after all, they played Blackjack there. They also played poker. Although she knew the basics, Shawna had never really played much poker. She knew of Texas Hold'em but had never played in a game. She did however have a quarter of a million dollars and she loved to be in action. Shawna did not ease herself into playing Texas Hold'em; no, she jumped right into one of the biggest No-Limit games in town – a game in which all the big boys of Las Vegas played. With some of those big boys, she even took them on in heads-up matches for $10,000 per match. Days later when the dust settled Shawna found herself on another airplane headed to Reno, Nevada with her bankroll cut in half.

Down to $125,000, she arrived in Reno more than a little shaken trying to come to terms with having lost half her fortune, in such a short time, playing a game with the world's best players, in a game she really did not know at all. She checked into a room at the Sahara Reno and made a beeline for the poker room. This time, she proceeded with caution. She started playing in a small Limit Hold'em game. She bought in for $100. She wanted to learn the game.

It's not clear how Shawna hooked up with Tyler Beatty. Probably because she was an attractive lady in her early thirties sitting in a poker game in a room full of mostly men. Tyler was a handsome man, with the look of one who might play a heartthrob attorney on a daytime soap. He was quite fit with jet black hair and kind eyes. In addition, he had a good sense of humor and a gentle demeanor. He was a friend of mine and not at all a scoundrel like a pretty lady with lots of money could easily attract in a poker room. Tyler was a good dude. Tyler and Shawna became a quick item in Reno's poker community. It was through Tyler that I got to know Shawna and learned her story. They seemed good together. With Tyler's mentoring, Shawna began to learn to play Texas Hold'em; however, she still did not play well. She was way too eager. She quickly stepped up her game and wanted to play in the biggest game in Reno, which at that time was $30/60 limit. With Shawna at the table, the games picked up steam and the tempo of the increased action manifested in the size of the many large pots. Tyler played, but Shawna was the attraction. One evening Tyler introduced her to his friend Missouri Dave. They all had dinner together and after the meal, Shawna challenged Dave to a heads-up match. That did not go well for her.

Shawna's bankroll was in a swiftly moving downward trajectory.

Shawna and Tyler didn't do a lot of things as a couple. They didn't go out dancing or attend any concerts. They never went to the theatre or even see a movie together. They did remain in the hotel at the Sahara Reno and upgraded to a suite. They would play poker late each night, sleep in until the afternoon, have a nice meal and return to the poker room. Because the $30/60 game was so good since Shawna started playing, more players started coming to Reno. The word was out.

One night, as the inevitable was getting closer and the end of Shawna's bankroll was in sight, I was hanging out in their suite and talking with Shawna. Tyler was occupied, playing Backgammon for some serious cash. It was then that Shawna, totally cognizant that her run was about over, confided in me that she wasn't remorseful about going through all that money in such a short period of time. She was only sorry she never took the opportunity to really enjoy any of it.

Tyler and Shawna were not to last as a couple.

*****

Shawna was one of many, in an endless line of people, who have journeyed to Nevada and found themselves broke and in a bad situation. They come to The Silver State from all over the world. Many lose their money and some lose their way. Some folks pass through and others come full stop. Shawna, like so many before her, found herself with no cash and no lifeline out. With no cash, Shawna did not have the bankroll required to play Blackjack. Perhaps her experience in Asia left her with little desire to ever play Blackjack again. Shawna, too, had come full stop. For many of those people stranded in Nevada, survival becomes a daily grind.

*****

I used to run into hometown champs from poker games in cities from Somewhere, USA. They'd have a string of successful trips to Nevada and figure they'd take the leap: quit the job, uproot, move to Reno or Las Vegas and become professional poker players. Most did not succeed. Years after the leap, I would run into a few of them here and there. The lucky ones scored a job dealing poker or Blackjack; some hustled everyday to find a buy-in in a poker game in which they couldn't make a livable wage. If they could afford it, many returned to from where they came.

The first time I cashed out of a poker game in Las Vegas, I was followed by 'a sad story' needing a bus ticket back to nowhere. I bit and gave the guy $30 and my address, which he never used to mail me the 'money order' he promised.

There are low-limit, hard-core gambling junkies that get jobs in restaurants: cooks, dishwashers, porters, bussers and the like. On payday, they pay the rent, they buy their cartons of cigarettes and because they work in restaurants, they can gamble away the rest and always eat at work.

I've seen the same people walking through the same casinos each day checking slot machine trays for coins or seeing if credits have been mistakenly left on a confusing modern slot machine. They pocket the coins or cross their fingers and play the credits. I was told those people were called silver miners and that was a job for them.

Missouri Dave once lent a total deadbeat poker degenerate (his words) $100. I asked Dave, "Why did you lend that guy money when you know you have no chance of getting paid back?"

"That's okay," he told me. "Since he owes me, he'll never ask again and I probably just got off cheap."

Those gambling towns are strange places filled with people just trying to get through the day. Some fare better than others but each person has their story. These are places full of those stories.

*****

It had been a few years since that night in Tyler and Shawna's suite and I had not seen either of them. I had been playing some poker in the El Dorado Casino poker room. It was a small No-Limit Hold'em game, but the only no-limit game in Reno at the time. One trip I played late and spent the night in a room in the hotel. In the morning, I passed through the casino on the way to the valet parking and that's when I saw her. It was Shawna, she was still in Reno and she was dealing Blackjack. I stopped at her empty table and said, "Hello old friend, it's been a long time." We conversed for a few minutes. She told me she and Tyler split up quite some time ago and that Tyler returned to Los Angeles and took a job outside of poker. She said she had a new man in her very normal life and she was carrying their child. She said she was good. She was one of the lucky ones. From her fall from grace, she had landed softly.

A player sat down in her game, which was my signal to leave. "It was nice to see you," I said. As I walked away, I thought again about all the stories people have. It's stories that make us who we are. I looked back at the guy who sat at Shawna's table, a guy certainly with stories of his own, and a guy without a clue that he was in the presence of such a huge story, both fascinating and tragic, the story of The Lady from Macau.

Rick Ketcher

It had been a routine patrol, another day trying to stay alive in Vietnam, when Rick's squad was ambushed and everyone ran thirty yards in retreat for the nearest cover. In that scramble for safety, Phil Klien became detached from his helmet. That, in its self, was not such a huge loss but Phil kept his address book, which had all his contact information for everyone back in the real world, in the lining of his helmet. War, I'm sure, does strange things to a soldier's head and this was one of those times. Phil, in his insane attempt to retrieve his helmet, had been hit and was stuck in no-man's-land with no chance of getting home on his own. So, there was Phil Klien, screaming in agony, when from about thirty yards away, and in the gaze of his squad's disbelieving soldiers, Rick Ketcher said, "Fuck it!" and sprinted as fast as he could while keeping low to the ground. All in one motion, Rick grabbed Phil, lifted him onto his shoulders, and, amidst the chaos of a firefight, brought him to relative safety. For that, Rick Ketcher would be given the Bronze Star with the "V" device, awarded for heroism in combat, the fourth highest military decoration for valor. He'd also get paid the $1,000 Phil owed him from the poker game two nights prior. When I heard this story, jokingly, I asked Rick if he would have saved Phil if there hadn't been a poker game. He grinned and said, "Nah, money had nothing to do with it." That was the first story Rick related to me about his tour of Vietnam.

Rick was born and raised in the small town of Nevada, Iowa. He was from a tight Midwest family and was raised with traditional values born of the American heartland. He was a three-sport athlete and went to Simpson College on a football scholarship. After college, where he was affectionately known as 'two hundred and twenty pounds of twisting, turning steel,' he was given a tryout with the San Francisco 49ers. The 49ers found they didn't need all that 'twisting, turning steel' and the tryout was short-lived. While in college, Rick discovered he had a knack for poker and a strong propensity to gamble. He told me of a game of that went on for days at a friend's house near the university.

In the game, Red Dog, each player puts up a pre-determined amount of money in the pot. The first player is dealt four cards face up; the object of the game, with suits counting, is to cover the next card dealt; for example, the very best hand is all four aces, then the player covers all cards in all suits. The player can choose to bet any amount up to the size of the pot on the fifth card being covered by the four up-cards. If he wins, he takes that amount wagered from the pot; if he loses he puts that amount into the pot. At times, the pots can become various degrees of huge. In Rick's telling of this notorious game of Red Dog, he was dealt the Ace of hearts, the Ace of clubs, the Ace of spades and the Jack of Diamonds when the pot was monstrous and had been growing for hours, now weighing over ten thousand dollars. There were three cards, and only three cards, Rick could not cover; those were the Ace, King and Queen of diamonds. Rick, feeling the pull of that pot, put up the pink slip to his car. In poker terminology, the Man with The Axe is a King depicted holding an axe; that King is the King of diamonds. Rick will forever feel the shock when the axe came down and he lost his 1968 Ford Mustang.

"When was that game of Red Dog?" I asked.

"That was in the year nineteen hundred and sixty-eight!" Rick responded. When he was only twenty-one years old, Rick did, in fact, lose a brand spanking new Ford Mustang on a most unfortunate turn of a card.

After his brief tryout with the 49ers, Rick was ordered to report to his local induction center for his physical exam. Having been deemed physically fit, he was loaded on a bus and sent off to boot camp with a load of fellow Iowans to serve as more fodder for the war in Vietnam.

Rick's second story about Vietnam was his transformative experience as a soldier. Even though the Vietnam war dominated the news cycles prior to his going into the army, Rick did not have a firm grasp as to the reason he and all his comrades-in-arms were being asked to fight and possibly die for their country. Surrounded by so much chaos, bloodshed and death, Rick and eight other members of his squad began questioning why they were there. After many deep heartfelt discussions, seeing the constant futility of both sides killing each other, and finally realizing the whole war was a lie based on deceptions, they concluded that they needed a new approach to the war. Revelation!

Based on their performances under fire, Rick and his guys all had a high degree of respect amongst their peers for being fierce warriors. From that point on, they decided they would continue to do their jobs but would only kill when absolutely necessary and, moreover, would dedicate themselves to having each other's back so they would all make it home. Eight of the nine did get home alive. Rick had his own close encounter with death. He was in a massive firefight in which their perimeter was overrun. A week after the battle, Rick came out of a coma in a hospital in Japan and found, for his gallantry in action, he had been awarded the prestigious Silver Star, a medal just below The Medal of Honor. He was returned to the States. The big take-away for Rick after his tour of Vietnam was, although he loved his country, he would never again trust a politician.

After arriving home from Vietnam, Rick took a job in Los Angeles working for an airline. Time passed and, attracted to the beauty of the Sierra Nevada, but mostly to the casino's bright lights, he took a leap of faith and moved to North Tahoe. Still possessing a propensity to gamble, Rick played poker and Blackjack. He bet sports, he shot craps and he would play most anything except Red Dog.

For a while, Rick took a job as a pit boss in a local casino.

I met him in 1976 when he was trying to limit his gambling to the one thing he could beat: he was trying to make a living playing poker. We met at the North Shore Club in the Sunday dealer's choice game. We took a liking to each other, and being as how we were both at the early stage of playing poker for a living, a friendship was struck, one that still runs strong to this day.

When Karen and I split up, Rick said, "This is for you any time you need it," as he handed me a key to his house.

When I needed investors in my casino game, High Country Poker, Rick and our close friend, Dan Giovanni who also entrusted me with the key to his Berkeley house, decided to invest $10,000 each.

Rick was an outstanding softball player. We both shared a passion for the game. He and I played together on an assortment of teams for thirteen straight years. It was midway through our softball careers that I first met the girlfriend of our right-fielder, a sixteen-year-old, wearing a tie-dyed shirt, named Eve, who would go on to become our families' nanny, and, eventually, a college writing professor and the editor of this book. That path from the softball diamond led to the local bars and that led to the sharing of many stories.

One such story that Rick told me took place in the boarding lounge of the Los Angeles International Airport. Rick was working for the airline at the time and was waiting for a delayed flight to Des Moines, Iowa and a Christmas reunion with his family. He met a fellow traveler, a woman many years his senior who was also traveling east. She asked where he was going and he responded that he was flying to Iowa and then going on to his hometown of Nevada. She told him that quite some years ago she was in Nevada, Iowa. A strange thing happened she said, as she drove through a neighborhood, looking for a friend's house. A child on a bicycle flew out of a blind driveway into the street and although she slammed on the brakes, she hit the bike. She frantically jumped out of her car and there looking up at her was this wild-eyed, frightened child who screamed, rolled out from under the front of her car and ran up the driveway and into a house. Panicked and with her heart racing, she ran after him. She followed him into the house where the child's mother joined the parade that led to an upstairs bedroom. The child's mother demanded to know what happened. The woman said she ran into the boy with her car. She recalled staring, with his mother, at a child in tears, who had crawled under his bed.

As an airline employee, when in the terminal, Rick was required to wear his employee badge with his name on it. The lady, seated on Rick's right, had gone quiet. Rick turned so that she could see the badge on the left side of his shirt. He asked, "Does this name mean anything to you?" Facing her, he could see that she had turned pale, her mouth was open but there were no words; she was indeed speechless. He confirmed what she was thinking, "Ma'am, that child was me all those years ago."

Bonded by that traumatic event, the woman and Rick's mom remained in contact for years after that eventful day.

In 1985, Rick quit playing poker for a living and went to work as a shift manager in the Hyatt Lake Tahoe poker room. In 1995, Rick sold his lake-view home high on the mountain and moved to Las Vegas. He spent a year and a half there playing Limit Hold'em, earning a decent living. From there he traveled to Tunica, Mississippi where he took up residency in Binion's Horseshoe Tunica Hotel and Casino. Most professional poker players have the freedom to choose their own path. The one Rick chose was fairly unique. From the day he checked into Binion's Horseshoe Tunica he left only for his infrequent trips back home to Iowa or to visit various friends around the country. He lived in the hotel, played poker every day, sometimes two sessions a day, for just over five years and beat the largest Limit Hold'em games to death. He stayed for free as a guest of Binions, and his meals were comped, so Rick had no need to spend his money. Each week he would take his earnings and send a cashier's check to his father to deposit into an Iowa bank account for him. Whenever his father was asked, "What's Rick doing?" he would respond, "He's sending home so much money, he must be robbing banks."

Rosie was the housekeeper that made up Rick's room everyday at the Horseshoe. She was a large, older African American lady with a good smile and a great attitude. Some mornings he'd hear Rosie admonishing the other housekeepers, telling them to keep the noise down because "Mr. Rick plays poker all night and sleeps late." One afternoon, Rick found some of his clothes missing and thought, 'Oh well, somebody must have needed them more than me!' The next day Rosie brought in all his laundry, washed, fluffed and folded. She said she was concerned Rick didn't have enough clean clothes. At other times she brought him home-cooked meals; according to Rick, her fried chicken was the best he'd ever eaten.

One late afternoon, Rick was driving into town when he saw Rosie walking in the rain. He stopped his truck and offered her a ride. Rosie said, "No need, I'm just going to the bus stop." Rick insisted on giving her a ride to that bus stop and ended up taking her home. She lived in an old, run-down Mississippi neighborhood but had the brightest, best kept home on the block with a groomed hedge around a well-manicured lawn and lots of flowers. Her husband Harold, a local handyman, was working in the garage on his old beat-up truck, which Rick would later learn, was always a challenge to keep running. After that day Rick became a frequent visitor to Rosie and Harold's home.

In 2002, Rick decided to give up playing poker in Tunica. He was sitting in his last game when a fellow card hustler who was also packing it in, wanted to sell his Toyota pick-up for $7,000. With only 60,000 miles on it, Rick offered him $5,000. They settled on $5,500. Rick cashed out of the game and drove that truck over to Rosie's and handed her the keys. Totally stunned, she said she could not possibly accept a gift like that without talking to Harold. Rick said he was leaving Mississippi and insisted that truck was for them. Rosie stood in the driveway in tears when Harold left to drive Rick back to The Horseshoe. The last thing Harold, a stoic man of few words, said with a tear running down his cheek, was simply, "Forever grateful, Rick." It was the final time Rick ever saw either of them.

Rick returned to Iowa where he had inherited the old family home. He took up playing some poker on the Internet. He was a true grinder. Though he never set the world on fire with huge wins in those six plus years in Las Vegas and Tunica, he put in his hours, and he made enough money to retire quite comfortably.

Nevada, Iowa was a farming community and lots of the guys he'd known since childhood were still there and still farming. Rick would set his alarm each morning for 6:00am. He'd put on his jeans and suspenders or his overalls, his John Deere hat and scoot on down to the local diner for coffee, breakfast and conversation about anything from the price of wheat to hog futures to the weather to Mary Higgin's cow. Men would then go off and fire up their tractors or put up some fence while Rick would go home and play Texas Hold'em on his computer.

In 2007, Rick started claiming horses, training them and running them at the track. Horse racing became a passion late in his life.

As the years have gone by, Rick and I have always made sure to reunite. We would meet back up at our yearly Super Bowl gathering, and one time, Dan Giovanni, Rick and I rendezvoused in New Orleans for a week of music and a 49er/Saints football game. I'm sure not many people plan a vacation in Nevada, Iowa, but Dan and I once joined Rick at his house for a week watching basketball on his television during March Madness.

I've been blessed with the friendships of many extraordinary people in my life. Rick Ketcher is one who has always stood with me through my ups and downs. True friendship is special. We shared our history just like we shared our most intimate and personal stories. It was my great fortune to have him as a partner at home and on the road. As old Harold from Mississippi once said, "Forever grateful, Rick."

The Bank Robber

If ever there was an interest in playing in a poker game where the skilled player's advantage was so marginally small it was comical, $10/20 Limit Crazy Pineapple* with small blinds ($5 & $5) as once played at The Hyatt Lake Tahoe was the perfect game. It was, in my opinion, the worst limit poker game ever played. But in North Lake Tahoe it was the only game in town.

On weekdays, locals made up most of the Hyatt Poker Room's clientele. On weekends and during the summer there came a host of out-of-town regulars. Over the many years it became like one big Crazy Pineapple family. It is fair to say I hated the game but was very fond of the players. Amongst the regulars we had a wealthy casino owner, an ironworker, a bookie, a municipal judge, a pot dealer or two, a successful tech entrepreneur, an ex-NYC cop, a bartender, a world renowned attorney, a shopping mall developer, a woodcutter, bar owners, drunks, a tennis pro, Blackjack dealers, poker dealers, wealthy retirees, married couples, and just a whole magnificent assortment of people; all friends and all equals at the poker table. One day I realized we could add to that list a bank robber.

His name was Bart. He was in his early twenties and he showed up with a lot of money and was splashing it around in the Crazy Pineapple game. Bart was pleasant enough and seemed like just a regular guy with way too much money. It didn't take long for people to piece together that he was a trust-fund baby. It had been rumored that he was cut off from the family trust. He soon began courting a Hyatt cocktail waitress. The locals around the Hyatt make up a small community where everyone knows everyone and their business, so the story got around that Bart had just flown the cocktail waitress to Hawaii for lunch. When they returned that night, more than a few eyebrows were raised. People also noticed when Bart bought a new motorcycle, a dirt bike. He continued to court the cocktail waitress with flowers and expensive dinners. In the poker games, all that mattered was that the guy was friendly and he kept the money coming.

I read about the bank robberies in the local newspaper. Several local banks on both the Nevada side and the California side of Lake Tahoe had been robbed and the robber was getting away fast and clean. Police would set up roadblocks right away but were coming up empty. One edition of the paper had a photo from the bank surveillance camera showing the suspect. He had black uncombed hair, a black moustache and he was wearing Bart's 'number 42' Oakland Raider's poker-playing jersey! Just like Sherlock Holmes, I put all the clues together and solved the case. Bart wore a fake moustache and he would make his escape from the banks through the woods, rather than the roads, on his new dirt bike, thus avoiding the roadblocks.

Once I figured it out I called the local sheriff's office to be told there was a $10,000 reward. I had a plane ticket to London for a flight that left inside of twenty-four hours. I hesitated, as I had mixed feelings about turning the fool in: I could use some extra money, he was certain to be caught fairly soon, I was flying away the next day and I wasn't clear on the morality of turning in a bank robber with whom I was acquainted. I decided to go see my good friend Rick Ketcher who managed a shift in the poker room at the time. I explained to Rick the whole thing and told him the only thing that was iffy was that the hair didn't match. Rick said that even Bart was probably smart enough to mess up his hair before robbing a bank. I left it with Rick to turn Bart in for the reward if he felt like it. We agreed that we could split the reward money.

When I returned from England I asked Rick if he turned in the bank robber. He said, no, he couldn't bring himself to do it and that Bart had been arrested two weeks after I left. He was later convicted and sentenced to twenty years in prison.

Carmen & Stan

Carmen and her husband, Stan, moved to Lake Tahoe shortly after Stan retired from an executive position at a large Bay Area corporation. After Stan took his retirement and cashed in his company stocks, he was able to bank over a million dollars. Stan was in his 70's and Carmen was in her early 50's. They made a down payment on a condominium in the upscale community of Incline Village, Nevada, close to The Hyatt Lake Tahoe. Stan immediately discovered the Hyatt had a sports book. Stan was not completely healthy and, in fact, was semi-invalid and spent much of his time in bed. Three maybe four nights a week Stan and Carmen would drive the short distance to The Hyatt, have a posh dinner in one of the Hyatt's high-end restaurants and, before going home, Stan would make one or two $20 sports wagers so he could sweat his bets at home in the comfort of his bed. The Sports Book was located between the poker room and a lively little bar frequented mostly by locals. Carmen would have a cocktail at the bar while Stan made his small sports wagers. She became friendly with the bar-staff and some of the locals. After a short while, the much younger Carmen began remaining at the bar while the older Stan would return home to snuggle up in bed and watch sports.

Carmen was not a gambler. In fact, she may never have bet a dime on anything in her life. Now she was living in Nevada and many of the folks Carmen was hanging out with were playing the video poker machines that were embedded in the top of the bar. Carmen began to join in the fun.

When Carmen first made the very short walk from the bar to the poker room, she was given a quick tutorial on Crazy Pineapple. Carmen was always dressed well in a conservative style and certainly not casual like so many Tahoe locals. Every hair on her head was in its designated place. Her make-up was perfect. She wore a moderate assortment of jewelry. Her appearance was almost like that of a Sunday school teacher. Her smile and demeanor immediately endeared her to most everyone in the club-like atmosphere of the Hyatt Poker Room. Carmen, though she did not grasp all the nuances of the game of Crazy Pineapple, understood the basics and enjoyed the game and the company of the other players. Fortunately for her, the winning margin in Crazy Pineapple was small. In other words, even the poor players had a good chance of winning now and then. Carmen was one such player. Carmen's routine visits to the Hyatt would look like this: dinner with Stan, a drink at the bar, say goodnight to Stan, play video poker, play Crazy Pineapple, finish the night with some more video poker and catch a cab for the short ride to her home.

In the poker game Carmen would buy-in for $500. About half the time she would add a second buy-in of the same amount. Just occasionally she would buy in for a third time. And, now and then, Carmen would win. A reasonable guess would be she probably lost, plus or minus, $2500 a week playing Crazy Pineapple.

Her trips to the bar were another story. The video poker machines were dollar machines. However, the machines offered progressive jackpots, which required $5 to be wagered each hand to qualify for the big prize. Carmen mostly played $5 a hand in her quest for the progressive jackpots. How much Carmen lost at video poker can only be speculated. I heard that one year she was one of the Hyatt's single biggest players. Stan, on the other hand, had little or no idea the extent of Carmen's gambling and was simply happy with the many perks the casino provided including invitations to their VIP parties.

Several years passed, perhaps three or four. The first awareness Stan had of his wife's gambling came one day when Stan and Carmen were awakened in the early morning by a loud knock on the door. Movers had arrived at the instruction of the bank (which had foreclosed on the condo in which Stan and Carmen lived) to move the occupants out. The night before, Stan had gone to bed knowing he lived a carefree life in beautiful Lake Tahoe, thinking he was a millionaire, only to wake up to find himself broke and about to become homeless.

All who knew Carmen in the poker room were in shock that such a thing could happen to such a soft-spoken, pleasant and kind person.

The story of Carmen and Stan is not entirely unique. Gambling in general, and poker specifically, has taken a lot of people down. I have witnessed businesses and homes lost, relationships compromised, bank accounts depleted as well as the loss of dignity and self-respect. It's not all grins and giggles and good times. At times poker becomes tragic. Ideally, people would play within their financial means. When I began to play successfully, part of my personal code was to play at a high enough level to avoid playing with people working for low wages. That was not always possible, especially in my later years, when I began playing for smaller stakes. It was at times a difficult standard to adhere to. Stories like that of Carmen and Stan tend to make a small dent in one's soul or at the very least, cause one to pause and reflect.

I never heard of Carmen and Stan again.

Playing by Phone From Hawaii

Late one evening on my way home I stopped in at the Cal Neva Lodge and Casino to see who was hanging around the poker room. There was a four handed, low limit game of Seven Card Stud going on. I was bored and lonely so I put up two hundred dollars and asked to be dealt in.

My friend, The Peach, was dealing. The Peach was an old-time rounder from North Lake Tahoe. He was a great card player and particularly adept at Pinochle, Hearts and Gin. When it came to Gin, he loved playing it but he liked drinking it way more. He was one extremely intelligent, incredibly funny, hard-partying, decent human being. I had only played a few hands in the stud game when the phone rang at the poker room podium. The floorman said, "No, Missouri Dave isn't here."

"Hey," I shouted. "Who's calling for Dave?"

It was Trey Vedova calling from Hawaii. Trey was one of Dave's lifelong friends who went back to their younger days in Columbia, Missouri and was also a close buddy of mine. I took the call and when Trey asked what I was doing I told him I was playing in a small Stud game. Now, Trey was perhaps one of the worst poker players I knew, but he had a lot of money and loved to play. "Deal me in," he said.

My friend Rose Murray had just gotten off shift as a Blackjack dealer and was walking by. Rose was a gorgeous, red headed, big heart-ed, fun-loving sister with an all-world smile. I asked her to sit down and play for Trey by way of the telephone. She agreed. I introduced the two, and then I bought $200 in chips as a loan to Trey.

Before the cards were dealt, Trey said, "Wait, I can't play without a drink. I'll have a scotch on the rocks and get one for Rose and whoever else wants a drink."

The Peach dealt. Rose informed Trey what cards he had and what the other players exposed cards were, and when it was her turn to act, Trey told Rose what she was to do. Thus, began the process of Rose and Trey's phone-in poker routine. When the drinks arrived, Trey, through

Rose, tipped the cocktail waitress who set Trey's drink on the table next to the Peach. The cards were in the air; the game was on. In the middle of the next hand the Peach, from the dealer's chair, reached over, picked up Trey's scotch and gulped it down in one smooth stealth-like motion. I had never seen a casino dealer toss back a drink while dealing. I was impressed and I couldn't stop laughing.

After only twenty minutes of playing, Trey was $100 ahead, having won it all from me. He asked to be cashed out then paid me back the $200 loan. He thanked Rose and told her to take the winnings and spend it on herself.

Aloha and game over!

Richard Pryor

Missouri and I had just come from a Moody Blues concert and we were sitting at the bar in Caesars Tahoe next to the poker room. We were hanging with friends while still maintaining that glow great music produces; great music, that is, along with a few beers.

Randy Takamoto, the poker-room manager, approached us and told us that Richard Pryor had been in town all week playing in the poker room trying to learn Texas Hold'em. He'd been playing in the smallest games in order to educate himself at the lowest possible cost. Now he was ready to play in a bigger No-Limit Hold'em game. Randy asked us if we were interested in starting a game. He said he had a few local players who might be interested but needed us to get it going.

As a young man I was a huge fan of Richard Pryor from the first time I saw him on the Johnny Carson show. The man was flat-out funny and had his own hysterical brand of comedy. I had watched his career progress to doing stand-up in major venues to the making of many good films: *The Wiz, Stir Crazy, Silver Streak, Harlem Nights*, a long list of great performances. Consequently, playing in a poker game with Richard Pryor left me with the feeling of being in the presence of comedic royalty.

Normally Dave and I would not have an ounce of hesitation but just a moment before seeing Randy, Dave and I had each ingested a Quaalude. Still, this sounded too good to pass up.

We determined we would play $10/25 blinds and have a $5,000 minimum buy-in. We had Richard Pryor, Dave, myself and six other players, most of whom had usually exhibited *nitty* behavior, all ready to sit down and start the game. Being *nitty*, by definition, meant these players did not play in big games but also were the type of players who would only play in games full of live ones. They each dug deep into their pockets or put together partnerships to either afford the buy-in or limit the risk to their bankrolls.

Both Dave and I had been drinking and were about to be coming on to the Quaaludes. I liked ingesting an occasional Quaalude, if it was pharmaceutical grade, but I seldom played poker under their influence. This was probably going to be a big disadvantage. We would find out.

The game began. Richard Pryor was a very likable man. He was engaging, yet way out of his element, and it went without saying, he was the target. The story we heard was that he was very ill and dying and he was on his way to Hawaii to spend some of his final days on the islands. Lake Tahoe was just a stop along the way and he had always wanted to play in a big Texas Hold'em game. He was fulfilling that desire. Whether that was true or not, I had no idea.

Within the first few hands of the game Dave had a big hand and busted Mr. Pryor for his initial $5,000 buy-in. He bought in again for another $5,000.

A few hands later a local player called the Martian opened for $25 with a pair of tens (**10/10**). Pryor called the $25 with a pair of Queens (**Q/Q**). I called with a nine/seven (**9/7**) next to the button. The small blind folded and Dave with a seven/deuce (**7/2**), in for the $25 big blind, asked to see the flop. There was $110 in the pot.

The Flop was: **9...7...2** rainbow. The Quaaludes just started to kick in. Dave: (**7/2**). The Martian: (**10/10**). Pryor: (**Q,Q**). Me: (**9/7**). The Board: **9...7...2.** Pot: **$110.**

Dave bet $125, Martian called, Pryor raised to $300, I re-raised to $1,000 with top two pair. Dave tanked* for a long time. He agonized over his hand with bottom two pair and reluctantly threw his hand away. Martian immediately released his pair of tens. Pryor had no idea what to do and decided to go all-in. I immediately called. The pot weighed about **$10,000.**

At this point, I asked the dealer to hold the deck while Mr. Pryor and I discussed *doing some business*. I explained the situation to him and told him what the price would be of his pair of Queens winning against my two pair, and how we could each take some money out of the pot. He was lost with my explanation, even though I was speaking in a slightly

Quaalude induced slow and especially deliberate manner. What struck me as odd was here was a man with obviously an exceptionally high intellect, whose mind was historically razor sharp and he could not, at all, follow what I was telling him. I wondered if it was his illness? Was I, perhaps, slurring my words due to that pill I swallowed? Either way, no business was done. The last two cards a ten and an eight were dealt. Board: **9...7...2......10......8**.

I won the pot with two pair.

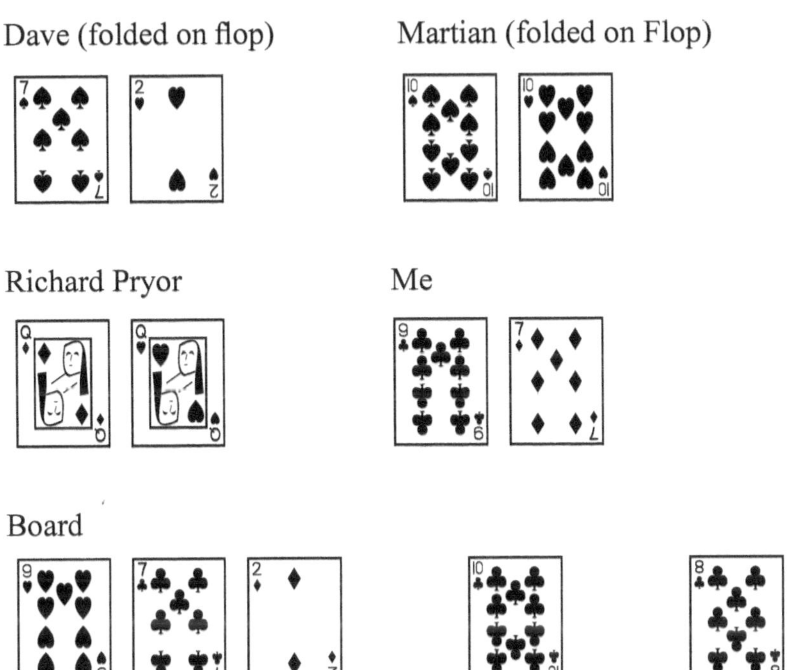

Richard Pryor graciously thanked us for the game, got up and retired. Dave and I played a couple of courtesy hands to allow him to leave the room and then we both cashed out winners. We went back to the bar, having only been gone for only about forty-five minutes, sat down just as the Quaaludes reached full impact, each with an additional $5,000 in our pockets.

Richard Pryor did not go off and die in Hawaii. He lived another 16 years until 2005 when he died of a fatal heart attack at his home in Los Angeles, California.

CHAPTER 5

PLAYING IN ENGLAND

In 1986, on the day Chernobyl began to melt down, I was flying home from London. It marked the end to a relationship with my Scottish sweetheart as well as the end of my close fifteen-year connection with England and Scotland. The UK was an important part of my life. I loved traveling to Manchester, London or Birmingham and playing poker with the Brits.

Howard Marks, Poker and a Hot Mercedes

I was driving through London late at night in a loud thunderous Mercedes Benz. The car did not have any paperwork and was possibly a stolen vehicle. What it did have was a broken muffler. London is an early-to-bed city; it was the late 1970s and pubs back then closed at 11:00pm. Other than coppers, there were very few cars on the road. The sound produced by a broken muffler reverberated off the tall city buildings, making my questionable Mercedes Benz on the streets of central London sound like a Sherman tank. I felt like a sitting duck. My paranoia had kicked in and I was trembling. How did I allow myself to get into this predicament? It started with Howard Marks.

I first met Howard Marks in Oxford. Howard, at that time, was reputed to be the world's biggest marijuana smuggler. He was a man wanted by the law. Howard would occasionally smuggle himself into the country to stay connected to his family and friends. I met Howard through Dr. Julian Peto, Howard's best mate while at Oxford University, and one of my dearest friends in England. Howard Marks was an extraordinary man. I respected that Howard only smuggled marijuana and hashish. He considered the dealing in hard drugs to be immoral. Occasionally over the years our paths crossed. During that time, we played some tennis, smoked some pot, drank a few pints and shared some stories. Howard was charming, extremely intelligent, funny and he had a remarkable zest for life. I found him to be a totally honorable man.

Howard Marks lived by his daring and his wits in an absurdly cavalier manner. I feel privileged to have known him. My favorite story, as it was told to me, involved his trial at the Old Bailey in London in 1981 for importing fifteen tons of Columbian marijuana from the USA into Great Britain. Howard's defense was centered on his claim that he was always acting for the good of the country as an agent of the British Secret Service. Howard claimed that in 1972 a mate of his from back at Balliol College at Oxford University, who was a British Secret Service agent, had made contact with him. Because Howard always ran in unconventional circles, Howard was recruited to seek and supply information on the IRA. The smuggling of marijuana was Howard's cover.

The British newspapers and tabloids picked up on this story and ran with it. Newspaper headlines inquired: *"Was Howard Marks a member of the British Secret Service?"* At the trial two things occurred in Howard's favor. First, for security reasons, no one from the secret service or the government came forward to deny Howard's story. Second, the prosecution conceded that Howard's Balliol connection was indeed real and Howard had been propositioned by someone from British Intelligence. In addition, Howard arranged for his support team to hire a Mexican actor that convinced his attorneys that he was a member of the Mexican Secret Service and he had dealings with Howard as his British counterpart.

At the eleventh hour, The Mexican, with no name and no credentials, testified for ten minutes in closed testimony that Howard had provided useful information on smuggled arms and drugs to the Mexican Secret service. Howard was to be found not guilty and was free to go. The following day, the headline in The Daily Mail read: *"15 Tons and What D'you Get?"*

Howard's infamy has been documented in three books: *High Time* (1985), *Hunting Marco Polo* (1991) and his autobiography, *Mr. Nice* (1997).

Soon after I first met Howard in Oxford we became friends. I knew Howard probably had some associates in London who, one might say, led alternative lifestyles. I asked if he might be able to find me a private poker game in England, and he did.

Howard arranged for me to play in a home game with some shady but trustworthy mates of his in a suburb of West London called Ealing. There was one catch. While in England, Howard had been driving an old Mercedes Benz he had borrowed and he wanted me to return it to one of the lads in the game. "No problem," I thought.

I was to meet his mates under the clock tower in the Ealing city center at midnight and we'd proceed to the poker game. When I picked up the Mercedes I found the muffler was broken and from it emanated a tremendously loud noise. Moreover, when I asked Howard about the car's registration, he said there was a slight problem. He said if I were to be pulled over by the police I would have to fake it! After I was about halfway to London I started putting the pieces together and realized I was driving what was likely a stolen vehicle.

My attempt to find a private home game in England is what led up to the mess I had muddled into that night. How I made it, I do not know. Finally at midnight, in the Ealing city center under the clock tower, I eagerly turned the Mercedes over to a mate of Howard's.

The poker game was Pot Limit Five Card Stud.* There were six players, plus myself. Howard's three friends turned out to be small-time thieves; to round out the field they brought their personal law-yers. The crooks were drinking and gambling and having a great time, while the attorneys were more subdued, drinking less alcohol and more coffee. The attorneys were less chatty and trying hard to build pots and then win them. In the end, the attorneys ended up with all the money and the crooks needed to set out in the morning to do more crooked things. I remember suspecting that perhaps the game was not totally on the square. My only evidence was finding a very small coffee smear on the back of an Ace. That was certainly not enough to obtain an indict-ment, only enough to raise reasonable doubt.

I had stayed about even all night and then won a decent pot as the game was winding down. That pot enabled me to leave with a small win. I caught a train back to London and then went on to Oxford. I was ecstatic to be a free man, no longer driving the Mercedes, and pleased with a few extra pounds in my pocket.

Perhaps the First Hand of Hold'em in London

At first I treated our yearly trips to England as a vacation, a break from playing poker as well as a chance to visit Karen's family and our friends. Eventually I started bringing what I thought was enough money to play cards.

When I played poker in the states, like most players, I wore what was comfortable. Most dressed casually, tracksuits seemed popular amongst card-players. I preferred a t-shirt, shorts, flip-flops and a ball cap in the summer and, in the winter months, a long sleeve shirt (often tie-dyed), blue jeans, cowboy boots and a straw cowboy hat. I was shocked to find that in order to play poker in a London casino I needed a membership and I needed to wear slacks and, at minimum, a sports coat. A membership was no problem but that attire thing was going to require a small investment.

I decided to play at the Victoria Sporting Club in London. The Vic was a fair-sized casino with Blackjack, Faro, Roulette and Baccarat on the first floor. The staff was decked out in tuxedos and bowties. The poker-room lived on the second floor and the costumes there were less severe. The first time I entered that poker-room, dressed in my newly acquired finery, I had the appearance of a hippie gone wrong. They regularly played Half-Pot-Limit Omaha* and Half-Pot-Limit Seven Card Stud. I became a frequent player at the Vic. I did happen to be there when they announced they were going to start what I believed to possibly be the first Half-Pot-limit Texas Hold'em game in London. It was scheduled for the following Friday night.

On that Friday, I traveled to London to play in the game. The Blinds were £5/5. Most players bought in for £1,000. I was really curious as to how these players played the game of Hold'em. The very first hand told me all I needed to know. The cards were dealt and five players bet and raised until they had each put in £420 (about $600 at the time) to see the flop. I don't remember the flop but it was fairly non-spectacular, something like: **8...5...2** rainbow.*

Three players checked and the fourth went all in. The fifth player folded, and so did all the others. As he was dragging in the pot, the winning player showed his hand, the **Jack/six of clubs**. If I had had that hand, not a shilling of my money would have gone into that pot. Furthermore, the player went all-in when he had a hand that had absolutely no connection whatsoever to the flop; it was a stone cold bluff. Now, here's the punch line: the player seated next to him who also put £420 in the pot said, "Hey mate, I had the same hand in hearts." What that hand told me was: 1) These players did not have a clue how to play Hold'em and, 2) The game could be dangerous but I could make a lot of money playing Hold'em here if my limited bankroll did not run out first. Not running out of money was the key.

Within a month the game moved to Baker Street at The Barracuda Casino. The game had gotten bigger as the Blinds were £5-5-10-20. The game had a good mix of strong and weak players. I was at a huge chip disadvantage because I was grossly underfunded for a game this size. Players were tossing around £1,000 chips like they were meaningless. In the end, I had to stop going to The Barracuda. I had to reckon with the fact that the game was far too big for my English bankroll.

I stuck to playing at the Victoria or going up to Birmingham to the Rainbow Casino.

"Look Mate, You've Taken All Our Readies"

Traveling to England was something I looked forward to. Karen's family lived in the north in a small village outside of Manchester called Hale Barns. The family home was an old coach house built in the late 1800s. Staying there was nice except I was always expected to work, starting in the very early mornings, in the family steel fabrication business. It was manual labor and because I was family, it was usually work without pay. So, I actually preferred to stay in Oxford where Karen had spent much of her youth. We had a good many friends there and I could sleep in late.

On one particular trip, as Karen and I were just wrapping up a lengthy stay in England, we were visiting friends and saying our goodbyes when I met a mate of Karen's who had just come down from the North Sea where he worked on the oil rigs. He explained that they would work for two weeks, earn high wages and then get one week off. When they were off work they would have a pocketful of money and they would be hankering for a good time. From Aberdeen they shipped to and from the oil rigs. I asked if there was any poker played in Aberdeen. He assured me there was. He said there were always a bunch of Texans contracted to work on the rigs who liked to play as well as a bunch of Brits who played. As far as he could tell the games were big.

Upon returning to the States, I had a plan, which I presented to Mark Porter, a friend and fellow poker player from North Tahoe.

Within ten days Karen, Mark and I flew to Manchester. We spent the night with Karen's family, hired a car and we were off to Scotland, Aberdeen bound. On a lark, we bought a book called *Castles of Scotland*. Our first night into Scotland we consulted our new book and found a castle located along our route. Next to the castle, we found a charming country inn to stay in. We had drinks in the local pub, had a great dinner and a good sleep. In the morning we took a tour of the castle. From then on, *Castles of Scotland* provided the template for the next month and, although we found a poker game in Aberdeen, it was small and our interest in playing was trumped by the joy derived from good food, lively pubs, historic accommodations and castles. We returned home having never taken a flop. Karen and I would return to Scotland some years later after I had started playing poker in Birmingham.

*****

Birmingham sits between Manchester to the north and Oxford to the south. At the Rainbow Casino in Birmingham, No-Limit Texas Hold'em was played. I had played there quite a bit and had a couple of friends there who were top players in England. One of them was Derek Baxter, who had told me about The Rainbow when he and I played heads-up at The World Series of Poker. The other was Derek Webb, who would go on to create the casino game called Three Card Poker. He would one day become my mentor in the development of my own casino game, High Country Poker. It was in Birmingham, on a trip down from Manchester, that I had a most memorable night of poker.

On this particular excursion, Karen had decided to join me. We traveled south by train and checked into a small boutique hotel recommended by the poker-room manager, Tony Saracine. He told me the two owners of the hotel played in the Rainbow game. For me, poker had not gone well this time over. I had started the trip with a playing bankroll of £2,500 sterling (about $3,800) and was down to my last £350 when I started playing that night.

The poker game went until the casino closed. One of the players, a partner in the hotel, said if anyone wanted to continue playing, we could go to his hotel and play a private game. I was about even for the night, and since I was staying there and I loved a short-handed game, I was excited to play. We were to be joined by this very friendly, young Greek who was a local backgammon hustler. We were playing No-Limit Hold'em; the blinds were £5/10 and we took turns dealing. The Greek bought in for a couple hundred quid and went broke in the first hour. I bought in for 350 quid and was winner when the Greek busted out.

After that, the hotel owner and I began playing heads-up. I knew I was in a good situation. I was a way better player and my opponent was not only a poor player but also an out of control gambler. I kept busting him and he kept going to the safe and coming back with more cash. After the sun rose, many trips to the safe later, we took a break. The safe was now empty and my opponent owed me £400. At that point, we needed to wait for the banks to open so he could settle his debt and reload, then we could continue playing.

Karen came downstairs and asked how I was doing. Karen grew up thinking a five-pound note was plenty of money, and when she saw the huge quantity of five, ten and twenty-pound notes in my possession her eyes popped out of her head. That's when Frankie came and introduced himself to me as the other owner of the hotel. He told me the game was over. OK, it was over but, as I explained to Frankie, I was still owed the four hundred quid that I had lent his partner. I will always remember Frankie's words to me: "Look mate, you've taken all our readies (ready cash), can you let us off the hook for the four-hundred we owe?"

And I thought why not? I had made a pretty big score and I wanted to be certain we could get out of Dodge with the dough. So I said, "Sure, we're good." I put all the money in a large paper sack, retired to our room and went to bed.

When I woke we emptied the sack. The biggest denomination at that time in the UK was a fifty-pound note; I had started the game with seven of them. The rest of the sack contained notes of £5, £10 and a few of £20, thus, the stacks of bills were fairly large in volume. Besides the seven £50 notes I started with, we counted £5,650, all in smaller bills, which would not all fit into the shoulder bag I carried. We packed up and caught the train back to Karen's family home in Manchester. We felt overwhelming relief that I had turned a disappointing poker trip into a success.

*****

The Edinburgh Fringe Festival (The Fringe) started in 1947, as artists from around the world were attracted to the Edinburgh International Festival. The Fringe is the world's largest celebration of arts and culture, with over forty thousand performances in over three hundred venues. Karen and I celebrated our newfound wealth by making a bed in the back of a hired van and treating ourselves to three weeks of international artistic creativity, enjoying the good life in the heart of a very festive Edinburgh.

*****

About twenty-five years later, Missouri Dave was traveling around England and while playing in a poker game at the Rainbow Casino he met Frankie. Dave told him he was from Lake Tahoe, prompting Frankie to tell him that many years ago a guy from Lake Tahoe stayed at his hotel and beat his partner out of a lot of money. "Yeah," Dave told him. "I know both the guy and the story well." A few years after that, I met Frankie again when he came to visit Dave and we spent a few days in Lake Tahoe together hanging out on Dave's boat and telling old war stories. When Frankie first showed up at Dave's house, before I even saw him, I recognized his voice when he walked in the door and said, "Look mate, you've taken all our readies." We both had a good laugh!

CHAPTER 6
COCAINE & POKER

Cocaine & Poker

I woke to find a cord around my neck. I was confused as to where I was. The cord wasn't choking me but it was nevertheless wrapped snugly around my neck. I traced one end of the cord to the telephone on the overnight stand. Under the covers I located the telephone handset, I then unwrapped the cord and re-assembled the telephone. Slowly my whereabouts began coming to me. I was at the Reno Peppermill in a hotel room. I had been in a poker game, a very long and drug-crazed poker game. It came to me – sixty-five straight hours. I remembered doing the math when I finally stood up and left the table. Then came the jolt. It was the huge, unsettling jolt of reality I experienced nearly every time I woke after having lost a lot of money in a poker game. I didn't know how much I lost but I knew it was a fairly big sum for a moderate size game. Clues to the number in question could be attained by looking through the pile of dirty clothes lying by the bed. In that mess would be a list I kept of all the people I lent money to and borrowed money from to keep that train of cocaine induced insanity chugging along for all sixty-five hours. Between that tally sheet, my check ledger, which recorded the checks I cashed, and the cash in my extremely thin money clip, all the bad news I could stand would be provided.

I came to Reno not planning on spending the night in the hotel. On Thursday I sat down in a \$15/30 Limit Hold'em game at 5:00pm. I stood up from the game for the final time at 10:00am. on Sunday morning. The poker room manager arranged for a room from which I must have made a phone call. I must have fallen asleep with the phone in my ear, which would explain the cord around my neck. I was positive it was not an attempted suicide; no, those thoughts have never entered my mind.

Sixty-five hours in a poker game was, and still is, my personal best, or personal worst, depending on one's perspective. I choose to go with personal worst. The \$3,200 I lost was nowhere near a personal record, but for mid-limit poker game in 1980 dollars, it was slightly stunning and very depressing. The game was a foggy memory. I'm sure certain hands haunted me (the bad ones always did) but I had absolutely no recollection of any of them. What I do recall is many trips to the men's room to suck white powder up my nose-holes. For those trips, I paid a big price monetarily, as well as with my health and in the loss of countless brain cells.

This story goes back to 1972 when Karen and I had accepted an offer of a room in my pal Joe West's house in Davis, California. One evening a friend came by and we found ourselves staring at some scraped up lines of white powder on a mirror. I was handed a straw and told to go for it. I naively asked what it was and was told it was cocaine and that it wouldn't hurt me. I had very little idea of what cocaine even was. That soon changed. We, like so much of America, were about to become quite familiar with the tsunami of white powder that was simultaneously about to sweep over the United States and also transform many South American countries into violent, broken, narco-states.

Fast-forward about three or four years and cocaine had become far more prevalent. At first, I was an occasional user. My focus was on being a successful poker player and there was not a big place for cocaine in my world. However, as poker success and readily available cash became the norm, my cocaine use became more frequent. I started playing longer white-powder-fueled hours. Games would go around the clock and often I would go with them. I also found I would have great success in playing cards starting early in the mornings in games that had gone through to the next day. These games were usually short-handed and that was one of the places where I excelled. I would be fresh and my opponents would have been transformed into crazed gamblers. Sometimes the opposite occurred and I was the all-night crazed gambler. In those instances, I usually had the wherewithal to pick up and go home when the fresh players started to arrive.

Cocaine, for the most part, had a devastating effect on the poker economy. An untold amount of money was withdrawn from that economy, one gram at a time. When playing, it was so easy to go in on a gram of coke with another player. It only required each removing a green chip or two from his stack and contacting one of the many coke dealers hanging around. Often, they were in the same game with you. So many players, wherever one went, were playing poker under the influence of the drug. For a while it was energy-packed fun. Playing for hours and hours with strangers and friends, drinking and gambling, hooting and hollering, stacking chips, or going broke and desperately borrowing money to stay in action and eventually finding your bed to sleep forever.

I played a lot at Caesar's Tahoe. The poker room was situated close to a very large men's room. One evening my friend Dale returned from that men's room, handed me the bindle we shared and told me matter-of-factly that he was quite upset. "Can you imagine," he said with a grin, "someone had the nerve to come in and take a dump in the cocaine lounge."

One morning my friend Joe B, one of the best heads-up players around, had played through the night with a good, established, older player. The older player, who had never so much as smoked a joint, told Joe B he was getting really tired but wanted to continue to play and he knew some of the guys did something to help them stay awake and alert. He wanted to know if Joe B could help him out. It so happened Joe had just purchased a gram of coke and told his opponent to follow him to the men's room. Reaching under the stall Joe B handed him the full one-gram bindle and a straw. The guy snorted some and left the men's room. Joe B caught up with him at the table and asked for the bindle back. He was told he thought he was supposed to do it all and had thrown the empty bindle away! Joe B's opponent was a super tight player, that was, until the game resumed. The pace of the game, according to Joe B, picked up mightily.

At another time, Missouri Dave and I thought we would host a home game. We covered our dining room table with a blanket, invited a bunch of players and held a good $5/10 No-limit Hold'em game. Amongst those we invited was our favorite cocaine dealer. We started taking $10 out of each pot that held over $200 and putting that $10 into a jar. When the jar held $100 we would buy a gram of coke from our in-house dealer. We would then pour the coke on the plate that never emptied and passed it around the table as the game went on. About three or four hours into the game the cocaine dealer took me aside to thank me for inviting him to the game. I responded, "Hey man, you are losing over $4,000."

He replied, "Yeah, but business is great." That was the nature of the drug; everything was twisted and convoluted but business was great.

On the upside, games often lasted for days and days nonstop. Action was incredible.

On the downside, players started going broke. People changed for the worse. The rest is well-documented. Mortgages, rents and bills went unpaid. Relationships suffered. Families separated. Jobs were lost. Nations were destroyed. Crack. Ice. Crystal meth. It was a steep fast downhill slide over the edge into the dark side.

As for me, I lost my way.

After a time, snorting cocaine ceased to be fun. It started to make me feel bad rather than good. I became way too emotional, way too temperamental. I became a sore loser, often a raging jerk in poker games. I stopped treating the game with respect.

I eventually came to the realization that I needed to break the grip cocaine had on my life. Quite often amongst our group of gamblers, a person would make a bet that was meant to help them make an adjustment in his lifestyle. For example, stop smoking bets were a very lucrative source of income for me. Weight bets were common. Overall, weight bets were pretty much a cinch for the person not on the diet to win. So, I decided to make a cocaine bet. I made a $500 bet with Rick Ketcher: first one to do coke paid up. I lost the bet once and had to pay the $500. Then we renewed our bet. However, I often made the effort to locate Rick by telephone, and I would then bargain for a one-night pass. Passes cost $25 to $50. I paid him plenty for one-night passes over the next year or so. He never paid me a dime. In the end, I managed to stop doing cocaine completely. What I found then was, in the local poker games, I started getting all the money. Eventually most of my cocaine-snorting pals followed suit and quit too.

The poker economy recovered. I did too. People may or may not still imbibe while playing poker. I really don't know. It is an absolute certainty that the current crop of players, if they do it at all, do not involve themselves with cocaine on the scale that players did through the late 70's and well into the 80's. That was indeed a crazy time. There are periods during that time that remain a cross between hazy, out of control dreams and total nightmares. That all passed. I was one of the lucky ones who came out the other side.

CHAPTER 7

BINION'S WORLD SERIES OF POKER
(WSOP)

Binion's World Series of Poker (WSOP)

One evening in 1949 a famous gambler and poker professional named Nick 'the Greek' Dandalos visited Binion's Gambling Hall, a casino owned by Benny Binion. After dropping several thousand dollars at the craps table, Nick engaged Benny in conversation and asked where he could get a heads up, high limit poker game. Benny thought it over and said he'd try to arrange a game under the condition that they play in public as an attraction for the casino. Nick agreed.

Benny telephoned his old friend Johnny Moss from Odessa, Texas, a top professional poker player, and persuaded Johnny to come to Las Vegas and play heads up against Nick. For five months Nick and Johnny publicly played nearly every form of poker. Johnny hardly ever slept but Nick, it has been said, never slept. The match was billed as the 'game of poker giants' and folks flocked to Binion's Gambling Hall to watch them play. Five months after the legendary match began, with Johnny ahead somewhere between $2 and $4 million dollars, Nick famously said, "Mr. Moss, I have to let you go."

That match put poker on the map and planted the seeds for the World Series of Poker that began twenty years later in 1970. That first year, by vote of the players, Johnny Moss was declared the winner.

The World Series of Poker;
An Overview

Nothing I've ever been a part of could produce the stimulus or match the intensity and the grandeur of Las Vegas and playing at the annual World Series of Poker. Each year, for nearly a decade, it was the most anticipated activity in my life. It bolstered my confidence and defined, for me, where I fit amongst the larger community of poker players. And, I had a hell of a lot of fun.

* * * * *

It was good to have wheels when staying a month in Las Vegas so I usually drove from Lake Tahoe. It was also good to stay at the Golden Nugget because that's where the very best rooms in downtown Las Vegas were, and, after all, Binion's would pick up my entire room bill. After I valeted my car, checked into my room and had my bags brought up, I would immediately head down the elevator and make a beeline for the Nugget's front corner exit. In an instant I'd feel the warmth of the desert breeze accompanied by the familiar rush of adrenalin as I crossed the neon-lit Fremont Street at the heart of downtown Las Vegas and made my way towards the glittering wall of lights of Binion's Horseshoe.

Upon entering through the open-air front of the casino, my senses would be jarred by the familiar sounds of gambling: the distinct clang of coins banging against the metal trays in the sea of slot machines, the shouts from the craps table, the hum of loud talk and ongoing parties around the bar, bells and whistles and whoopin' and hollerin.' Welcome to Binion's Horseshoe Casino, home of The World Series of Poker! It was easy to sense the constant excitement in the air competing with the ever-present smell of tobacco smoke and yesterday's beverages left to marinate in the carpet. At the long oval bar in the middle of the casino I would be greeted by a constant procession of old friends from around the country. The poker community in the 70's and 80's was a small one and it seemed like I knew an awful lot of players and was aware of so many more. Each of those familiar faces represented a relationship, a story or a hand once played. I always felt it an honor to be a participant in The World Series of Poker. To play with both the very best players from around the country as well as some of the biggest 'producers.'* For every hometown champ there were all the hometown wannabes who would come to take their shot at poker fame and fortune.

After a short stroll beyond the bar, I would begin to hear the unmistakable cricket-like sound of the shuffling of poker chips. I would walk towards the small cramped poker room, a room that I would spend much of my time throughout the next month; there the socializing slowed as the focus and concentration was directed at the green felt tables. My feelings were simultaneously familiar and exhilarating. This room would be central to the many highs and lows I would experience in the days ahead with fortuitous cards and cards so torturous I would question why I even played this game. It would also be central to the many stories soon to be lived and then talked about in the months to come. In that moment I would become anxious to take a seat and begin competing, but my personal rule required me to sleep a night on a travel day before playing. It would be my first night in town and at that point my self-discipline would be strong enough to send me to bed.

There was a great book written about the 1981 WSOP, called *The Biggest Game in Town* by Al Alvarez. It was one of the best poker books I had ever read. It captured the immersive feel of being in and around the biggest games and the best players in that incomparable environment of Binion's Horseshoe.

At the WSOP, there were players from across the country and from around the world. The southerners, particularly from the gulf states of Texas and Louisiana comprised a big faction of the top players. They were, for the most part, colorful characters. Some wore cowboy hats, some wore suspenders, some carried coke bottles to spit their chew in. They had their own hilarious expressions (like, "Bank frogs don't croak," meaning if you're on the rail* watching the game then you shouldn't say anything about the hand in progress). So many of these guys had been raised playing Texas Hold'em. Among them was a Cajun named Junior Prejean. Junior seldom played in the biggest games; he was content applying his skills in medium level contests, but, to me, he was one of the toughest players I ever played against. There were so many good, jam-up players from that part of the world: Jack Straus, Crandall Addington, Bobby Hoff, Carl McKelvey, Bill O'Conner, Steve Lott, the great Dody Roach, Jessie Alto, Bob Hooks, Betty Carey and Bill Smith, just to name a few.

From Florida came Dewey Tomko, a kindergarten teacher who discovered he could sit in a poker game with the best players in the world.

New York and the east coast had a lot of big games, mostly private, and had its share of elite players, among them: Jay Heimowitz, Eric Seidel, Mickey Appleman and Dan Harrington.

The Pacific Northwest had a good poker contingent with stars like Yosh Nakano, Tom Hood, and Ralph Morten. The Razor came from Montana.

Las Vegas was the home of big-name players, who collectively might have been the best in the world. These were the marquee players, the big stars. Many were Texas transplants, like Doyle Brunson, Johnny Moss and Amarillo Slim. There was Bobby Baldwin from Tulsa, Oklahoma; Stu Ungar from New York; Bones Berland from Los Angeles; Chip Reese from Ohio and Johnny Chan, born in China but a Las Vegas resident since he was 21.

Then there was our contingent from Reno and Lake Tahoe. Missouri Dave and Flyer were already known and well respected. Aside from my other cronies there was Hans 'Tuna' Lund, Brad Daugherty, Young Scott and Railroad Mac. Some of us were relatively new and had begun to get some recognition as decent players.

From abroad there came a few outstanding players, like Donnacha O'Dea from Ireland and Derek Webb from Derby, England. One night I ended up playing heads up with a strong British player named Derek Baxter. From Derek, that night, I learned of the games in London and Birmingham. More European and South American players were starting to make the trip to Las Vegas.

Back in the day, the WSOP was so extraordinary because of the incredible hospitality extended to players by the Binion family. Binion's Horseshoe either comped player's rooms in The Horseshoe's hotel or picked up their room bills at nearby establishments. Furthermore, Binion's provided an excellent and exclusive breakfast and dinner buffet for players at no charge. The dinner buffets were nothing short of a culinary sensation with a steady stream of gourmet delights, such as wild game, rattlesnake, live Maine lobster and a plethora of international cuisines. As guests of Binion's, players could sign for comped meals in the coffee shop. After so many years, my mouth still waters to remember the world's best chili made with filet mignon at the snack bar.

Back then, the small poker room for live games had, as memory serves me, only seven tables. Later it expanded with a huge outdoor tent that accommodated the constantly growing popularity of the event. With so few tables, games were, at times, hard to get into. That meant that the poker rooms across the street at the Golden Nugget and The Four Queens were booming with overflow. At those places the games were always smaller than at Binion's, but players of all levels of skill and size of bankroll were able to make the trip and rub elbows with poker's best and most storied players.

Another popular hang for our crowd was a small bar at the Golden Nugget that was located on the way to the hotel elevators. There we could gather after playing to drink, process and unwind. We would discuss the tough river card that knocked someone out of a tournament or cost one his bankroll. We would relive winning big pots or bring up old friends we ran into. We'd talk story. We'd flirt with the cocktail waitresses.

The first week the cash games at the WSOP were always fantastic. After that a lot of weaker players went broke and headed home.

Some players only took that first week off from work and then returned home. In weeks number two and three, the games would tighten up and became a whole lot tougher. I usually played a few tournaments and less in live games during that time. About the fourth week more players started arriving in town in anticipation of the Main Event. The lights would get brighter and the games again picked up steam.

The Whuppin' Room

During The World Series of Poker days and nights would often be turned upside down. It was one of those nights. I had just awakened, showered and meandered into the poker room. I locked up a seat in a $10/25 No-Limit Hold'em game by putting down a $500 stack of green chips in front of my seat. I told the dealer I needed a cup of coffee and a bite to eat and I headed downstairs for my breakfast before the closing of the player's dinner buffet.

About midway through eating, Blackie Blackburn came running downstairs and found me.

Blackie was a Las Vegas fixture, both as a poker player and as one working in some capacity of management. We did not run in the same circles but Blackie knew me. I remember when my friend Paul Parker, a poker player and a dedicated world traveler, came to me one day and asked if I knew Blackie Blackburn. He said he had been traveling in Nepal and had found a casino in Katmandu that had a poker room being run by a certain Blackie Blackurn. When Blackie discovered Paul was from Lake Tahoe, Blackie asked Paul if he knew Missouri Dave or me. What a small world it is.

That night in the basement buffet of Binion's, Blackie approached me and asked, "Glen, did you put $500 down on the table in the $10/25 game?"

"I did."

"Well some guy came by, grabbed the chips and was walking away with them. A couple players raised the alarm. You should get up there right away."

I shot upstairs to find Jack Binion himself and a security guard detaining the would-be-thief. Jack was the President and General Manager of Binion's Horseshoe. He was also the eldest son of Benny Binion, the reputed former Texas outlaw and the legendary founder of Binion's Horseshoe.

I recall the first time I saw Benny Binion. He came in from a cold rainy night directly into the poker room. He was wearing a huge fur coat, blue jeans, cowboy boots and a Stetson so large it made his head look small. He wasn't a big man but he had a huge presence. There could be no doubt as to who he was. He sat by himself away from the poker games, and was immediately brought a shot of whiskey.

Unlike his father, Jack was a suit-and-tie guy. He was also a highly respected leader in both the gambling industry and the poker community. Jack was a down-to-earth, good human being. Like his father, Jack loved poker and the folks that played it. Jack himself would often sit in one of the bigger games. He was a formidable opponent and needless to say, to him money was no object. Jack went out of his way to get a sense of who was who amongst the poker players and he always made a point of saying hello to me and welcoming me back to the World Series.

So, that night, Jack asked, "Glen, did you put $500 down on this table in the #4 seat?" When I told him I did, Jack pondered the situation for a bit and then told the thief that he was going to give him a break. He was to be immediately escorted out the door and off the premises and told to never step foot in there again.

I sat down in the game and the consensus was that the thief had dodged a major bullet. Thieves were usually not able to walk away from the Horseshoe so easily, if they were able to walk at all.

Sitting across from me in the game that night was a highly regarded player called Ironman. He was an owner of a jewelry store and an old poker player from Arlington, Texas. Although Ironman was rather diminutive he had a big reputation. Curiously, when playing poker, he always looked over his wire-rimmed glasses that were usually sliding down his nose. He was called Ironman for his preference of irons over drivers when playing golf, though it could have just as well been because his poker game was solid as iron. He never got out of line, he never gave away a dime and he was a master of No-Limit Texas Hold'em. I hadn't played much with Ironman but I had been told plenty about him from friends who had. When asked how the games were back home, Ironman said, "The games were really good; the players bet when they have something and they call when they don't!" Curtis Skinner, aka The Ironman, was a fixture at The World Series and at Amarillo Slim's Super Bowl of Poker. I decided I would always *play around* the gentleman (meaning, I would not play in a pot he was in when I could avoid doing so).

An interesting thing about Binion's was that they hired incredibly large human beings to work as security guards. Certainly, they were not the type of people one would want to tangle with. And, like many old school casinos, Binion's had a reputation for being a place where one absolutely did not want to fall into its bad graces. There are stories about people who crossed over the line that did not end well.

About an hour after I joined the poker game, someone pointed across the room and said, "Look over there, it's that thief Jack kicked out." There he was walking through the casino. And directly behind him, closing in fast, was the biggest security guard I'd ever seen, and ten yards behind that big security guard was an even bigger one. The Ironman was a soft-spoken man of very few words and when he spoke people listened. I will never forget his words, "Oh, my," he said in his slow Texas drawl, "They're going to take him to the 'whuppin' room.'"

Top Hat Ken Smith

Of the many unforgettable characters I have run across, the visual of Ken Smith stands out. Ken was a Texan from Dallas, a Master Chess Champion, who once prepped the International Grand Chess Master, Bobby Fischer, for one of his most important international matches. Ken was a skilled poker player. Twice he made the final table at Binion's World Series of Poker with a third and a fourth-place finish in the World Championship event. He received bracelets for winning several other events at Binion's as well. He also won tournaments at Amarillo Slim's Super Bowl of Poker. Ken, like many other geniuses, was an eccentric.

Ken was a large man, a really large man. He had a trimmed white beard and wire-rim glasses. Ken's signature look, when playing poker, included a black silk top hat, a bow tie and a black tuxedo. He was quite easy to spot in any poker room already crowded with characters. The capper was every time Ken won a decent pot he would stand up, lift his top hat above his head, flutter that top hat and say loudly in his high-pitched, squeaky voice, "Oooooh, whatta player!"

That was, Oooooh, whatta sight to see!

The Best Laid Plans

I stood on the rail anxiously watching the last four players at the final table of a 1982 WSOP tournament event. For two reasons the event stood out to me. First, extraordinarily, two of the players had 95% of the chips on the table; the other two sat mortally wounded with so few chips, each was trying to hang on and outlast the other long enough to move up a place to third and an extra $12,300 payout. Second, and exciting to me, one player was my good friend Art Jungblut and I had a 5% stake in his winnings in this No-Limit Hold'em tournament. First place paid $123,000 and I stood to be paid $6,150 if Art finished first. The two chip leaders had almost equal stacks

Art was an attorney from New Jersey, who had built a home in North Lake Tahoe. He would spend most of the summers at the lake. Art was an excellent poker player and we played together a lot. One year we made an agreement that any time the two of us were both entered in the same tournament we would automatically exchange 5% of our action. This was to be a lifetime arrangement.

With $246,000 in chips in action, Art and Ralph Morton, a top player from Yakima, Washington, each had over $115,000 in chips in front of him; the other two had under $16,000 between them. The buzzer had just gone off for a 15-minute break.

The way tournaments work is, as each player "in the money" is eliminated, that player wins the amount of money designated to the respective rank of that player's finish. With four players left the prize money breakdown went as follows: 4th place: $12,300, 3rd place: $24,600, 2nd place: $49,200, and 1st place: $123,000.

Art came out of the men's room with ten minutes left in the break. I grabbed him and we went for a walk. First I told him how well he had been playing. Then I wanted to talk to him about what I was certain he already knew; he and Ralph were almost guaranteed first and second place unless one of the other players caught lightning in a bottle and managed to run his chips up. This was highly unlikely as both were at such a massive chip disadvantage. The other two players were so low on chips that they could barely make the huge blinds that were coming around fast. As each player was eliminated, the ensuing payout went way up for the remaining players. The most important thing for both Art and Ralph at this point in the tournament was to avoid, at all cost, playing a big pot against each other until the two players with small stacks were eliminated. Period. Art understood without question. It should not take long to be down to Ralph and Art. At that point, they would have the option of making some sort of "deal." For example if they both had about the equal amount of chips then they might decide to split the prize money of the top two spots giving them each $86,200. That would be a pretty good payday. Memo to Art: **Do not play a significant Pot with Ralph Morton until the two small stacks are eliminated.**

We returned to the tournament area. I went to the men's room. When I came back to the poker table I could not believe my eyes. Art and Ralph had gone all-in against each other. They had almost identical size chip stacks. One player was destined to win $123,000 and the other $12,300.

Ralph had been dealt two Aces (**A/A**) and Art Ace/Jack of spades (**A♠/J♠**). A Jack and two small spades flopped and, absurdly, all the money went in.

Ralph   Art

Board

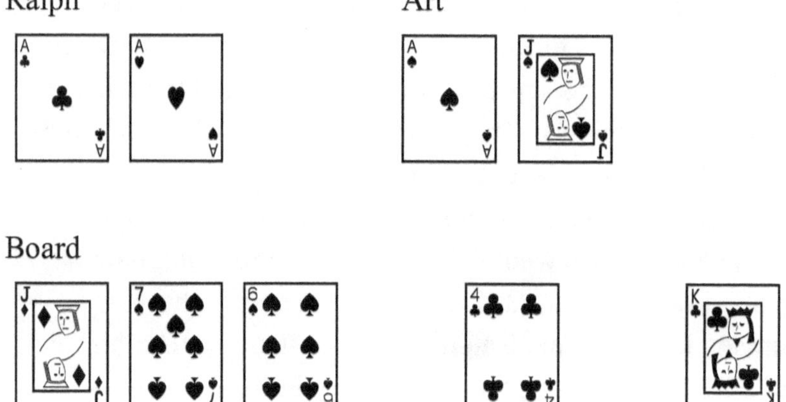

If Ralph and Art had played the hand like it should have been played, Art would never have called Ralph's raise before the flop. If he had called and they both had seen the flop, they both would have checked the hand down. Then neither jeopardized their standing relative to the two players with almost no money left, both of whom were destined to go broke within a few hands.

Art, unfortunately, took down fourth place money, $12,300.

Within five minutes of that hand the tournament was over. The two players with almost no money left each moved up a pay station. What a gift they received!

Suitcase Jimmy

I've played poker with Suitcase Jimmy.

I've sat with Jimmy at the bar where we drank and shared stories.

This is how I imagined his work in South America: somewhere in the jungles of Peru or Bolivia a hardworking American called Jimmy went about his business of setting up another site for the drilling of oil. He handled all the logistics required for the construction of the site: the cutting of trees, excavating the site, bringing in running water, dealing with sewage and doing whatever else would be required to make a small city in the jungle function. He coordinated the arrival of equipment and supervised the assembly necessary for a great deal of machinery. He oversaw the construction of the kitchen, the dining hall and the housing for the many workers, mostly men, he would employ. When he completed those tasks, he settled into the on-site administrative office for the global petroleum corporation that extracted oil from the jungle and dispatched it to their refineries. This man worked ten or eleven months a year and made a shit-load of money. When his downtime came, he headed to Las Vegas for The World Series of Poker.

*   *   *   *   *

Jimmy stepped out of the cab and checked into a suite at The Golden Nugget. After a shower and a shave he entered the poker room to many greetings, handshakes and hugs. "Bienvenido amigo!" "Welcome, Suitcase Jimmy!"

Jimmy was a solidly built man about 5'11" tall. His shoulders were a bit rounded and the lines in his face spoke of a man who had worked outdoors for many years. Jimmy wore a white short sleeved, button-up shirt and a gray short-brimmed hat that was not quite a cowboy hat and yet not a fedora. He had a warm smile and the eyes of one excited to be right there, right then. And Jimmy carried a small suitcase or *maleta* as it's called in Spanish. Jimmy's *maleta* was always completely stuffed full of bundles of $100 bills. Over the next few weeks, Jimmy intended to enjoy his cash as he played poker with some of the best players in the world.

When Jimmy sat down in a poker game there would be a rush of eager players who scrambled to get a seat. The noise created by feet rushing to the new game sounded like a herd of buffalo. The game immediately filled and a long waiting list formed. All of this hasty jockeying for position spoke to just how much money Jimmy might lose each time he sat. To the poker novice, the sound of buffalo in a poker room could be a gigantic source of curiosity. But, not to those who were in the know.

I remember one session when I was the first up on the list. While I played in a game one table away from Jimmy's game, I had to keep one eye on his game and the other eye on the list. After several hours a seat finally opened and the floor-man started to seat another player ahead of me. I made a big stink and was awarded my rightful seat. Then, the other player demanded the floor-man give him his $100 bribe back! That was the way it was. Over the years I played a few times with Jimmy and his suitcase was always in action. When he would go all in, he would yell: "*Maleta*"!

One particular night I played one big pot with Jimmy; it was for all my money. I held **A/10** and Jimmy held **A/7**. The flop was: **A...A...10**. All the money went in. A five slid off the deck on 4th street. **$8,000** sat in the pot and Jimmy was down to being able to catch only one of the two remaining tens in the deck for a tie. Out of the forty-four remaining cards up popped one of those foul looking tens to give Suitcase Jimmy half of that $8,000 and me the other half along with some instant poker nausea.

Me   Suitcase Jimmy

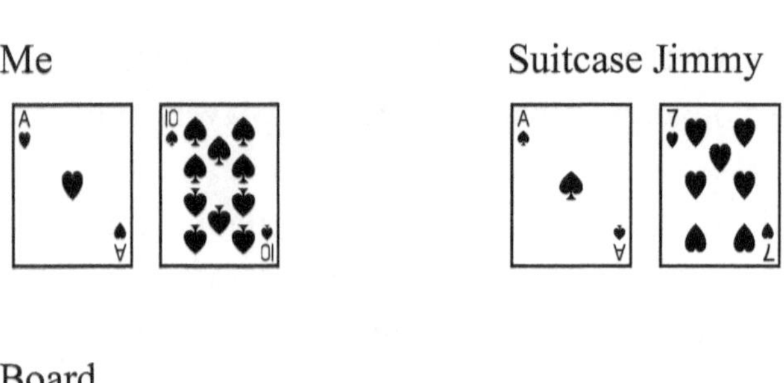

Board

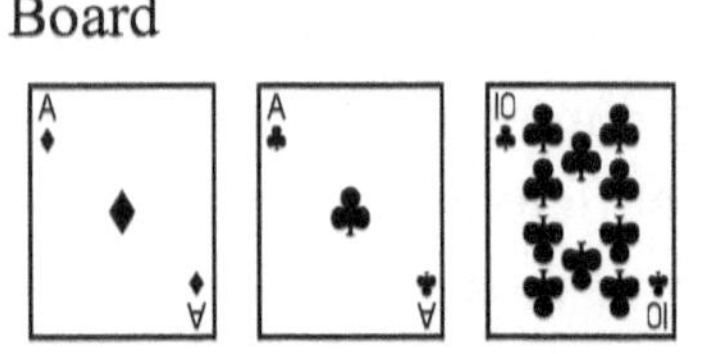

The pot was about $8,000 when we both had made Aces full of tens.

I enjoyed playing with Suitcase Jimmy above and beyond the fact that he lost a lot of money. He was a sweet man and, as he did every year, he really loved his down time in Las Vegas. He was hugely interesting, eager for conversation and maintained an exceptionally good outlook on life.

As he did every year, Jimmy left Las Vegas with a big smile and an empty suitcase.

Thanks for the Opportunity

Missouri and I were at the World Series of Poker one year when I ran into him at breakfast.

Dave told me, "I've got some good news and some bad news for you."

"OK, give me the good news."

Dave said he got in a game last night with a certain Robert T. This guy was one of the biggest 'producers' in the mid-size No-Limit Hold'em games at the tournament. Without a doubt he was one of the guys we definitely wanted to play with.

"The good news," Dave informed me, "is that you had half my action. The bad news, however, is we lost $5,000 and you owe me $2,500."

I thanked Dave, sincerely, for the opportunity as I reached in my pocket, counted out twenty-five one-hundred-dollar bills and handed them to him. No questions asked.

"Gentlemen, This Poker is All Right"

Missouri Dave, his sweetheart Mindy and I had been in Las Vegas for the World Series of Poker for about a month. I had played a lot of poker over that month and I was out of energy and out of cash. Dave, on the other hand, had not played a lot of poker. In fact, he spent most of the month traveling with Mindy between the swimming pool, the nicer restaurants and their room in the Golden Nugget.

Towards the end of the month-long gathering when Dave was finally ready to play he hopped into a big $25/50 blind No-Limit Hold'em game with some of the world's biggest and best players. Woefully, Dave kept running into bad luck and began borrowing money to keep playing. He was making a good comeback when a most unfortunate hand came down. Before the flop the pot was raised and re-raised. The flop was: **Q...8...4**. All the money was in the pot. The pot was big enough to get Dave even and make him a small winner. Dave held **two Aces** and his opponent had an **Ace** and a **Queen** giving him a **pair of Queens** with an **Ace kicker**. The pot held over **$32,000**. On 4th Street the board paired fours. The river brought a **Queen**, one of only two cards in the deck with which he could lose that monstrous pot.

Dave was stunned and Dave was broke. He was a $30,000 loser for that play and for the trip. He stood and walked away.

The next afternoon, we were at the front desk of the Golden Nugget checking out. Our plan was to drive my VW Van back to California and on to Fresno where we would visit Mindy's cousin, Tony, on his ranch and vineyard. Our hotel rooms were comped so we only had to take care of incidentals, that is, items charged to the room. Thus, I paid less than $100 for a month-long stay. Even though Dave's room was also comped and they could have eaten every meal at Binion's as guests of the Binion family, Dave and Mindy had, instead, chosen to charge most of their meals to their room and to also utilize room service. The printout of one month's charges started spitting out of the computer. Page after page after page, the computer rattled on, expelling a massive stream of paper documenting over $1,700 worth of food and beverage charges. Mindy covered it all with her credit card and now all three of us were broke-broke.

We were standing in valet parking, poised to hit the road when Dave said, "Wait a second," and headed straight out to the swimming pool area. Word had gotten around that Missouri had lost all his money, was broke and was borrowing. Thus when Dave approached two of Tahoe's tightest, non-lending poker players and said he needed a small loan, those two guys, who were expecting a request for five or ten thousand dollars, went into a complete state of paralysis. Dave, upon seeing that they both had gone pale and were stuttering, told them to relax, he only needed three quarters for the coke machine. Never had two souls been more relieved or a loan more eagerly extended. The valet brought the van. Dave had his Coca Cola and Mindy put a bottle of champagne to chill in my ice chest. We were on the road.

It had just gone dark when the check engine light went on in the van. At that point, after a month in a casino, my brain was not at its peak. I thought the problem was my generator and that I should probably keep driving so that the headlights would remain on. That was really a big mistake. The van soon sputtered and died. Since this was long before the advent of cell phones, we had to wait in the dark on this rarely-used highway for a passing car to stop and respond to my frantically waving arms. Finally, a car did stop. The driver agreed to call Triple A from Tehachapi and send help. The tow truck arrived and the driver hooked us up, hoisting my rear bumper to the back of the tow truck. We stayed and rode in the front of the VW. Mindy suggested we open that bottle of champagne. So, there we were, the three of us each dead broke, totally burnt out on Las Vegas, riding down the road backwards, looking out the front windshield in my broken-down van, each with a plastic cup of icy cold champagne when Mindy raised her cup to ours and said, "Gentlemen, this poker is all right."

In Tehachapi we checked into a motel using my credit card. We went to the room. I put the key in the door, opened it, switched on the light and we were greeted with a voice that said, "Put up your hands and no one gets hurt." We froze. Our hands went up! Then it dawned on us that the TV was turned on by the light switch and Humphrey Bogart was talking to the bad guys!

The next morning, we arranged for a garage to diagnose the problem with my van. We rented a car on my credit card and headed on to Fresno. We were about an hour outside of Tehachapi and Dave said, "Pull over, I have to take a dump." As I was driving, I went on the lookout for a service station on this desolate stretch of the interstate. "No" yelped Dave, "I mean I have to take a dump right now! Forget the service station! This is an emergency. Please pull over!"

I obliged. I stopped immediately on the roadside of the desert highway with some light traffic going both ways. Dave spotted one small bush thirty or forty yards off into the desert. I grabbed some paper that was lying between the seats of the rental car and handed it to a quickly exiting Missouri Dave. His pants were undone and were down nearly to his knees. His left hand held the make-do toilet paper I had handed him, which was starting to unfurl. The same hand was also clinging to the back of his pants that he was barely holding up. He was bent over at the waist and waddling unsteadily out into the desert in an absolute panic, trailed by the longest printout of a hotel bill one could imagine. He looked like some sort of large, majestic bird, hop-skipping along with a fifteen-foot long white tail feather blowing in the wind. Mindy and I were laughing hysterically. Moods were picking up.

A few hours later we arrived at Tony's place in Fresno.

It was the following morning, after an extraordinarily long sleep, my body was pleasantly shocked by fresh air, cool country morning fresh air; air pure and unflavored by cigarette smoke or dried and processed from the constant recycling by air conditioning. That amazing air flowed as a gentle breeze through the open window next to the cozy, soft bed where I found myself. I was on a vineyard in the central San Joaquin Valley of California. I was greeted by the melodic cooing from Tony's homing pigeons. That was one of the most welcome sounds I had ever heard. It was gentle and grounding; gloriously therapeutic. And it brought me back to earth from both the incredible intensity of a month playing poker in a Las Vegas casino and sleeping in a stuffy hotel room with windows that did not open. All was good with the world again.

We drove back to Tehachapi a week later to pick up my VW van with a rebuilt engine. All three of us were thankful that my credit card still had credit.

We returned to Lake Tahoe, borrowed some money and were back in action. Within a month or so we had paid off our credit cards and our poker debts. Just like that dark night riding down the highway backwards in the Tehachapi desert, we were thinking, once again: "This poker is all right."

Tuna

The dude was a very large human being; he stood well over six foot tall, probably weighed about 260 lbs. and was built like an NFL linebacker. He saw the world through large dark horn-rimmed glasses with huge coke bottle lenses. He looked like a cartoon character. He had the DNA of a super card sharp, the 'aw shucks demeanor' of a country bumpkin, and the instincts of a cold-blooded alligator. The man had a great laugh and talked a good game. He was called Tuna. His mama didn't give him that name at birth; no, she had called him Hans, Hans Lund. Mama, gentle and also large, was playing stud that night in 1976 on the table next to ours. She often accompanied Tuna on the trip to Reno from home in Carson City. I became immediately aware of Tuna that first time we played, not only because of his physical presence but because he played really good poker.

Tuna was a dangerous opponent. We squared off against each other in countless games over many years and we busted each other more than a few times. Early in his poker career Tuna began entering poker tournaments. He proceeded to make a name for himself as an accomplished No-Limit Hold'em tournament player. He racked up quite a few wins in some prestigious tournaments as well as nailing way more than his share of local events. In 1978, he earned his first WSOP bracelet, awarded to tournament winners, for winning a $1,500 buy-in No-Limit Hold'em event. In 1983, Tuna took first place in the $10,000 buy-in No-Limit Hold'em Main Event at Slim's Super Bowl of Poker. He won his second WSOP bracelet in 1996. He became a player who could flat-out play tournaments like nobody's business. Tuna had absolutely one goal in life that he coveted more than all else: it was to win the WSOP $10,000 Main Event and be crowned World Champion. Many players dream of climbing that mountain, some come close but each year only one amongst them reach the pinnacle. Tuna's focus in his poker life was to be that one.

Prior to the convening of the 1990 WSOP, Tuna approached Missouri Dave and myself and asked if we would be interested in joining him and a couple of other northern Nevada players in prepping for the tournaments. I was never quite sure what prepping meant but Dave and I being rather lazy, passed on the offer.

The 1990 WSOP main event had a first-place prize of $835,000 and the coveted WSOP ring. The tough final table included two former World Champions, Stu Ungar and Berry Johnston. It also included Carson City's finest, Hans 'Tuna' Lund, whose ultimate goal in life was possibly within reach. As it came to pass, Tuna ended up being one of the final two players for the Championship. The other was Iranian born Mansour Matloubi. The key hand, one that would be talked about for years to come, came with Tuna having a chip advantage of about $1.1 million to $800,000 for Mansour. Tuna limped on the button with **A/9 suited**. Mansour raised to $75,000 with a pair of tens **(10/10)**. Tuna called. The flop was: **2...4...9** rainbo.
Mansour: **10/10**.   Tuna: **A/9**. Board: **2...4...9**.

Mansour bet $100,000, Tuna raised $250,000 more, Mansour thought forever and then moved all-in for an additional $382,000. At that point Tuna also tanked. Finally, after several minutes, Tuna called. The hands were turned face-up on the table for all to see, and Mansour's two tens were about a four-to-one favorite over Tuna's pair of nines with an Ace kicker. The dealer turned the next card and the large crowd roared when the Ace of spades appeared and Tuna had drawn out, making two pair, to take the lead over Mansour's tens. Mansour could only win with one of the two remaining tens. Tuna was now slightly over a twenty-to-one favorite to win the hand, bust Mansour and achieve his life's goal of being the World Champion.

There was just one card to fade. There was just one card between Tuna and his dream of glory. There was just one card for $835,000 first place money as opposed to $334,000 for second place. The crowd was hushed and ready to erupt in celebration for the crowning of the new 1990 World Champion. The dealer gently tapped the table with her fist, a signal that the final card was about to be turned up. The card was delivered in soundless slow motion. And, there on the river, the fifth and final card sat the Ten of Spades, trembling, defiant and saying, "Not tonight Mr. Tuna–man, not tonight."

The collective groan from the large gallery sucked the air out of the building where Tuna stood, shocked, pale, in stunned silence. Anguish. Disbelief. Oh ye river! Oh ye cruel, cruel river!

Three tens had just beat two pair.

Mansour   Tuna

Board

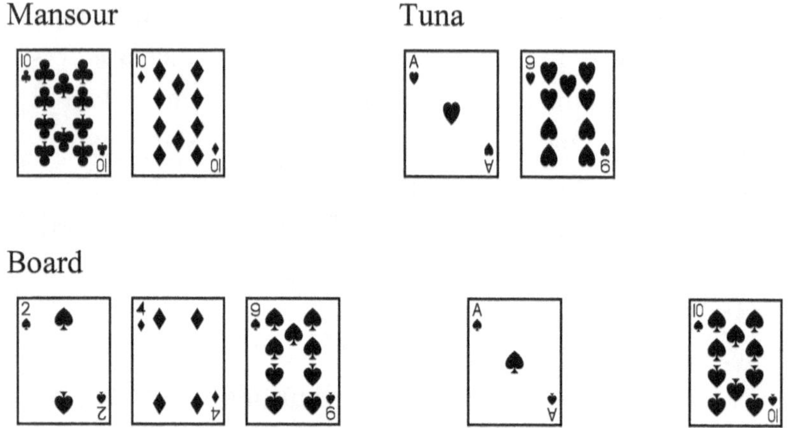

There is a phenomenon that involves one part self-assurance, one part grit, one part determination mixed with a whole lot of backbone. The scholars might call it fortitude or character. The Brits call it bottle. We call it heart. Think of Mohammed Ali and Joe Frazier, two exhausted, battered warriors each refusing to lose; each battling with nothing left except a massive amount of heart.

Tuna always played poker tournaments with tons of heart. He still had $300,000 left to work with, but, facing an emboldened Mansour with a better than five-to-one chip advantage, Tuna had a lot to overcome. Unfortunately, the cards had already spoken. Later that evening, Mansour Matloubi was crowned the 1990 World Champion.

* * * * *

Tuna's best friend in the poker community was Brad Dougherty. Tuna had taken Brad under his wing and taught him a great deal about No-Limit Hold'em and about tournament play. Brad was an excellent student and became a fierce tournament competitor as well. As astonishing as it was, in 1991 Brad surpassed all odds and won the WSOP Main Event. After being so close to a championship, Tuna now had extra incentive to achieve his life's goal. But that was not to be. Amazingly Tuna finished third in 1992. Making it to the final table against the very best poker players in the world is a terrific accomplishment in itself and Tuna managed it two out of three years and was one lousy ten on the river from being the World Champion he so wanted to be.

In 2009, Tuna passed at the early age of fifty-nine. He was a good man and I enjoyed competing against him for nearly thirty-five years. He earned over $2.9 million in tournaments over his lifetime. His accomplishments in so many tournaments made him undeniably one of the all-time great tournament players. He had come such a long way from commuting from Carson City to Reno, accompanied by his poker-playing mother, so many years ago.

The 1985 World Series of Poker

The Las Vegas casinos are far removed from most people's concept of the real world due the city's many highlights and distractions: the themed facades, the shows, the dancing ladies, the extravaganza of gourmet food, free drinks, instant credit and the startling loss of the value of money. It was in that environment that I would live and play poker for a month each year. The games required a level of skill, patience, concentration, creativity and self-control far beyond any other of my life's endeavors.

There are many poker players that play an eight or ten or sixteen-hour session, cash out and find their way to their bed. When their heads hit their pillows they go to sleep only to wake up eight hours later refreshed and ready to start a new day. I was not one of those guys. Sleep has never come easy to me, especially after a poker game. Following a few beers and often a quarter of a low dosage Xanax, I would be awake for hours, adrenaline still coursing through my body as the cavalcade of hands from the day's session would parade around my mind. I processed the day's play at the expense of my rest. This sleep disorder has always been part of my particular genetic make-up. At the WSOP my body remained adrenalin-charged for hours after playing; getting to sleep was near impossible. When I did sleep, my dreams were permeated with the sounds of poker chips and the awareness that games downstairs were still in progress. Staying asleep was difficult. Days became nights and nights became days and the weeks melded into each other. Through the many days of mental haze, the sleepless nights, the extended plays, my mind grew foggier. The energy would be slowly sucked out of me. It brought out the worst in me: eating poorly, drinking more beer, sleeping crazy odd hours—when I slept at all—and the dabbling in cocaine. It would take a huge toll on my body and my mental acuity; my play would deteriorate accordingly.

After years of a month-long stay at the WSOP, I was keenly aware of the toll the tournament took on my wellbeing. A month at that

level of intensity could burn a person out. In 1984 I arrived with a new
strategy. I brought with me my bicycle, my racquetball gear and a new
commitment to maintain my stamina and focus. The first week of the
tournament Joe B and I played racquetball a couple of times and I rode
my bike at least every other day. I ate healthy and slept fairly well. The
second week, racquetball was out; however, I still rode my bike, and I
remained generally healthy. Week Three, the bike never moved; I ate
terribly, slept worse and woke nearly everyday with a hangover. By
week four I had full-on alcoholic tendencies. I was snorting cocaine
and I had started smoking cigarettes.

But that was 1984.

The next year, 1985, I kept it fairly well together even though I
was a loser from day one. My earnings were non-existent as my losses
mounted. Some time in the middle of the second week things began
to turn around and I began making dents into my accumulated losses.
It wasn't until the night before the Main Event, after a month of playing poker at a very high level, that I finally managed to win enough
to get myself even, and declared winner for the tournament. In that
session I played through the night and early into the morning and on
the very last hand of the night, I busted a guy in a pot of considerable
size. After a month of playing from behind, I was a significant winner
and I was elated. I decided to enter a ten-person satellite tournament
for an entry into the $10,000 buy-in World Championship event. Ten
players ante up $1,025 each. The house keeps $200, and the remaining
$10,050 pays for an entry into the tournament. Over the years, I had
entered a few satellites and had never won a seat into the Main Event.
This satellite on that morning got down to two of us: me and a player
I'll call Mr. X. I had **two Jacks**, Mr. X had **A/Q**, all the money went
in, the dealer never put out an Ace or a Queen, the Jacks held up and I
had a seat in the main event. I was even more elated. In fact, I was eu-
phoric.

In spite of my elation, I was exhausted. I had been up the entire
night. I didn't even have a clean shirt left in my depleted wardrobe. I had

about an hour to buy a new t-shirt from the gift shop, take a shower and attempt to get my head together to play in the biggest tournament of my life. An hour later I was ready. At least I was sort of ready, inasmuch as I was clean and so was my shirt. I was still sleep-deprived, exhausted and a bit off kilter.

Dave had won a seat in a satellite early on in the month. He had managed to fly home, rest for a few days and get himself mentally prepared. I wished him luck and vice versa. Names were drawn. Seats were taken. The cards went in the air.

The very first hand I was dealt was the **Ace of hearts** with the **ten of hearts**. I raised on the button and I was called by none other than Mr. X, who had put up $10,000 of his own money, purchased his entry and ended up at the same table as me.
The flop was: **10...8♥...7♥**.

I had a big hand with top pair, Ace kicker* and the nut flush draw. Mr. X bet into me and I raised. He re-raised. I was contemplating whether to call or go all-in. I already had put nearly $1,400 in the very first pot of the event and I did not want to go broke having played just one hand. But before I could act the dealer turned the next card prematurely off the deck. It was the deuce of hearts (**2♥**). There it was! A card that made me the nut flush, and it had just been taken back, set aside, so it could be shuffled back into the deck after the next card was dealt face up. It was the proper decision but I felt sick. I still needed to act on my opponent's raise. I decided to flat call. Then, like a miracle, the next card was the King of hearts (**K♥**). I couldn't believe it. For the second time in the hand, I had made the nuts.

Me

 Mr. X

Board

Mr. X bet, I moved all-in, he called. The final card was a blank, (meaning it did not affect the outcome of the hand), and I had doubled up on the first hand of the tournament. Mr. X showed the Jack and nine of hearts (**J♥/9♥**). He had flopped the nut straight with a straight flush draw. So, in two consecutive hands dealt an hour and a half apart, I had beat Mr. X for a $10,000 buy-in and won his $10,000 starting chips in the tournament. To be fair, after the flop, Mr. X's hand with the **J♥/9♥** was more than a two-to-one favorite against my **A♥/10♥**. I got very lucky to win that pot. At that point, however, after one hand, amongst the 140 entrants, I was the chip leader.

Being incredibly exhausted, I decided my strategy was to play as tight as I possibly could. Unless lightning struck, I would try to make it through the day, get a good night's sleep with some chips left to play with the following day. I never won another pot of any significance; thus, I was left with $13,500 to start day number two.

I was so jacked up on adrenalin and in spite of three or four beers, a massage, a Valium and me being totally and completely exhausted, I was unable to sleep for more than a few winks.

Day number two was a complete blur. I went broke with a combination flush draw and an inside straight draw; therefore, despite my previous day's success, I no longer had a seat in the tournament.

It's a strange, almost surreal feeling going broke in a major tournament. A player is part of and partly consumed by the action and the excitement of the tournament. The level of intensity is sky-high, and a player's focus and concentration have been raised to a maximum level. Then suddenly you get busted. You have to stand up and leave but your legs are weak. Standing becomes difficult, and, as you walk away, you look back and your game is still being played, only you are no longer part of it. It's over for you and no one misses you. Your adrenalin still flows through your body; you feel dazed, you feel lost and you feel alone. You may feel you got very unlucky; you may feel anger. You may think, "If only?" And all those players you have battled with, stared at, studied, looked for clues that might betray their blank poker faces; all those players whose heads you have entered for so many long hours: they are still in the game and you are now merely a spectator. A spectator if you can bear to watch at all.

Ultimately, I finished in 55th place. Dave, who had been moved to the same table as me, exited just twenty minutes before me at 60th. We met at the bar.

That night I was able to sleep for a very long time.

Leaving Las Vegas

In 1986, about midway through the tournament, Missouri Dave and I flew down to Las Vegas for the World Series of Poker. We were both on short money and needed to book some quick wins in order to be able to stay and play.

The night we arrived, we checked into our rooms, had a couple beers at the bar and retired for a good night's sleep. After breakfast we ambled into the poker room. As there was only one $10/25 No-Limit Hold'em game going, and it had been going all night, Dave and I both took a seat in it. A hand developed that was to have dire consequences for the home team. Bill Smith was in the game and he was in the crucial hand.

Bill Smith was a Texan who could flat out play poker. Bill was tall and pale and looked like he had never seen the sun and if he had seen it, it was probably right before going to bed. He was a throwback to another era. He usually wore a sports coat often accompanied by a loose and wrinkled cravat around his thin and wrinkled neck. He constantly smoked cigarettes that were held in a plastic filtered cigarette holder. He could have been confused for an aging gangster from a classic Bogart film. Perhaps he was from the same tribe as The Adams Family. I never saw Bill play without both a cocktail in his hand and his very attractive sweetheart, who was as pale as he was, seated behind him. But as I said, he could flat out play poker. He was a particular marvel to behold when playing short-handed.

On several occasions I watched him play in a short-handed game. He was beyond super-aggressive. Acting with speed and without any hesitation, he would check and raise, lunge and parry, and move all-in when he smelled weakness. He'd make great laydowns when he sensed he was beat, he'd bob and weave, weave and bob, and just when his opponent doubted him, he'd attack and destroy. Bill would continue to stack his chips higher and higher as the empty cocktail glasses multiplied in his vicinity. He was really something special to watch. He was an early pick on Dave's and my imaginary 'all-star-drinking-and-playing team.' In 1985, the year Dave and I both played in the Main Event at the World Series, Bill Smith was the last man standing and was crowned the World Champion. That year I ran into Bill early in the morning on the second day of the event as we were about to start and I asked him: "You drinking already, Bill?"

He replied, "The sun's up isn't it?"

There was a story that went around about Bill after he won the $700,000 first-place prize money. It was said some six months after his big win a couple of thugs tried to rob him on the street in Las Vegas and he suffered a brutal beating when he stood his ground and refused to give up his cash. Bill was a good man and it made me sad me to hear that story.

Our crucial must-win pot at the '86 WSOP was played like this: I limped into the pot for $25 with two eights. A player from Louisiana called $25. Bill made it $125. Dave called. I called. The player from Louisiana made it $325. Bill called. Dave called. I had about $1,100 left and I felt like I might have the best hand at that point so I went all-in, hoping I could win the pot right then and there. Louisiana called. Bill went all-in for more than I bet. Dave thought hard for a bit and called all his money, which was about $600. With the last of his money, Louisiana called Bill's raise. It was immediately obvious to me I had clearly made a huge bonehead mistake.

Because all the money was in the pot and there was no further betting, the dealer dealt out all five cards. It looked something like this:

Me	Louisiana	Bill	Dave (?)

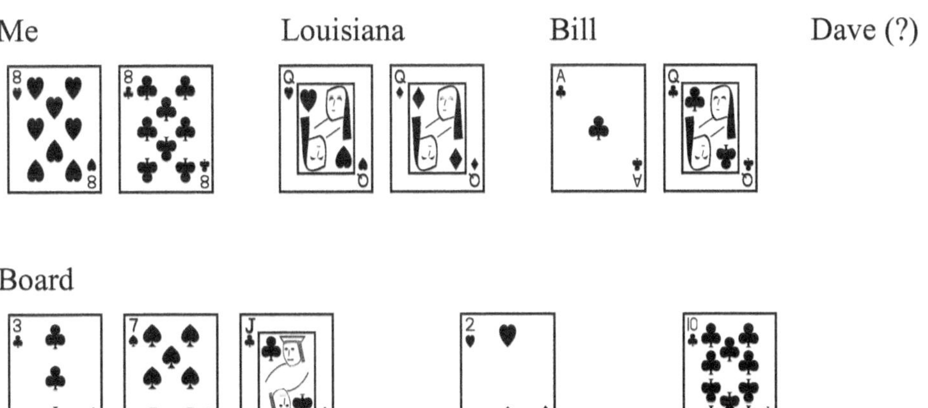

Board

Louisiana turned over a pair of Queens (**Q/Q**). Bill Smith turned over the Ace Queen of Clubs (**A♣/Q♣**) and had made the nut flush. I threw my two eights face down in the muck. Dave threw his hand face down in the muck. Bill busted three players with an Ace-high club flush.

Dave and I went to the bar. We were both broke. We booked a flight for later that afternoon.

* * * * *

We checked out of the hotel and boarded a plane back to Reno. When we were taxiing down the runway, Dave looked over at me and asked what I had in the hand we both went broke on and as the plane lost contact with the earth, I told him, "Two eights."

He looked at me, shook his head and stated, matter of fact like, "Well, you weren't going to catch another eight." He knew because he held the last two eights.

At a time when we desperately needed to beat a poker game, we both put all our money in the same pot with each of us holding two eights, the same ridiculous hand. It was a major effort getting to Las Vegas only to go broke, essentially drawing dead. After a very quick turnaround, we had a most miserable trip home.

* * * * *

Beyond a doubt, The World Series of Poker has always been the most spectacular gathering of poker players. The players honored, the game celebrated. The entire month-long event as well as the generous hospitality of the Binion family was a true wonder in my world. I loved playing poker with some of the best players on the planet. I had made friends with so many players from within the larger poker community. I loved the excitement, the adrenalin rushes, and being treated like a celebrity. Eventually though, after some serious soul searching, I had two major realizations. First, for my financial health I could manage my money and play better poker away from the WSOP. Moreover, for my physical health, considering my sleep disorders, I needed to eliminate the WSOP from my life.

Every year after the painful decision to stop playing poker at Binion's, when The World Series was about to begin, I would get anxious and I would stay anxious knowing what was transpiring down south. I had to fight the urge to get on an airplane and fly to Las Vegas. I always remained unsettled for the month until the final hand was dealt, and only then I could relax. It took me many years of using all my will power before I no longer felt drawn to the special camaraderie of kindred spirits, to the turning of cards, to the chatter of shuffling poker chips, to the bright lights in the desert of southern Nevada.

CHAPTER 8

AMARILLO SLIM'S SUPER BOWL OF POKER

Amarillo Slim's Super Bowl of Poker

In 1972 Thomas 'Amarillo Slim' Preston won the championship event at the WSOP and managed to parlay that win with multiple appearances on television talk shows and a couple of cameos in films (including *California Split* in 1974) into being considered the national spokesperson for poker.

Recognizing that players wanted a major poker tournament beyond the WSOP, in 1979 Slim created and hosted Amarillo Slim's Super Bowl of Poker at the Las Vegas Hilton. Over the years, that very successful tournament was hosted at numerous locations until the last hand was dealt in 1991. Slim's tournament was an important part of my year from 1980 to 1984 when it was hosted in Reno and Lake Tahoe.

The Little Lady from Houston

Betty Carey looked like the girl next door. Yes, she was very attractive. She dressed in western style: jeans, vests, cowgirl shirts, and silky blouses. Occasionally she sported a Stetson. Betty wore make-up in moderation. Her good looks and gentle personality would invite attention while her smile and country charm would disarm many tough opponents across the green felt tables. Behind the smile was a skilled laser-focused assassin whose legacy was defined by the trail of empty wallets, smashed Stetsons and broke buckaroos left in her wake.

I first became aware of Betty Carey in 1982 at the fourth annual Amarillo Slim's Super Bowl of Poker at the Sahara Tahoe. Players I knew had been talking about an incredible poker-playing lady that had established a big reputation playing in Texas with some of poker's biggest stars. There were lots of stories about Betty Carey that left no doubt she was an accomplished opponent. She once challenged a highly regarded professional player from Texas to a heads-up match for some seriously high stakes. The kicker was Betty would spot him the button every hand. That is an enormous spot. Her offer was turned down. It was said that Betty was at that time, hands down, the best woman playing No-Limit Texas Hold'em.

I took notice of her as we were both playing nearly every day at Slim's tournament and on a couple of occasions I found myself looking across the table at Betty.

Early one evening she played a hand that remains locked in my memory. At a table or two away from the game that I was in, a crowd had begun to form, a sure sign a big pot was brewing. I got up from my game to take a look. All the cards were out:

The Board

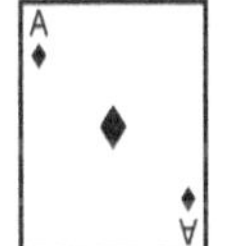   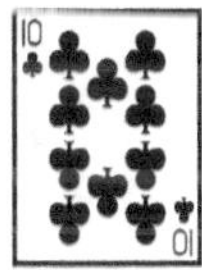 

Betty Carey had checked. Her opponent was a fella with a cowboy hat and he had just bet about $8,000 at a pot that already held about $6,000. For somewhere around five minutes, Betty studied the board and she studied her opponent. Finally, in a thick southern drawl, the fella said, "Dealer, put the clock on the pretty little lady from Houston."

When the clock is put on someone the player is given one minute plus ten seconds to act on their hand and if the opponent has failed to act, the hand is dead.

The floor-man was called over; the dealer started the clock. Betty continued to study. She took the full minute. The floor-man began the countdown: ten, nine, eight, seven, six ... Betty said to the dealer in a calm and very direct manner, "Dealer, take the clock off the little lady from Houston and put the clock on the nice gentleman from San Antonio, I'm all-in." With that, Betty called the $8,000 and moved in about an additional $15,000.

A small bit of moisture appeared on the gentleman's forehead; it formed into a bead that ran down his face and then that bead's cousins appeared and they too ran down his face. Soon his face was wet with sweat. He was in that place, the unenviable place where all one's money was at stake and there was no clear choice as to what to do. At this moment, all one's strength is required – strength to call or strength to throw the hand away. He sat frozen, in shock, disbelief and indecision. Betty just sat there smiling. A full minute later the dealer began the countdown: "ten, nine, eight ... "

"I call," said the gentleman. Betty turned over the **J/8**, making the nut straight. The gentleman from San Antonio showed **8/6**, making the second nut straight. The crowd that had gathered around the table, now three rows deep, sighed in unison.

Betty   The Gentleman from San Antonio

As the pot was pushed to the 'little lady from Houston,' the crowd dispersed and the nice gentleman from San Antonio, who was barely able to rise up from his chair, quietly limped off into the night.

The Clone

David Sklansky was a household name in the poker community, mainly for penning *Hold'em Poker*, the best-ever book on Texas Hold'em. Sklansky was an accomplished poker player and a very bright mathematician, who went on to write other respected books on poker as well.

Sometime in the early 80's an eccentric young man showed up in Reno looking like a smaller version of David Sklansky. Though he was a few inches shorter and about fifty pounds lighter, he physically resembled David Sklansky. Because of the eerie similarities he quickly became known as The Clone. He was a very upbeat yet quirky dude. He laughed a lot and enjoyed his poker. As a young man back then, he usually looked like he'd just spent the night on a friend's couch and had combed his hair with a pork chop. I liked the Clone; he was bright, funny, always pleasant, had a big smile and he viewed the world through his own unique set of lenses. Other players liked him and he had his core of good friends. The day I first met The Clone he was fairly new to the game but still an above-average poker player. His game continued to improve and in a relatively short span of time he became more accomplished and a man to be reckoned with in a poker game. In those early days he was playing a lot in Reno but ended up playing all over Nevada. The last I heard of him he was residing in Las Vegas.

It was 1984 at Amarillo Slim's Super Bowl of Poker at Caesar's Tahoe that a sequence of events involving the Clone left a lasting image in my head. The Clone showed up at the tournament really pumped-up. It was rumored that prior to coming to Caesar's, he had taken on a progressive slot machine and hit it for a big number, perhaps over $100,000. He came to Slim's with a substantial amount of cash.

During the course of the tournament, I played in several No-Limit Hold'em games with the Clone. The last game I played was a four-handed $25/50 game with two World Champions (Phil Hellmuth and Jack Keller) plus the Clone. The last hand I played was an interesting one.

Before the flop, I raised, the Clone re-raised on the button, Phil called on the big blind, I called and three of us took the flop.

Phil (folded)   Me   The Clone

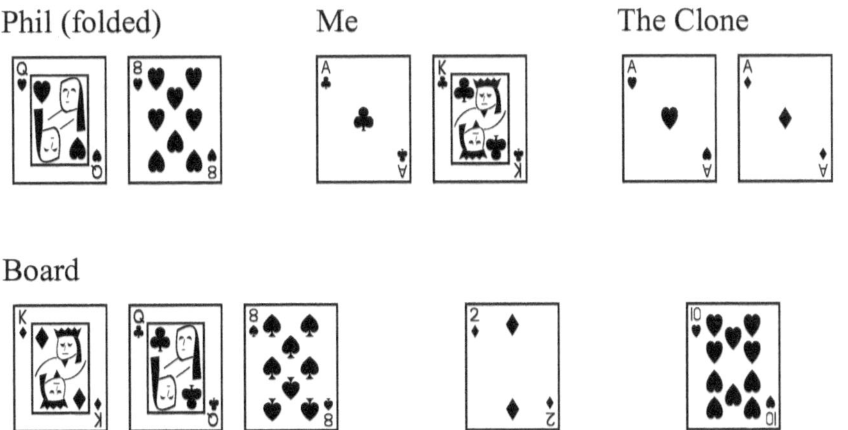

Board

Phil bet. I raised. The Clone re-raised. Phil tanked for several minutes.

It's been said many times in poker circles about bottom two pair, "You usually win a small pot or lose a huge one." In a pot that both Phil's opponents raised before the flop, with a **K...Q...8** flop, and both were eager to continue to play for considerable money, Phil was very likely up against a set of Kings or Kings and Queens or maybe even a set of Queens. Phil tossed his hand. Even though he did have the best hand on the flop, it looked like a wise laydown on his part.

I called for the rest of my money and went home broke.

The real story about the Clone from that tournament is one I only heard about because it happened after had I left, though the seeds were planted while I was still there. It all started when a player, who was in a couple of the games where both the Clone and myself were also at the table, kept baiting the Clone. He kept pulling out more money and challenging the Clone to do the same. He continued challenging the Clone to play him heads up. It seemed obvious that this guy wanted to play against the Clone, and just the Clone, for a lot of money. It seemed to me that this guy knew the Clone had made a big score and he wanted the Clone to put that score in action. It felt odd to me for I had played with this guy a few times and I had played with the Clone a lot and the Clone was a superior player. Until the time I left the tournament, the Clone had managed to not take the bait. From the story that swept through the poker community, I learned how that all had changed.

This is the way I heard the story of their match: apparently, the Clone agreed to tee it up with the guy. They played heads up with each putting up somewhere in the neighborhood of $100,000. For a time, they traded chips back and forth. Then it all came down to a most extraordinary hand. The Clone held a **pair of tens**. The guy held a **pair of nines**. Dealer placed **10...9...9** in the center of the table.

The Guy   The Clone

Board

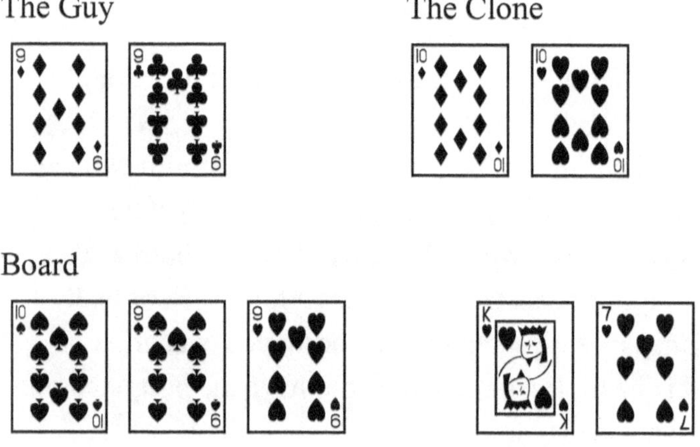

The Clone had tens full of nines and the guy had four nines. The money, around **$200,000**, all went in the pot and the Clone was out a lot of dough.

End of Story.

CHAPTER 9

CHARLATANS & THIEVES

Charlatans & Thieves

Everywhere I played poker charlatans were to be found. The most basic, of course, were those who borrowed money with no intention of paying it back.

I was in a game when a player repeatedly shoved a rubber-banded brick of one-dollar bills covered by a single one hundred-dollar bill into the pot representing a much larger bet. He was exposed the final time he bet the cash when his opponent requested an exact count. What was assumed to be about five or six thousand dollars turned out to be only one hundred and fifty-three dollars (a one hundred dollar bill covering fifty three one dollar bills.)

A player I knew accepted a large gold bar as overnight collateral for a loan during a game only to discover the next day he held a baked bar of clay painted gold.

I was told of the Vegas player who was caught red-handed as he brought a five thousand dollar bundle up from his lap and placed it behind his stacks of chips **after he flopped four jacks**. The kicker to this story is he checked quite forcefully by pounding the table with his fist. Without a bet people began to fold and the cheat looked down to see his pocket Jacks had flipped face up following his emphatic check.

A Las Vegas player/dealer I knew, while dealing a very big game at the WSOP, stood to move to his next table when a handful of one hundred dollar black chips he had palmed from the many sizable pots and stuffed beneath his dealer's cummerbund, rattled to the floor next to me like a slot machine gone wild. I was the only one to see it happen and he whispered to me "keep quiet and I'll split them with you." To which I responded "thanks but no thanks."

* * * * *

In Reno and Lake Tahoe I never worried about being cheated. I could not say the same for some other places I played.

I've witnessed a person standing on the rail peering into a player's hand and signaling information to his partner in the game.

In a heads-up match, I heard of a card mechanic dealing his accomplice's opponent the same two cards his accomplice held and discarded the hand before; the accomplice, therefore, always knew his opponent's two-card Hold'em hand.

I've read of Omaha players seated next to each other trading a key card under the table as they palmed them and then placed the cards on their knees for the exchange.

Some forms of cheating were more sophisticated. Carl McKelvey was cheated while playing heads up, by an opponent in cahoots with the operator of the overhead security camera. They utilized cards marked with invisible ink, freeze-framed camera work and communication through headphones that were supposedly the source for music.

At a major Northern California card room, in a good-sized weekly game that was live-streamed on screens, the in-house commentator was allegedly communicating to his accomplice the cards his opponents held (it was believed through his phone the player held in his lap). Suspicions were reinforced when the alleged cheat only ever lost when the commentator went on vacation.

There has been a wide variety and certainly enumerable stories of unscrupulous behavior since people began playing poker.

Taken Down in Las Vegas

When a particularly good poker game is going the word quickly gets out. Sometimes it's a daily game, other times it could be a once-a-week game or perhaps a game that began three days ago and is still going strong. What makes a good game could be the structure or size of the game, the amount of money involved or who might be playing and losing large amounts of money. In short, if the action's good and the game is juicy, it is a good game. Most often good games don't last long. They only last as long as the loose money flows.

Once I heard about a No-Limit Hold'em game at a major Las Vegas casino. The game was said to be juicy, action-packed and very live. Though I was leery of playing in Las Vegas in no-limit games away from the World Series, I knew the two guys who had leased the card room and were hosting the game. I figured I would be safe playing there even on the off chance that the game might not be totally on the square. I flew to Las Vegas, checked into the hotel and headed to the poker room.

The blinds were $5/5/10. The buy-in was $500 but most everyone had larger amounts of money in play. I bought in for $1,500.

Now there was an oddity to this game. Generally, when a new deck is introduced into a game it is **spread out face up** so the dealer can check that all the cards are accounted for. Next, the cards are turned face down and then they are mixed together before the shuffle. In this game, however, the deck was brought into the game, and the dealer went directly to the shuffle, then cut the cards and dealt the hand. Curiously, I was told that it was being done like this to save time.

The game was as advertised: lots of action, big pots and a couple of very live players with tons of money in front of them. The game was going my way and I was rapidly accumulating chips when a big hand came down. I held the **A/K of spades** against one of the live ones. Before the flop, I raised and the live one raised me back. The Flop was: **A...6 spades...3 spades**. I had the top pair of Aces with a King kicker along with the nut flush draw against a live one! My hand, in knowledgeable poker circles, would have been considered huge. All the money went into the pot, about $2,500 each. The Pot was over **$5,000**.

Me   My Opponent

Board

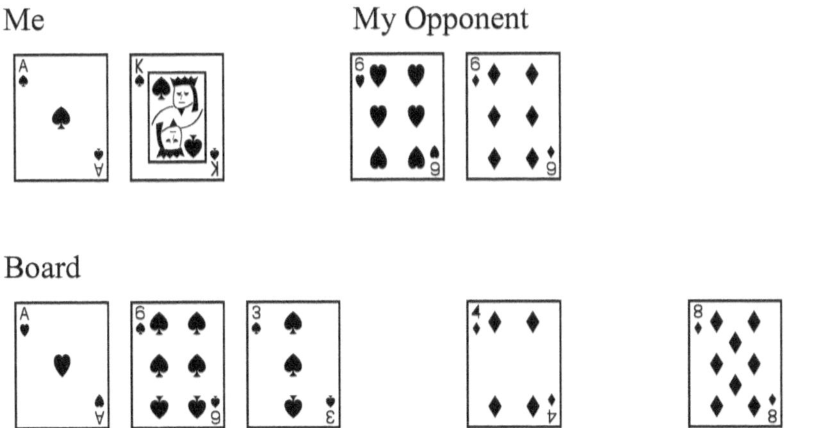

My opponent had surprisingly re-raised me with two sixes and flopped a set. I missed the flush draw and I was busted.

I bought in for $1,500 more. Again, I was playing well, making hands and staging a comeback. Then another big hand came down with the same guy who had previously busted me. He raised, I re-raised and he called. I held: **A/A**. The flop was: **A...2....3**. I made a good size bet. My opponent moved all in. At that point something freakishly strange occurred; I felt someone kick my foot under the table. I thought little about it until it happened again. Then I heard someone say in a very soft and low voice: "That was me." I froze. It was said again. I recognized the voice. Sitting right next to my opponent was a local player from Las Vegas who I had been friendly with for years and the voice was his. I thought he must have caught a glimpse of my opponent's hand and he was probably telling me the old guy had a really big hand. But so did I and, besides, I didn't operate that way. Consequently, all the money went into the pot, over $5,000 in the center of the table. Two cards, that did not pair the board, and I was broke again. This time my opponent had surprisingly raised with **4/5**, then flopped the nut straight.

Me   My Opponent

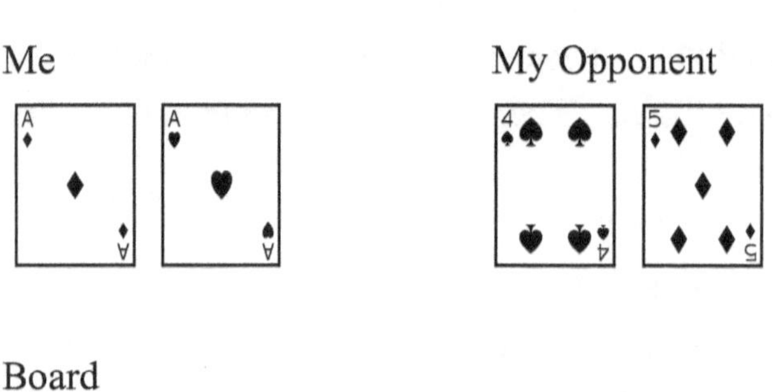

Board

I left the game and headed straight to the bar. The next morning I flew back to Reno.

Two days after I returned from Las Vegas, I saw Missouri Dave and I told him of my short stay in Las Vegas and the hands I played against the live one. A week or so later Dave came to me and said that he had made plans to go to the same casino I had just frequented; however, when he spoke to a mutual friend in Las Vegas who was playing in the game, the friend told Dave the game was not on the square. The friend went on to explain that he was **in** and that Dave could also be **in** if he wanted to be. Dave told him, he did not want to be **in** or **out**; in fact, he was no longer going to Las Vegas. Dave was told that the card room hosts were running up (stacking) the decks and bringing them into the games. The dealers, all excellent card mechanics, were giving the cards false shuffles and cutting the deck perfectly to deal out the cold decks,* of which I presumed I was twice the victim. The live ones who were winning the money were 'take off' players, meaning they played like suckers but were designated to take the money off the marks, such as myself. At the end of the week, or whenever, the money was split between the hosts, the dealers and all who were **in**.

When Dave told me this, I was reminded of a warning about cheating in Las Vegas that my friend The Razor had once given me.

Then I remembered what The Razor said a couple of weeks ago when I told him about the no-limit game and asked, "Do you want to go Las Vegas?" He had replied, "No and neither do you."

Whoa! Whose Button Was It?

The definition of 'gobsmacked' is "a British expression meaning astounded; overwhelmed with wonder, surprise or shock."

The previous hand was over, the next was in progress and as I put together the clues from that 'just played hand' I was quite suddenly gobsmacked. This is my story.

It was in the mid-seventies playing at the WSOP in Binion's old funky seven-table card room where, at times, the big action was simply jaw dropping.

I was seated in a great $10/25 No-Limit Hold'em game in the first week of the gathering. The action was good and a very live player with tons of money sat in the #8 seat. In the room that evening were many well-known players from all over the country, and at that time I was just getting to know who was who. Often I would be in a game with someone I knew was an established veteran player but I did not know much about them. Such was the case that evening with a certain Mr. Knight sitting on my left in the #4 seat. Mr. Knight was a 'big name player' from Arkansas.

The dealer had just gathered the cards, shuffled, cut and was about to deal when the player in the #5 seat said, "Hold it, the button* is in the wrong place." He said it was his button and that the dealer had moved it twice as it now sat in the #6 seat.

The dealer replied: "No, that did not happen, the button is correct."

The player in the #6 seat chimed in and said, "No, the button is wrong, I just had the big blind, the button belongs in the #5 seat."

Again, the dealer took issue and another player was adamant that the dealer was wrong.

The dealer was not going to give, but he realized he had no choice, as it was obvious the button belonged in the #5 seat. I had never seen a dealer make such a huge issue of where the button belonged, I thought it very out of the ordinary and made a mental note of it. The dealer shifted the button back one seat and dealt the hand from the deck he had already shuffled and cut.

Two players entered the pot for $25. When it was my turn, I looked down and saw **two Queens**. I raised to $150. Everyone folded behind me until the player with the big blind, a very tight player, re-raised $450 more. One of the players who entered the pot earlier went all-in for about a total of $125. Now, it was my turn to act. I put the raiser on **two Aces**. I did not have enough money in front of me to justify a $450 call in hopes of catching a Queen. So, I threw away my two Queens.

The dealer's nametag said Homer. Below his name it said Arkansas. Homer from Arkansas put out the flop: **Q...5...6**. I thought: "Oh shit, I could have won a good pot." Instead, with two Aces, the player in #7 seat won a small pot against the all-in player. It was time to play another hand.

Then it hit me. Oh my God! Did that just actually happen? If the button had been moved one to the left, Homer, the dealer from Arkansas, who had just made a huge issue about the button belonging in the #5 seat, would have dealt Mr. Knight from Arkansas in the #4 seat (with loads of chips in play) the two Queens that I picked up and the two Aces would have been in the possession of the live one in the #8 seat (who sat with tons of money and mountains of chips in front of him), instead of the tight player in the #7 seat. And Mr. Knight from Arkansas, after flopping three Queens against two Aces, would be tipping Homer from Arkansas as he stacked up all the chips that had, moments before, belonged to Mr. Live One. I was the only one who had a clue as to what would have been, because I was the only person who knew I had the two Queens destined for Mr. Knight and threw them away; that is with the very possible exception of Howard the dealer from Arkansas.

And I was gobsmacked!

I got out of my seat, went to Missouri Dave who sat one table away and told him the story and asked what he thought. He shook his head and said to me, "Remember where you are."

There is a procedure, used by magicians and dealers who are card mechanics, called 'stacking the deck' or 'running up a deck.' A good mechanic can put cards in a certain place in the deck when they bring the cards in after the last hand, put the deck together, give the deck a false shuffle and cut without the players having the slightest idea what they were doing. Then, when the card mechanic deals, certain players receive certain cards to produce the desired result. I was once treated to an exhibition of 'stacking the deck' by a friend who was a decent card mechanic. He told me what he was doing as he was doing it. With my eyes mere inches from his hands and the deck of cards, I was unable to detect anything that looked out of the ordinary; yet, I was amazed at the results of the dealer's work.

In the case of Homer, the dealer from Arkansas, he only needed to collect and track five cards, three Queens and two Aces, and see that they were then dealt to the appropriate players. The other cards seldom mattered.

The takeaway for a poker player: unless you know how to spot a crooked dealer, it is important to trust the places you play and the people you play with.

'Lenny the Levitator' and This Pot Be Rising!

One of the great aspects of The World Series of Poker is you were introduced to so many new players. They were players from different parts of the world, some wild and flamboyant, others, strong players hidden and disguised as *everyman*. When you sat in a game, part of the challenge was to quickly identify who was who and how they approached the game. In some games you knew, or knew of, all your opponents. Other games held up to eight total strangers, with some stranger than others.

I had taken a seat in a live game, the blinds were $10/25 and I bought in for $1,000. I sat in the #9 seat next to the dealer. To my right was a guy named Lenny. He called himself 'Lenny the Levitator.'

Lenny was from one of those New England states. He had long curly shoulder length black hair, a long black beard, earrings and lots of jewelry. He looked like someone from the same tribe as myself. And Lenny had chips. He had lots of chips, piled high, as well as a bunch of $100 bills, mixed with more chips, all scattered around the space in front of him. It was a small fortune and totally untidy. It looked as if a money bomb had gone off and it was obvious that Lenny had been winning a lot of pots. Squeezed in amongst the clutter in front of Lenny were also a pack of cigarettes, an ashtray, a glass of whiskey and a bottle of beer. Lenny was loud and played poker with a drunken, care-free manner. I presumed he called himself the Levitator because of the numerous pots he raised and for his aggressive style of playing poker. He would announce his numerous raises by calling out, "I'm Lenny the Levitator and THIS POT BE RISING!" He was the focus of the game; he built big pots and won way more than his share of them.

Lenny continually bullied the game and went all in over and over. Since I was sitting next to him, he kept trying to verbally engage with me and I was fine with that; after all, he was proving to be one of those outlandish characters that made poker both interesting and fun. I entered a few pots with him and folded or lost them all. Not counting the pots I played with Lenny, I was doing OK and I had built up my stack of chips considerably.

There were two things to note that Lenny was doing. First, he was lifting his cards too high, right in my field of vision, and often I was seeing his hand. I told him at least a half of dozen times to keep his cards down, that I could see them. Second, he would look at his cards and then slide them under the scattered mess of chips and bills in front of him so as to more or less bury them under his money.

About two hours into the game a hand came down like this: I watched the players look at their cards and as the action came around to Lenny and then myself, I looked to my right and Lenny was holding a **6/4** in his hand, high enough for me to see, when he announced, "I'm Lenny the Levitator and THIS POT BE RISING!" He raised the pot $50 and made it $75 to enter. I looked down and found two eights (**8/8**), so I thought, *hell with it, I've told him enough to keep his cards down.* I called the raise. Just he and I took the flop and the flop did nothing for either of our hands. Lenny made an oversize bet of $300 into a pot that only weighed $185. I called. On with 4th Street; with the pot holding $785, he bet $700 and I called. The river helped no one. "I'm all-in," Lenny announced. I called with the money I had left, which was just over $1500. Lenny then searched around for his hand and pulled it from under his scattered chips and turned over **two Aces**! I was in shock. I could not get my head around what had just happened and how I had gotten busted. I stood up, bewildered and completely dazed. I left the game weak-kneed and feeling dizzy.

I thought about that hand for days after. The best explanation I could come up with is Lenny must have seen the two Aces he was dealt and slid them under his chips before he came into my view. He then must have had two personal cards he brought in from his jacket pocket or from who knows where, which were the ones that he held too high, knowing I would see them. Then, with a sleight-of-hand, he made it look like they were under his chips. He then disposed of them somehow, somewhere on his being. Or, perhaps, he did bury them under his mess in front of him and they remained there. This all sounds elaborate but I could not come up with any other explanation other than I did not see what I was certain I saw.

Perhaps my Karma got me for playing a hand after seeing my opponent's cards. I did know two things for sure: first, calling him out and saying I saw his cards was not an option; I could not have said, "Wait, I saw his hole-cards and those Aces weren't what I saw;" and second, I had been had by 'Lenny the Levitator.'

* * * * *

When writing this story, an old black and white film from 1933, called *Tillie and Gus* came to mind. The great W.C. Fields, as Gus was on trial accused of assaulting the gentleman who was seated next to him on the witness stand. The guy was bandaged from head to toe and had the look of a mummy. He had his crutches at his side. Gus says to the judge something like, "Your honor, we were having a friendly game of poker…yes we were… and I don't mind a man having four Aces when I have four kings… no, no I don't. But, I do mind when it happens when I dealt and I knew what I dealt him."

155

Larcenous Behavior

Tom Tourist stood up from the table, shook his head and said, "Well, you got me mister."

Champ tipped his cap and said, "Thanks for the game. I know I got lucky!" As Champ was stacking his chips, he looked up and gave a nod to Big Sam who had been sitting a couple of empty tables away from where Tom Tourist and Champ had just finished playing. Once Big Sam got the nod, he stood and followed Tom, catching him just before he exited the casino.

"Hey buddy, I saw you playing that fella heads-up and I think you got really unlucky," Big Sam said.

"Yeah, he did get lucky against me a few times," Tom Tourist replied.

"Well, I watched you play and I really think you are much the better player"

"Really?"

"Yeah, most definitely. I really think you can beat him. In fact, I'd like to put up some money, say $2,500 for half your action if you wanted to have a rematch."

"You'd do that? You really think I'm that much better of a player?"

"I do and I wouldn't put my money up if I didn't."

Champ was still sitting at the table when Tom Tourist returned and asked for a chance to get his money back. Champ said, "Sure, why not." They each bought in for another $5,000 and the game was on.

As he stood for the second time, Tom Tourist apologized to Big Sam for losing his money but thanked him for his confidence in him.

Tom Tourist was out the door before Champ and Big Sam divided up the spoils from a profitable evening. Tom Tourist had no idea he had just lost two $5,000 heads-up, freeze-outs to one of the most talented young players in Las Vegas.

Champ, Big Sam and their pal Truck Stop were a three-man wrecking crew. They had more scams and more moves than most in a city full of grifters and hustlers. The prevailing motto for some in Las Vegas was: *never give a sucker an even break.* Some of their hustles, like what was done to Tom Tourist, were not illegal, only unethical. Other things this bunch did from time to time did cross the line. What I never understood was the fact that all three were winning poker players; in fact, Champ had established himself as one of the game's toughest players and an up-and-coming superstar, so they didn't need to cross that line.

One of the scams Champ would run involved big-money tournaments. Champ would buy in a tournament and then trade a percentage of his tournament action with other players. Because he was such a gifted player, other players were eager to swap for a piece of him. He would trade 5%, 10%, 20% of himself for an equal amount from his fellow player. When two players trade a percentage of each other, should one of the players finish in the money (called cashing), he pays the other guy a percentage of his prize money based on the percentage they exchanged. The key to Champ's swaps was that he'd swap as much over 100% of himself as possible. Sometimes Champ would have over 200% total from other players. Then he'd play in the tournament and at some point, before he finished high enough to receive prize money, Champ would lose all his chips and would exit the tournament before he cashed. Obviously, if he cashed he'd owe way more than he won so he could not afford to cash in the tournament. If the circumstances were right and they managed to get to the same table, he'd lose his money to Big Sam, Truck Stop or another tightlipped scamming confederate. In that case they'd settle up later if that partner, whose chances increased greatly with the infusion of Champ's chips, cashed. Once he exited he only had to wait to see if any of his many horses finished in the money.

Another move his crew would make involved palming large denomination tournament chips and stealthily taking them off the tournament table. If and when they progressed far enough in a tournament where the smallest chips were valued at, say, $500 or $1,000, they would remove a few to use in the next tournament they played. At the early stage of a tournament, those chips, when snuck into their chip stacks, would have far greater value when people had far less money.

Cultivating friendships with whales (wealthy players with huge bankrolls) was another of their hustles. Truck Stop usually had his whale put him in big games or big tournaments. Truck Stop and his wealthy pal would be inseparable. Truck Stop played in a lot of really big poker games with his backer's cash.

I met Champ when we played in tournaments together, and we became friendly. I was quite aware of his reputation as a scammer, so I kept my guard up. One year he moved to Reno. We played a lot together. I liked Champ; I learned a lot about Hold'em playing with him; he was always straight up with me.

However, he wasn't always straight up with my close friend Joe B. One time in Las Vegas, Champ approached Joe B just before a tournament got underway. He told him that Mr. Tucker, Champ's backer, who was putting him in the tournament, was running late and would be down in thirty minutes. According to Champ, he needed Joe B to front him the $500 buy-in for just half an hour. Joe B bit and gave Champ $500. A year later, in spite of Joe B's many attempts to get his money back, Champ still owed him.

Big Bruce was a good friend, a poker player and a massive man from our circle from South Lake Tahoe. Big Bruce was big because he was a manic bodybuilder, unlike Big Sam who was big because he ate too much. Big Bruce stood 6'2", his muscular arms were as big as my legs and his legs were large and rock solid. His chest was huge. Bruce was a very sweet man but did not shy away from what he perceived as wrong.

One day in Reno, Champ was sitting in a Hold'em game with several stacks of green chips in front of him. Big Bruce took stock of the situation and knowing full well what Champ had pulled on Joe B, he walked up behind Champ and, towering over him like some giant muscle-popping human monolith, reached over Champ's shoulder and counted out $500 in green chips. He then told the stunned Champ, as he removed the chips, "This must be the money you were planning on paying Joe B."

The best a shaken and stammering Champ could come up with was, "Yeah, well, tell Joe B, Mr. Tucker never did bring me down the $500 he was supposed to."

That borrowing with a promise of a quick repayment must be a thing amongst some of the more unscrupulous. It happened to me one night during one of Amarillo Slim's tournaments. A very well known poker superstar, who I'd known for ages, told me he needed $300 until his wife brought his cash down from the hotel room. I, like Joe B, bit and handed him $300. He proceeded to put the money in action on the craps table. After over a year and numerous attempts at getting paid had failed, I was on the verge of writing the money off when, while in Los Angeles at the Commerce Casino, I got a call from Missouri Dave. He told me my man was down to the final two players in a big tournament at the Bicycle Club. I jumped in my car and scooted over to the Bike, as it was known, just as my guy was collecting $60,000 for first place. I stalked him until I could get his attention.

"Hey buddy, congratulations and do you think I can get the $300 you owe me?"

"I can't pay you out of this, I have a backer."

"Yes you can, you sick bastard, now pay up!"

With great reluctance he did peel off three $100 bills out of one the six $10,000 bundles he was holding.

Then I asked myself: *If a man has trouble paying you $300 when he cashes for $60,000 when can he ever pay you?*

It's strange that such people, who have larceny ingrained into their being, somehow seem to think nothing of conning people, even people they know, and do so without a hint of conscience.

Poker, to me, has always been a world inhabited by some of the most honorable people on the planet and, also, some of the least honorable. The fact of the matter is that your word and your reputation for integrity are sometimes all that separate you from the others. I've gone to banks to borrow money. They always require references, credit checks, reams of paperwork and sometimes weeks to process all that you provide them in order to give you a loan. In poker games, I've lent as much as twenty thousand dollars and borrowed more, simply on a handshake and one's reputation. That's not going to happen when that reputation has been tarnished.

CHAPTER 10

ROAD TRIPS

Freedom! That's what playing poker for a living is all about and nothing brings home that truth better than a road trip.

My First Road Trip to Las Vegas

It's a truly exhilarating feeling to be driving down the open highway with a good pal at your side, a pocketful of money and some good poker in your future, especially when one is young and in the early stage of a life's dream.

And bam, in one awful instant my car's engine blew and that exhilaration was suddenly dampened.

Skinny Denny was a dealer/player at the North Shore Club in Crystal Bay, Nevada, the current home of the weekly Dealers Choice game. It was 1977 and we decided to take a road trip to Las Vegas. This was to be my first time in Las Vegas as a professional poker player. I had less than 500 miles on my newly rebuilt engine in my Volkswagon Beetle when, ten miles short of Tonopah, Nevada, that engine conked out. We had the car towed into Tonopah and our ride was with the tow-truck driver.

We tried to rent a car but not one was available. We tried to catch a bus to Las Vegas but had just missed it and the next one didn't leave until the following afternoon. We tried to get a room and every place in town was sold out. That dampened feeling of exhilaration was turning into despair. The only thing left to do was go to the bar, which we did. At that point in time every lonely heart that entered that Tonopah, Nevada bar played Kenny Roger's *Lucille* on the jukebox.

We began drinking and struck up a conversation with Donna the bartender. We told her of our situation and after a while she offered us floor space at her house. Since we had sleeping bags, this seemed to be our best option by far.

Now we each had about $5,000 for our trip and, unlike myself, Denny kept flashing his money. It was so obvious that I had to tell him to stop. As the night went on, Denny and I made the rounds in Tonopah, visiting all the local bars. At the Mizpah Hotel and Casino we met Donna's boyfriend, who had been terminated from the Los Angeles Police Department for the use of excess force. He was working as a security guard at the Mizpah. He had a large burly presence and was not at all friendly. Now, my persona was pretty much that of the Northern California Cosmic Cowboy. I had long hair and a beard, and wore a straw cowboy hat, jeans, cowboy boots and a hippie necklace. Denny was a clean-cut Jewish boy from Los Angeles with curly black hair, a thin build and an innocent smile. We were particularly ripe for the plucking.

From making the rounds that night we learned how hitchhiking in Tonopah was illegal and we were told tales of the local police treating hippies in a very harsh manner. We needed to hang out until Donna got off shift, which was 2:00am, when we would meet up. Denny and I ended up getting pretty drunk. At closing time we were at Donna's bar, ready for her to take us home so we could crash on that floor-space. We walked to her house, then Donna quickly departed and went to meet her boyfriend. We laid out our sleeping bags and fell asleep.

At first sun, they came home. I was barely awake but I distinctly heard him say, "Should we shoot them here in their bags or should we take them outside?" My ears began to burn. Did I really hear that? Did I really, really hear that or was I dreaming? No, I was not dreaming and I really did hear that! They went into their bedroom and in one single movement I was out of my sleeping bag and dressed. I woke Denny and said, "Things are not right and we must get out of here immediately!" Denny grabbed his toothbrush and headed for the shower, so I grabbed him. "Listen to me, we must leave immediately. I'll be outside." A minute later we were running with all our gear towards downtown and Highway 95.

Several blocks from that surreal encounter with darkness, we planted our gear on the highway and prepared to hitchhike south. Denny walked across the street to get coffee and I stuck out my thumb just as a cop drove by going in the opposite direction. Now the penalty for possession of marijuana in Nevada in those days was one to six years in prison and/or a $2,000 fine, a penalty immensely more severe than California. I couldn't imagine what lay in store with one found in possession of cocaine. So there I was, a California hippie standing in the middle of Tonopah, Nevada, illegally hitchhiking, trembling from what I perceived was a near death experience, with an ounce of pot in my bag, a gram of coke in my sock and that cop had just made a U-turn and was heading back my way. I was still shaking from the dose of early morning panic; now with the addition of a strong measure of dread, last night's despair had degenerated into a sense of impending doom. Yesterday's exhilaration was relegated to history. Standing there as the cop approached, the situation I found myself in seemed only slightly better than being shot in my sleeping bag. Nonetheless, I had no doubt that I was pretty much screwed!

The cop started by asking where my friend went and then proceeded to write down my personal information. Denny walked casually back with coffee and gave his vitals to the officer too. I told the officer my car broke down and we had no way out of town until later in the afternoon. Then, as if by miracle, he told us we had to hitchhike outside the city limits and to walk on down the road a quarter mile.

We caught a quick ride and were in Las Vegas by noon.

* * * * *

In many older Nevada casinos, there would be a stage facing out towards the expanse of gaming tables, fronted by a bar below the stage. When musicians drove their music across the casino, the atmosphere was festive and the party was on.

In my life, I've been struck with a few impactful moments that I still recall with undiminished clarity. Like most of my generation, I know exactly where I was and what I was doing when news of JFK's assassination penetrated my brain. I can visualize the entire scene at the army induction center when I received my draft deferral in the middle of the Vietnam War. Such was a most glorious moment in my life at The Union

Plaza Hotel and Casino that evening in Las Vegas. I had just cashed out a $200 win in the first Las Vegas poker game I ever sat in and I had begun a slow exit from the casino, my whole being was totally puffed up. I was bedecked in my cosmic cowboy attire; I wore my straw Stetson, my head held high, my shoulders back, a triumphant grin across my face. As I passed directly in front of the stage, I looked up at the pretty country singer as she belted out *Mammas Don't Let Your Babies Grow Up To Be Cowboys.* I smiled at her and she smiled back, and for just a brief second, our eyes locked and she gifted me the sweetest 'country-singing-gal' wink of the eye, a wink that I would never forget, a wink that still marks a most impactful moment in my life.

I was absolutely on top of the world. Exhilaration was back.

Off to Montana

The car packed, our spirits high, our pockets full of dough, we headed east in the direction of Montana. Bruce Springsteen and the E Street Band were rocking *Thunder Road* on the stereo.

It was in the late seventies when Roy Ritner, Rick Ketcher and I took a road trip to Montana. It was State Fair week and we had been told of a big poker game where the best players in Montana would gather at "The Playground Casino" in the city of Great Falls.

* * * * *

On our first evening on the road we stopped for the night in Winnemucca, Nevada. After dinner we decided to check out the poker in the Bank Club Casino. The poker-room was empty except for the dealer. His name was Giuseppe and he said it was slow but if we wanted to play some No-Limit Hold'em he'd deal and play out of the rack (meaning he'd play with the poker bank that sat in the metal rack in front him), and perhaps, he continued, a few more players might stop in. Playing out of the rack was unheard of but this was Winnemucca on a slow night and the rack contained a substantial sum of money. We were young and cocky, definitely foolish, but we felt good about ourselves as poker players. Hoping some players would show up, we sat down and played against each other and Giuseppe and his rack of nearly unlimited chips.

We each bought in for $500 and Giuseppe began dealing. Within the first fifteen minutes Roy's original buy-in had shifted over to Giuseppe. Roy not only lost his $500 but he may possibly have allowed his ego to cloud his normally sound judgment; he pulled out his entire bankroll for the trip, maybe another $5,000. It was a minor miracle that Roy left Winnemucca with us instead of taking a bus back to Lake Tahoe because twenty minutes after his losing his first buy-in to Giuseppe a potentially disastrous hand came down. Roy raised with **Ace/Jack**. Giuseppe called with **Ace/Seven**. The flop came: **7-4-2**. Roy bet and

Giuseppe called. The turn card was an Ace and Roy thought he really had something and bet again and Giuseppe called. The river brought the **'case Ace'*** (meaning the last Ace in the deck). Now Roy really, really thought he had something: **three Aces** with a **Jack kicker**; but Giuseppe had **Aces full of sevens** the absolute nuts.* Roy bet about a $1,000 into a pot that already held $1,000.

Roy   Giuseppe

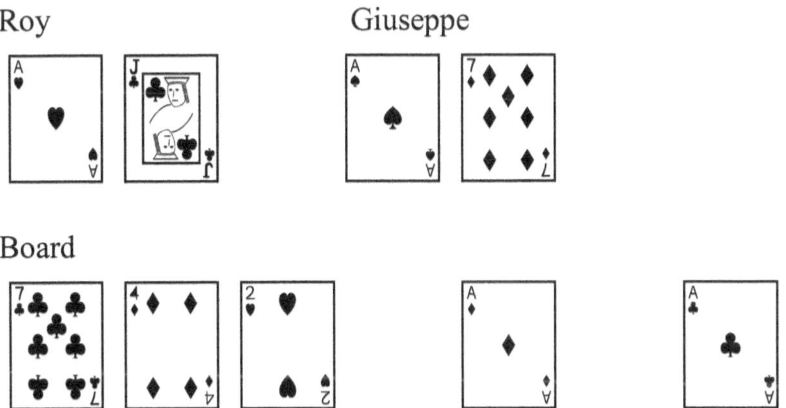

Board

Giuseppe called! That is correct. Giuseppe just called and did not raise with a hand that could not be beat. Roy, who I do believe at that point in that night, might have called a raise for all his money, was spared a bus ride home. I recall, at the time, scratching my head and wondering if Giuseppe was just feeling charitable or he didn't know he couldn't be beat. The game was over for us.

After the near-disaster in Winnemucca, we resumed our journey with our energy (especially Roy's) rather deflated. Once we left the desert of Nevada and entered Idaho the landscape became more interesting. By the time we entered Big Sky Country with the excitement of a road trip and the sheer beauty of Montana, our spirits were lifted once again.

* * * * *

We arrived in Great Falls, found a motel room and immediately sought out The Playground. This establishment was truly an adult entertainment center. This was where the poker games were to take place. There was bar with a pool table, a Chinese restaurant, a discothèque, a full menu coffee shop and, of course, the casino (though calling it a casino was a stretch of the imagination). There were two poker tables and an electronic Keno game that had a pay-off so bad that one couldn't beat it if one had been given the numbers in advance.

It was Montana State Fair week and players were supposedly coming from all over that part of the world. I met Frank Schend, who was reputed to be a top player in Montana. In years to come, he and I would often butt heads in Las Vegas at the WSOP. Others showed up, a few of whom I had previously played with in Reno or Tahoe. The big star, however, was The Razor. The story goes that he had become an accomplished Hold'em player on the east coast and had moved to Las Vegas, where he solidified his reputation as a premier all-around player and a respected authority on 'all things poker.' He left Las Vegas and moved north just as Hold'em was catching on in the northern states. The Razor was said to have left an impression on every big money player in and around Montana. Consequently, there were not a lot of sizable games left in the state where people were willing to risk a lot of their cash playing poker with The Razor.

Over the course of the week, The Razor and I became quite friendly. He spoke to me a lot about Las Vegas. Eventually, The Razor cautioned me about the danger of playing there. He was, of course, speaking of cheating, something that had not yet entered my way of thinking about playing poker for a living. Years later I would encounter precisely what The Razor had spoken of in Las Vegas.

And just perhaps, my traveling companions and I may well have already experienced that about which we were being cautioned. Although Rick, Roy and I had never had a conversation about our encounter with Giuseppe, in retrospect the three of us in our innocence and naivety had entered into a situation that would have certainly raised 'red flags' years later when we became more seasoned professionals.

* * * * *

The games at The Playground were good. The results were mixed and we thoroughly enjoyed our time in Great Falls. I liked the people of Montana and the Big Sky Country was beautiful. In fact, Montana had just become my favorite state.

Mostly, what I took away from that journey was the knowledge I could travel, see new places, meet new people and pay my way playing poker. That road trip in 1978 opened up a new dimension in my life.

It also taught me to never play poker against a guy called Giuseppe, who played out of the rack and dealt the cards.

Eventually, The Razor moved to Reno where we met now and then at the poker table.

St. Croix via Kansas City

It was after Karen and I had separated for good. Followed by an explosion of epic proportions, Dave and Mindy's relationship had completely blown apart. It was quite possible that irreparable damage had been done. Dave and Mindy were both devastated.

For some time, Dave and I had been talking about shipping his boat down to the Caribbean and having a nice vacation cruising the islands. With Dave in a bad mental state it seemed like it would be a good time for such a trip. Thus, Dave arranged for a shipping company to pick up his Bayliner, put it on a trailer, haul it cross-country to Florida and send it off to St. Croix where we planned to board it and do some island-hopping. When we booked the airline tickets, there was a flight that required a change of planes in Kansas City, Missouri. One of Missouri Dave's oldest and rowdiest friends, a gentleman called Shad, lived in Kansas City. It made sense to pay him a visit and, besides, another old Missouri pal, Phil Matthews, had a poker game there. The trip was set when we booked the flights. We each brought along enough money to play poker and to enjoy being on the boat. We had roughly $12,000 each.

We arrived in Kansas City. Shad met us at the airport and took us to his classic old three-story brick home in a nice historic neighborhood. Each of us had our own room and we settled right in.

It was extremely hot and humid so we immediately attacked his antique Coca-Cola vending machine filled with icy cold long-necked Buds. When empty Budweiser bottles littered the downstairs and all good sense was totally lost in an alcoholic haze, Shad and I thought it would be a swell idea to head to downtown Kansas City and seek some female companionship. Dave had slid into a massive post-Mindy funk and was barely functional. We left him sitting in a chair in the living room with his head hanging down on his chest.

Shad and I arrived at 12th Street and Vine and thinking of Dave, contracted three Kansas City working girls to come to Shad's party house. It turned into a disaster. Dave remained totally dysfunctional. The lady we thought would cheer up Dave sat around reading a book. Shad went to his room and I went to mine. After a short bit of time passed I heard Shad yell, "Get back here, HELP, she's stealing my watch!" I ran downstairs in my shorts just after the gal with the watch went out the front door. Shad stood at the door and was able to stop the other two ladies from exiting. A car pulled up out front and the gal that bolted got in the car. The car sat idling. In my inebriated state of mind, I grabbed a broom and held it like a rifle and yelled at the car, "Give the watch back, I have a gun!" Shad almost slapped me in the head saying, "Don't be completely stupid, they have the guns, we have the broom." Shad quickly diffused what could have been a nasty situation by sending the two other ladies out the door and they and the car with the watch drove away. Dave had barely moved a muscle the entire time.

The next day we did two things that would prove to be consequential. We arranged to play in Phil Matthew's poker game and Dave decided he would try to salvage his relationship. He called Mindy and after a long emotional conversation, she agreed to fly to Kansas City and join him. I called a lady in Tahoe I had been seeing and she thought it would be fun to come along with Mindy and join the festivities.

We went to Phil's to play in his No-Limit Hold'em game with $5/10 blinds. Phil ran a good game and had a great caterer that set up a massive buffet with gourmet offerings. He had lots of icy cold beer and plenty of hard liquor. I don't remember much about the poker game because Dave and I thought it would be a swell idea to take Quaaludes and play poker. When the dust settled and we walked out in the morning light, I had won about $3,000 and Dave, still thinking about Mindy, and under the influence of a Quaalude, had lost about $10,000.

The film *Casino*, starring Robert DeNiro, Sharon Stone and Joe Pesci, is about the evolution of Las Vegas. The Kansas City Mafia is prominently featured in the movie, depicting these guys skimming money from casinos they owned in Las Vegas. The real guys that the movie is based on got busted by the Feds and were sentenced to prison. Before going to prison, where they would spend their final years, the real guys had a poker game in Kansas City and they were blowing off as much dough as possible. At the time we were there, the big guys were away in *The Big House* but the poker game was still going. Phil said he could get us into the game.

Several nights after Phil's game, Dave and I showed up at a suite in the Kansas City Howard Johnson Hotel to play in a Mafia poker game. The players were all very welcoming, quite friendly and they seemed like players in any ordinary poker game. The night, however, did not go well. We managed to lose all the money we had. We called Shad for a loan and because the game was finished for the night we sat there for hours waiting for Shad and for the game to begin the next day. Shad needed to wait for the bank to open, so when the game fired up in the morning, we were unable to play for lack of funds. The game was going for about an hour when Shad showed up with a huge two-liter bottle of red wine and a doggie bag stuffed with $10,000 in cash, which he tossed on the table and said, "Lets gamble." Between Dave and I, we lost that too.

Still in Kansas City, we were broke, in debt to Shad and feeling different degrees of miserable. This was a boating vacation in the Caribbean gone terribly wrong. Just before our ladies showed up, Shad called the house and told us we should each check for critters. It seemed one of the ladies from 12th Street and Vine had left Shad with a little gift of the crabs. Shad, in turn, gave them to his girlfriend of many years and he was now a single man. Fortunately, I never received the gift.

Obviously, St Croix was now off the itinerary. Mindy and my girlfriend arrived and I, at least, was cheered up. Dave and Mindy remained in total turmoil. Before the four of us flew back to Reno, Shad paid for a ten-day jaunt around Missouri to visit Dave's mom and several old friends. Just prior to leaving, Shad told Dave and I that this had been like the movie *Neighbors*. In that film, people moved in next door to some other folks whose life turned into total shit. Shad said, after we moved in, he lost his very expensive watch, got the crabs, lost his girl-friend, was out a large sum of cash and paid for everything for everyone for two weeks. In spite of that he thanked us for coming.

I got home and sent Shad a check for what I owed him.

Dave sent him the title to a boat docked in St. Croix. They did manage to motor around the Caribbean together a year later.

Shad and his girlfriend got back together and they one day married.

Dave and Mindy did not get back together.

Tahoe to Aspen to Denver

I had left our house on the North Shore to Karen and I was both couch-surfing and living in my WW van. With Dave recently becoming homeless, he and I rented a house in Zephyr Heights on the Nevada side of South Lake Tahoe. While hanging out on our deck with Joe B, soaking in the spectacular view of Lake Tahoe, Joe happened upon a full-page announcement in one of the poker magazines for a poker tournament in Aspen, Colorado. It was billed as The Aspen Pro/Celebrity Poker Tournament and was to last a few days in downtown Aspen right in the heart of winter. We immediately agreed that this could be an exciting combination poker and ski trip. As we talked, we formed an uncomplicated plan. We'd take the Amtrak from Truckee, California to Colorado Springs and then travel on to Aspen by bus.

It started with Dave, Joe B and myself. Joe B was a life-long winning poker player, originally from the San Francisco Bay area, but a long-time resident of South Tahoe. He was one of our closest friends. Like Dave, Joe B had offered me a safe harbor when my marriage to Karen had finally ended. Dave and Joe B's relationship went back long before me. The three of us played a lot of poker together. Joe B was one of the finest gentlemen to ever play the game. He was a stand-up guy, extremely bright, funny and brimming with integrity. This was the same year Joe and I began playing racquetball under the tutelage of our poker playing buddy, Dale Steward.

Frodo, a hippie card player and fellow Deadhead, signed on for the trip along with Mike "the Wig" and Flyer, all from the North Shore. Finally, our old pal Mark Peterson, who had friends in Aspen, decided to join us. Mark split his time living between Hawaii and Palm Springs where he majored in both tennis and golf and minored in poker. We booked a condominium in Aspen with three bedrooms that would accommodate six of us, while Mark planned to stay with a friend in Aspen.

A couple of weeks later, just as planned, we boarded an overnight train for a ride through Nevada, Utah and into the Rocky Mountains; we de-boarded at a station in Colorado Springs and took a shuttle bus to Aspen. We quickly got a feel for the place, and the bar at the Jerome Hotel became our gathering spot. The poker tournament was to take place in one of the larger eating establishments. There were lots of players in town with the majority being from Denver, Montana, Las Vegas and our bunch from Lake Tahoe. Unfortunately, although there were plenty of pros, there was only one who qualified as a celebrity. That was Jerry Van Dyke, a comedian and brother to Dick Van Dyke. Consequently, for lack of celebrities, the tournament was changed to a Pro/Am event. Each pro was to be auctioned off to a hometown amateur, raising money for local charities. That two-person team would tag in and out, playing the same chips in the tournament. It was a hoot; Aspen was totally welcoming and we communed with old friends and players. In the beginning, the cash games were really good and, although no one put on skis, the four-days in Aspen was one big party with poker mixed in.

While in Aspen we learned that poker was being openly played in Denver. This was a very recent phenomenon and billed as social poker, which meant the house running the game could not rake, or charge, for dealing the game. The players, therefore, were asked to generously tip the dealers and the tips were to be divided between the dealers and the local charity sponsoring the game that day. There were about a dozen bars, restaurants and hotels participating. Poker was alive and well in Denver.

When our time was up in Aspen, Missouri Dave, Flyer and I decided we would head to Denver. Mark Peterson was going to hang out in Aspen for a while and would join us later, while Joe B, Frodo and Mike 'the Wig' caught the train home. We flew to Denver and we were told that there were a bunch of poker games underway at the airport hotel. Dave and I took a room there together, while Flyer headed for the poker-room and was in a game before we were even in the elevator. The room we checked into was rather bleak. It was a typical no frills, downright grim hotel room. As Dave and I entered the poker room, we ran into a small-time hustler we knew from North

Tahoe who had been in Denver for a few weeks and he said there were good games going downtown. We immediately checked out of The Grim Hotel and took a cab to the Denver city center. We asked the cab driver for the best hotel he could recommend and he dropped us at The Oxford, a beautiful, recently refurbished turn-of-the-century luxury hotel. Flyer remained at The Grim thoroughly ensconced in his poker game.

Dave and I began playing in Craig Morten's Steakhouse, a short cab-ride from the Oxford. Craig Morton was a former star quarterback from Cal and then the Denver Broncos and one of the proprietors of the restaurant-turned-card room. The poker games were fine and with our wins there and from Aspen we were both well ahead. We heard of a big game in Boulder some miles outside of downtown Denver. Dave headed out there but needing some rest, I stayed in town.

Dave found the poker game in the bar located in the basement of a busy Boulder dinner house. He reported the game was really good with lots of money and great action. It was hosted by a guy called Shamrock. The next day, I joined Dave and headed to Boulder. From what we had heard, we learned Shamrock was a bookie with some rather erratic behavior and very shady connections. Even though he was very friendly towards us, his looks, his presence and his aura shouted tough-guy. We felt the need to tread carefully. Soon enough, Flyer found his way to Boulder as well.

Flyer, as always, was a phenomenon. When we were contemplating our trip to Aspen, Flyer was totally busted. He loved the idea of the trip but he needed to refinance; so, before signing up for our pending adventure, he entered into an arrangement with Mark Peterson. Mark would give him $5,000, half of which was a loan and the other half bought fifty percent of Flyer's action. Flyer did well in Aspen and settled up with Mark prior to traveling to Denver. Flyer re-paid Mark his initial $5,000 investment, plus he gave to Mark half his winnings, which amounted to an additional $5,000. Now Flyer had his own $5,000 bankroll and was playing for just himself. Flyer had fared well in the card room at The Grim and now had his money up to over $7,000. At the hotel gift shop, Flyer bought Del, his sweetheart of many years, two stuffed pink flamingos as a memento to celebrate his good fortune.

For a week, Flyer, Dave and I all played at the basement card room in Boulder. Between sessions, Dave and I returned to downtown Denver and to the Oxford. We enjoyed Denver; we were eating at good restaurants and patronizing some cool city bars with live music. Flyer continued, steady on, playing in the basement in Boulder.

Shamrock, who had the same sleep patterns as Flyer, played hour for hour with him. It was during this long session in which Flyer and Shamrock were both playing that Shamrock came completely unglued. Shamrock had been up for many days and nights pounding Grand Marniers and very likely snorting cocaine. He was becoming increasingly more paranoid, delusional and angry. Though I was not there, Dave was at the bar waiting for a seat in the game when Shamrock convinced himself that someone was cheating in the poker game by holding out cards. He really lost it when he threatened to kick the shit out of anyone that refused to strip down to their undershorts so he could search them for what he thought were cards being held out. So there, in the basement poker-room in Boulder, Colorado, stood Flyer, Cowboy Wolford and six other players as well as the dealer, in their underwear, as Shamrock searched them all to no avail.

Shamrock's girlfriend was skinny, really skinny. She had multiple rings on her fingers and perhaps even bells on her toes. Much of her body was heavily tattooed and her head was covered with body piercings in her ears, nose and lips with a stud or two in her cheeks. She went by the name of Dagger. She had a generally unpleasant disposition and managed to drink and ingest many of the same things Shamrock did, though, perhaps, not the same quantities.

When he failed to catch any cheats, Shamrock went ape-shit crazy on Dagger for no apparent reason, though the word reason no longer had meaning to the totally crazed Shamrock. He physically attacked

Dagger on the stairs going up to the restaurant. Missouri Dave, who, from the bar, had just witnessed the scene around the poker game in absolute disbelief, jumped up to try to prevent serious harm from coming to Dagger. On the stairs to the restaurant, a human chain formed. Dagger, weighing in at one hundred pounds of attitude and defiance, was screaming while simultaneously scratching and clawing near the top of the stairs hoping to find sanctuary in the busy restaurant above with two hundred and fifty pounds of a maniacal Shamrock holding her back by a few toes and maybe even an ankle; meanwhile, all one hundred and sixty-five pounds of Missouri Dave was wrapped around one of Shamrock's legs on the lower part of the stairs as he was trying his best to aid an extremely distressed Dagger. Simultaneously, just around the corner from the stairs sat a poker table with nearly one hundred and fifty thousand dollars in cash and chips, with eight players and a dealer all wondering if it was safe yet to get dressed; those standing around in their skivvies included Flyer and the professional card playing, former rodeo star, Cowboy Wolford. The overweight and bare-chested Cowboy Wolford stood in his white skivvies and still sported his ever-present, high crowned, wide brimmed, gray Stetson cowboy hat. This was not a scene from a typical poker room. Anyone entering from the street into that poker room, at that particular moment in time, would wonder if they had, indeed, entered into *The Twilight Zone* or some other alternative reality. Many hours later long after order and decorum had returned to the asylum, Dave checked out of the poker game. He left Flyer, still playing, with about $40,000 in cash and chips in front of him.

When Dave arrived back at the Oxford, he found that Mark Peterson had showed up from Aspen, checked into the hotel and was sitting in the bar with me. Dave joined us as we celebrated with a few victory drinks.

Mark had a 1981 VW Rabbit convertible, which I had long coveted, and which he was possibly interested in selling although we were far apart on the price. However, when I flashed a big wad of one-hundred-dollar bills, the sight of the money was too great a temptation and Mark agreed to my offer of $13,000. He took the cash, which was most of my winnings-above-expenses from the trip. In turn he handed me his airport parking claim check. I drove that Rabbit for the next fourteen years.

The following day it was time to head home. Aspen and Denver had provided a bucketful of fun and entertainment and certainly some good stories. The Oxford was special. The poker was good for Dave and myself. Mark had left earlier that morning. We met Flyer at the airport. Financially, Flyer found himself right where he had started the trip. He was flat broke. He boarded the plane without a dime to his name, carrying only his suitcase and his two stuffed pink flamingos.

A Tournament at the Frontier

"It's better to live a day as a lion than a lifetime as a lamb."
A version of an old saying, made popular in poker circles by 'Treetop'
Jack Straus, Texas poker professional.

Jack Straus won the championship event at the World Series of
Poker in 1982. His win turned heads and stood out for a rather startling
occurrence. A big hand came down where Jack pushed all his chips into
the pot. A player with more chips than him called his bet. Jack lost the
pot and was getting up to exit the tournament when he discovered a single $500 chip under a Keno ticket. After some discussion, it was deter-
mined that Jack bet but did not say all-in; his opponent only called and,
therefore, that chip was Jack's and he was still alive in the tournament.
Jack was then able to parlay that single chip into winning every chip in
the tournament to earn him the most unlikely World Championship as
well as the $520,000 first place prize money. It was from that scenario
that the expression *"a chip and a chair"* (meaning a player was still in
action) was born.

Dave and I were honored when the phone rang on that early
morning in 1983 for on the other end of the phone line was Jack Straus.
Though I didn't really know Jack, we would give one another the nod
when we saw each other. Dave, on the other hand, had played against
Jack on numerous occasions. Jack called that morning to say he was
sponsoring a poker tournament at the Frontier Hotel and Casino in Las
Vegas. Since Missouri and I knew most of the poker players in the Re-
no-Tahoe area he wanted us to help promote his event. I said we'd put
the word out.

Once again, Dave and I were both on the verge of being broke;
however, the bills were paid and we lived in beautiful Lake Tahoe in my
knotty pine home with a panoramic view of the lake. Life really wasn't
all that bad.

Jack's poker tournament at The Frontier sounded like it could be fun but Dave and I needed to do some refinancing. As was the way things so often happened back then, it took just a small handful of phone calls and we had a $5,000 bankroll and our flights were booked.

Frodo joined Dave and I and we flew to Las Vegas. Dave insisted we arrive in style so we hired a limo at the airport and headed off to The Frontier, arriving like we were financially better off than we really were. Dave and I had decided to do something we had never done before: we would play the same bankroll and we would split the win or loss from our overall play in Las Vegas. We checked into the hotel and headed to the poker room.

We made sure we each sat in a different poker game. Dave played in a game with Jack Straus. In the slightly smaller game I was playing in was a friend from South Lake Tahoe named Gary Messenger. When I first met Gary, he was the card room manager of Caesars Tahoe. That was a big-time job. Gary was a handsome man, sturdy, a strong swimmer, soft spoken, a kind and gentle human being and a capable poker player. I remember going into Caesars one afternoon a few years back to find Gary walking with a cane. He said his balance had been a little off but all was well. Fast forward to The Frontier that evening and Gary's seat in the poker game was a bed-like wheel chair where he laid with advanced multiple sclerosis. Gary's mind was perfectly functional; it was his body that let him down. Gary was in the company of his caregiver who we referred to as Nurse Ratchet. She sat next to his elevated bed and would tell him what cards he held and would read the board to him. He would tell her what to do in the hand. She would handle the cards and the chips and act accordingly. We had watched this process before, except this night was different.

The caregiver was pounding down cocktails.

Gary was losing and he was becoming as animated as a person who could barely talk and could not control his limbs could become. I grabbed Dave and told him something wasn't right. Together we concluded that she was not at all listening to Gary, but instead she was playing on her own with Gary's money. What she was doing was causing him to have out-of-control spasms from anger and disbelief. She was losing Gary's money and she was losing badly. Dave and I managed to put a stop to it. We spoke to the shift manager and insisted they deal around Gary. Then, in no uncertain terms, we told Gary's caregiver, who was then accompanied by security guards, to take him to the room. We called Joe B, who would call The Martian, who would call Big Bruce who was dating Gary's ex-wife. In turn, she called Gary's parents in the Midwest, who would arrive in Las Vegas the next evening. They would immediately send Nurse Ratchet packing and take Gary back to their home and assume the role of Gary's caretakers. Gary would be out of Las Vegas and the awful situation he had found himself in.

That night, after the first session, our bankroll was up to about $7,000. We decided to go to a favorite steak house and have a minor celebration. After dinner we headed back to the Frontier. I retired to the room and Dave took the money and headed back to the poker room to see what the games were like. Sometime in the very early morning, the telephone woke me. It was my old friend Mark Porter. He said I needed to get down to the poker room as fast as possible. He explained that Dave was drunk and out of control, and he was throwing away his dough.

I was beamed down there in a flash. I stood behind Dave, "How's it going?" I asked.

"Not good," he said. He had about four or five hundred dollars in front of him.

"Okay, give me the rest of the money."

Dave turned his head, put his hand over his mouth and in a low voice out of the corner of his mouth said "This is the rest of the money."

With that, I turned and went back to bed totally disgusted.

The next day when we caught up with each other, he told me he quit drinking, sobered up and had managed to get lucky and play his way out of the hole he had dug. Our money was up to $9,000.

We stayed for a week, had a great time and returned home no longer broke. We repaid the money we borrowed and split about $12,000.

We never saw Gary Messenger again after that night.

Jack Straus carried on having his tournament the next couple of years.

Missouri & Me

Like a few good stories, it started with a telephone call. Missouri Dave and I, being severely underfunded, were hanging out at home on a mid-October morning when the phone rang; it was Tommy Kosub, a long time rounder from an old gambling family. Tommy was calling to tell Dave and myself about a poker tournament he was producing. He was billing it as the Montana State Championship and it was going to be held in Sally's Casino in Livingston, Montana. I explained to him our current economic reality and told him our appearance there was highly unlikely. Tommy assured me that if we could just get there with a little cash in our pockets he would lend us some money should there be a need.

Dave and I had just been lamenting the fact that being broke always left us low on options as to what poker we could play and where we could play it. We agreed a trip to Montana would be fun but our pockets were empty and, besides, the mortgage and all the bills were due in a couple of weeks. Being broke for us, as well as many of the less disciplined poker players who derived their entire income from play-ing, was not really that unusual; it was only a temporary inconvenience. A player I knew, after being broke and then bouncing back in action, would declare, "There's no crime in being broke, only in staying broke!" Over the years Dave and I both had established strong reputations in the poker community; therefore, from a solid network of friends, we had very good borrowing power. So, we could play but we had to chase down some cash and that was never a lot of fun. Earlier in the year we both played in Binion's World Series of Poker Main Event, but that was then and this was now and now we were, so to speak, financially embar-rassed.

Then the phone rang again. It was Karl Fox calling from Santa Cruz, California. He told Dave, at that moment, he was in a poker game and he was winning and he had the $500 he owed Dave and that if he got down there fast he could get paid. Fast was the operative word, for he was still in the game and so was Dave's $500. The wheels began to turn! I had $300 stashed away for certain emergencies, such as eating. We formed a plan. We would pack our bags, get in the car and go to Santa Cruz, collect money from Karl, if he still had it, and perhaps play in the game. If we came home with money, we would go to Reno and play $10/20 Limit Hold'em, the biggest game going at that time in *The Biggest Little City in America*. Then, if we could beat the game there, we had Montana on our minds.

SANTA CRUZ, CALIFORNIA

It's a four-hour drive west, up and over Donner Pass, down the mountain, through Sacramento, across the valley, south to San Jose and over the coastal mountains to our destination. Santa Cruz is a picturesque little University town sitting right on the ocean with a beautiful beach. It's known for good surfing, great music and an abundance of folks living alternative lifestyles. The city's centerpiece is an oceanfront Boardwalk with a huge roller coaster, lots of thrill-rides, carnival games you couldn't beat, cotton candy, photo booths and a fun fair-like edginess. But we weren't there for a vacation. We were there to find Karl Fox before he could gamble away his dough. Dave and I had decided, for the time being, we'd combine our money and play the same bankroll.

We arrived at the card room in the Aptos Hotel not a moment too soon. There sat Karl. He had just lost a big pot but still had $400 in front of him. He said hello, gave Dave the $400 and went to the bar. Dave sat in the game and I joined Karl at the bar. In Nevada, Texas Hold'em was the main game. In California in 1985, however, only Low-Ball and Draw Poker were legal. On this day at the Aptos Club they were playing an illegal game of Hold'em. The way it worked was simple. A security guard sat by the door and watched for the police. He was to shout a warning if they showed up. Someone in the game always had to sit in the '#3 seat' to block the view of the community cards being used from the outside. Community cards would be a sure-sign of an illegal game of Hold'em.

Word got around that we were in town, so we were able to see some old friends. Two days later we left Santa Cruz. We arrived back in North Tahoe with an after-expenses combined bankroll of just over $800.

RENO, NEVADA

We returned home long enough to pack bags for Reno. Our plan was to take the $800 bankroll and to play in shifts until we either reached our goal of $3,900 or went broke. The goal we set was for $1,200 to pay the mortgage and the bills, $200 travel money, and a $2500 bankroll to get us started in Montana. We had $800 and just short of a week before we needed to leave for Montana to arrive in time for Tommy's Tournament. We decided not to get a room until we made our first play, just in case it went badly.

The grind was on. Dave got us off to a good start and late the first day we did check into a room. I played the next shift. Reno offered a variety of amusements, but most of what we enjoyed involved friends, food and libations. However, on this trip, none of those things were the focus of our attention. No, we were on a mission. We continued to play in shifts. We had some winning sessions and some losing ones. It was early Thursday evening and the tournament was to start in Livingston, Montana at noon on Saturday. I was about three or four hours into playing when Dave walked up behind me after having slept some and asked where we stood. I counted my chips and added that to the money in my pocket. "We're $200 short of $3900."

Dave responded, "Close enough, lets go."

With a big smile on my face, I cashed out and we headed back to Tahoe to pay the bills, pack clean clothes and replenish our box of cassettes for music on the road. Once back in Tahoe, the turnaround took less than an hour and we were back on Highway 80, this time heading east to The Montana State Championship Poker Tournament.

TRAVELING EAST THROUGH NEVADA

We both were feeling really good that our plan had worked well so far. It was mid-evening when we left Tahoe. We passed back through Reno and headed into the night and the open highway. Dave was at the wheel of my 1981 Volkswagen Rabbit convertible. Waylon Jennings set the mood, singing and playing his hard-driving guitar, coming in strong on the stereo. Even with Waylon and a few of his pals serenading us, I managed to get some sleep. We passed through Winnemucca. In Wells we stopped at a truck stop so I could take a turn at driving. I thought about Flyer and I looked into that truck stop to see if any 'eights' were at the counter eating "chili and chicken gumbo!"

We headed north towards Jackpot with Willie Nelson singing about mothers and babies and cowboys. Jackpot is one of those towns located on the state's border. It's the place where Idaho residents go, close to home, to legally gamble. Its equivalent in the east is Wendover, Nevada, for the residents of Utah. Both places consist of a small handful of casinos, housing for the workers, a gas station, perhaps a small diner, a grocery store and the requisite number of bars to make it all happen. Other than that, there's not much to these places stuck in an empty and barren part of Nevada.

We checked out the casinos to see what the poker rooms looked like and there wasn't anything going on, so we continued north into Idaho. Dave resumed driving in Idaho Falls. We motored through Twin Falls and drove straight through into Montana. On the final stretch, between Butte and Livingston, I woke to the music of Jerry Jeff Walker. I was treated to a full moon so bright I thought there was a fire on the other side of the mountain. As we passed through narrow canyons, sitting low in the passenger seat, I became mesmerized by the moon as it danced in and out of view, behind the jagged mountain ridges high up above us.

LIVINGSTON, MONTANA

Suddenly, we were in Livingston. We had traveled about a thousand miles in twenty-four hours. Dave had driven eight hundred of those miles. We stopped at Sally's Casino in the downtown. That was the funkiest casino ever. It should have been called Sally's Western Bar and Tiny Card room. The place had a long bar with a dozen barstools, a pool table and two poker tables. A surprised Tommy Kosub sent us to the Livingston Motor Lodge. It was about 8:00pm when we checked into our room. In the lobby we ran into Diane Wagner who wrote for *Card Player Magazine* and lived just up the road in Bozeman. Dave went to bed. I was well rested and went out with Diane. It was Halloween and everyone, just like most nights, was dressed like a cowboy, only more drunk. Drinking cold beer and hanging with folks dancing to a live country music band was a welcome change from the road.

The next day I got up, went to Sally's and played in the No-Limit Hold'em Tournament. Dave still slept. The pool table had been moved out and a third poker table moved in. All three tables were full. I finished 4th and made a little money. Later the real game started. We were playing $5/5/10 blinds No-Limit Hold'em. In the game were Big George from Denver and his buddy whom they called The Sheriff, known for keeping people honest by calling most bets. Folks who knew him said he'd never be bluffed; he was definitely a guy you wanted in the game. There was Young Todd, an action player from Bozeman, and Denis from Great Falls. From Billings were our good friends Eric Schultz and Barbed Wire. Then there was a gentleman, named Mike Art, with lots of cash. He owned Chico Hot Springs Resort and Hotel.

The game was action-packed and rip-roaring out of the chute. I got 'hit by the deck' (meaning I won way more than my share of big hands). I cashed out over $3,500 winner. Dave joined the game when I packed it in and he, too, beat the game. When we counted our bankroll, we had $7,000, and our room, which we updated to a suite, was paid in advance. We played for two more days but the games weren't nearly as good as on the first night. We had a hell of a good time, which we concluded with a big party we hosted in our new suite.

Our plan was to head to Billings and catch up with some old friends. But we were pretty wiped out from lots of driving and our brains needed a break from the intensity of playing cards.

CHICO HOT SPRINGS

We had met Mike Art while playing poker and he had suggested we come to his resort at the Chico Hot Springs just an hour south of Livingston. Folks we met in town highly recommended a visit, so we headed south. The resort sits at the western entrance to Yellowstone National Park. It's an old historic hotel, a solid structure built to withstand Montana winters. The lobby and lounge were western-themed with wood interiors, cushy leather couches and antique furnishings, lots of hanging plants, walls adorned with paintings from the old west and a fair number of animals who'd encountered the taxidermist. There was a great bar with a pool table and a gourmet restaurant that was a big attraction for people from all over the state. Keeping with the western motif, the two rooms we checked into had sturdy antique brass beds. We headed for the hot springs. There was one massive outdoor thermal pool and several smaller pools of various temperature ranges. After many miles on the road and way too much poker, a good soak was the ideal way to relax and spend our late afternoon.

The weather had turned while we were in Livingston. Our first night in Chico we were slammed with a massive snowstorm. As I was soaking in the hot pool, I recalled thinking fondly about Tommy's phone call and the special odyssey we were in the midst of. Quickly, the storm brought the freezing cold and heavy winds with almost zero visibility. We exited the pool, dressed and made our way to the bar.

The only people in the bar were two cowboys shooting pool and Sandy the bartender. I sparked up a conversation with Sandy. She was a cowgirl, a real cowgirl. Sandy worked at Chico in the winters but come spring she gathered supplies for a horse-drawn chuck wagon and would take it up to the very high country where, for two weeks at a time, she would cook for groups of hunters. She even packed a six-shooter.

We were getting friendly when the door opened and two more women, trailed by snow and the howling wind entered from the raging blizzard blowing outside the bar. They bellied up to the bar opposite us. A few minutes passed.

"I think I know one of those ladies," Dave said to me in a low tone.

"Missouri Dave, you're just dreaming. We're a thousand miles from home, in the middle of nowhere and in the midst of a snowy white-out. I don't think so."

Another minute passed.

"Excuse me, is your name Dave, Missouri Dave?" Inquired the young lady who'd just circled around the bar.

Her name was Vicki and she had been a girlfriend of Teddy Binion of the Binion's Horseshoe clan. Vicki's family and the home she grew up in were not far from Chico and she and her girlfriend were hanging with her folks while she recovered from her break up with Teddy. Dave hooked up with Vicki and I with Sandy, the pistol packing cowgirl bartender. The Chico Hot Springs had just taken on a new dimension.

After several days of dancing and romancing and a few good meals, punctuated with relaxing soaks and the magic of the hot springs, Dave and I were ready to take to the road again. We dissolved our partnership and split up our cash, ending up with just over $3,200 apiece. We said farewell to the ladies, packed our bags and headed east to Billings.

BILLINGS, MONTANA

I had played in Billings once before and I knew a few locals. We also had some good friends we had known for years from their forays into the poker worlds of Reno, Tahoe and Las Vegas. A few of them were around and we felt welcomed. Barbed Wire was one such old friend.

Barbed Wire was a full-time poker player. He was a mountain of a man, standing at about 6'3," weighing about 250 lbs. He had a huge mound of kinky, curly, reddish brown hair that sat under an extremely tall Native American style ten-gallon cowboy hat with a flat brim and a colorful hatband. With his height, his hair, his hat and his cowboy boots, he had the appearance of a western giant from a Zane Grey novel. He looked exactly like the type of outlandish character he actually was. He was an artist who combined ceramics and woodwork. He was a gentle giant, a kind soul and he traveled to many points south to play poker regularly. He had about a half dozen motorhomes parked in parking lots of casinos and card rooms all over California, Nevada and Washington; thus, when he flew or drove to play cards, he had his own digs waiting for him. He played a lot of cards and knew well the western airways and highways.

Another old friend was Monty the Gambler. He was a frequent visitor to Reno and Lake Tahoe. He was one of Billings' finest card players. Over the years, Dave and I had played a lot of poker, smoked a bit of weed and drank a lot of beer with Monty. When we rolled into Billings we found Monty to be the new owner of a 'happening' night-club and card room. It was a jam-packed local hotspot with a good sized poker room, (five or six poker tables), a restaurant, two bars, a poolroom and a huge dance floor with live music most nights. It was quite a joint. That night we checked into the Dude Rancher Motel. The next day we began playing poker at Monty's club. During our stay in Billings we would also mix in playing downtown at the Empire Club. Dave ran into an old girlfriend, a poker dealer he had met in Las Vegas and they began hanging out together. Sandy came down from Chico for two days.

It was cold in Billings, usually between minus ten and twenty degrees. Another week went by. We each had run our money up pretty good but with too much drinking and the 'been playing poker too long blues,' our mental acuity became stressed, resulting in our bankrolls beginning to lose heft. Then on a freezing cold, snowy Montana night, Dave, Monty and I went to a local brothel and we contracted all the available working ladies to spend the weekend with us at Monty's place. So, with three cases of beer, a bottle of tequila, an ample supply of pot and a small bag of cocaine, we headed to our impromptu party at Monty's accompanied by *three ladies of the night*. After an initial burst of energy, with the six of us snowed in, we passed much of the time the next three days cooking, sharing meals together and engaged in heated games of Monopoly, Scrabble and Hearts! When the extended weekend was over, we returned our new friends to the brothel. Then Dave and I looked at each other, fairly disgusted with ourselves from all the degeneracy, and realized we needed badly to go home.

THE ROAD HOME

We called Barbed Wire and asked about a shortcut to Nevada through Montana and Idaho that he had mentioned. When we left that night, it was minus twenty degrees, with the wind chill factor pushing it down to minus eighty degrees. The stars were out but it was just starting to lightly spit snow. We thought very little about it; we just wanted to go home. The roads were great to Bozeman. There we turned onto the shortcut and headed south to Ennis. When we arrived in Ennis, the snow was falling on that small western town. It felt, cozy and appealing; however, in a heartbeat, we had passed through.

When we were about twenty-five miles south of Ennis, the snow had become heavier and we hadn't seen a car in either direction since we passed through town. Off in the distance, we could see a few lights and signs of civilization. The lights diminished the farther we traveled. Then there were no lights, just us and the wind and snow and darkness. We started climbing uphill. It was so unbelievably cold out that the falling snow was feather light. The higher we climbed the more this super light snow began to surround us. When the snow started to float over the hood of my VW Rabbit convertible I gently stepped on the brakes. We pulled out the map.

Tracing the map with my finger, I said, "This pass peaks at seven thousand feet and then the road goes down into a valley and then

up the other side and over another seven thousand foot mountain pass."
I looked at Dave. "I've never seen snow do this, the way it's coming up
over the hood."

Dave responded, "It's different, lighter than Tahoe snow. It's
just so fucking cold. If we were to break down…I don't like your odds
of finding help and no one would know where the fuck we are."

"My odds?"

"Well, I wouldn't be leaving the car."

"You know you always read about people freezing to death, lost
on some mountain pass in Montana."

"Yeah. I read recently about a couple of Montanans who were
out hunting when the weather changed so fast they were caught by surprise? Found dead weeks later."

"Well, freezing is freezing and I don't want to be another tragic
story in the newspaper. Besides, we only have one sleeping bag and my
big heavy sheepskin coat. I don't know what's going to keep you warm
since getting all chummy with you tonight doesn't sound so great."

"You're driving, buddy, I'll leave it up to you."

I made a U-turn and headed in the direction from whence we
came. As we drove each passing mile toward Ennis, the storm's fury
eased up, as did the tension in the car.

We arrived back in Ennis in time to get the last room at the Inn.
Dinner, a couple cold beers, two warm beds and we were glad we did
what we did. We continued on in the morning. The sun was shining and
there were huge snow berms on the sides of the road for about one hundred miles. It seemed certain the decision we made the night before was
the correct decision. It was then we came up with our own wise words to
live by: *Never take a shortcut in a blizzard.*

NORTH TAHOE

We had been gone for about five weeks, when we arrived home
in late November. After we paid the bills that were due, I had a little
over $2,000 left; Dave had about $3,000. Since we started with almost

nothing, for certain, monetarily, we were way better off than when Tommy had called in mid-October. But our trip was about so much more than money. It was about so many things. It was certainly about the freedom that comes with our chosen profession; the freedom that enabled us to pack up on a moment's notice, venture out and follow a dream. We saw some beautiful parts of America, communed with a bunch of old friends, made some new ones, lived a story and shared a memory that would last forever.

Hawaii

When I first met Missouri Dave he was bouncing back and forth between Hawaii and Lake Tahoe. In Hawaii, Dave had a sporadic home game in Waikiki and at times that game could get quite large. When Missouri and I started running together, I accompanied him on a trip to Hawaii for a vacation and it happened that a poker game was on the agenda. From that time on we would occasionally get the phone call inviting us to come to Hawaii telling us the game was on.

When we got the call, we wrapped a great Hawaiian vacation around each poker trip. We had an ideal situation; one of Dave's oldest friends, Trey Vedova, owned a car dealership in Kailua and he had a beautiful home in Lanikai Beach. Trey would pick us up at the airport in Waikiki, drive us to his home where we each had a room and he'd set us up with a new loaner car from the dealership. Our walk was about fifty yards to one of Hawaii's most beautiful beaches and we were close to everything on the Windward side of Oahu.

One such trip was in the winter of 1987. Dave and I had just returned that day from skiing at Heavenly Valley in South Tahoe when the call came. There was a mortgage broker who lived near Trey in Koneohe. He was a mad poker player and had been hosting a game in his home. Real estate sales were on fire and this guy was rolling in dough. The caller said they needed a couple of players. The next morning, we were on a plane to Hawaii. Trey made a phone call to our friends Shad and Sandy in Kansas City, told them we were coming to Hawaii and a party began to take shape. We arrived and settled into Trey's house, thrilled to have gone from the snow one day to sand between our toes the next.

Dave and I showed up at the poker game. Three of the guys from Dave's old game we knew well. Jack, the host, and one other were new to us. We were going to be playing a $20/40 Limit Dealer's Choice game. That was directly in my wheelhouse. Jack, however, lacked not only basic poker skills but also absolutely all self-control. When the game started, Jack raked the game five dollars per hand. That was reasonable. After a while the five-dollar a hand was out the window as the more Jack lost, the more, each hand, Jack raked. That, too, was reasonable. Shortly the rake from each pot became a handful of chips, but it did not matter, as Jack would immediately put every chip back in action.

After a while Jack was losing so much money he would not even bother taking chips from the pot; he had lost all sense of control and no amount he could rake from the pot could make a dent in what he was losing. He was banking the game and he would constantly go to the chip box for more ammunition. When the game was over and it was time to settle up, Dave and I were the big winners. And, we were the only ones not to get paid. We were given our original buy-in back and Jack told us he would settle up at the beginning of next week's game. It was a substantial amount of money and we just hoped he was as good as his word. On the bright side, it meant a game was scheduled for the following week.

At the time, I was involved in an ongoing long distance relationship. My sweetheart, Linda Lamb, was a beautiful, bright, Scottish entrepreneur from London who was full of life and a joy to be around. I had been going to London three times a year, staying with Linda about six weeks at a time, and she had been coming to Lake Tahoe for most of two summers. Since I was bucks-up after our first poker session at Jack's and the game showed the promise of lasting a while, I called Linda and invited her to Hawaii. She put her very busy life on hold and boarded a plane. Shad and Sandy arrived. The festivities had launched. Every day was special: the white sand beach of Lanikai, ocean boating, great meals, old friends together again. Nightly, the magic of the islands flowed through Trey's house on warm Hawaiian winds.

At the poker game the next week we were paid just as promised and that game ended with the exact same results.

Dave and I had established a tradition for our poker trips to Hawaii in which the biggest winner would buy dinner the following night at an upscale restaurant. I was buying the first two weeks and with that bunch, dinners were not cheap. It was the second dinner I hosted when Sonia, Trey's fiancé, invited a girlfriend, who was in a terribly abusive relationship, to join us. Her friend who just had a huge blowout with her abuser, was upset and in hiding. We all sat at the table having drinks before ordering dinner. The girlfriend was sitting between Shad, who had been cocktailing all day, and Dave. I was sitting across from them. That's when I saw him, the guy. I saw the guy who had just entered the restaurant. By the way he looked around the dining room, by the way he zeroed in on us, by the fire in his eyes I knew it was the guy. I knew it was him, the abusive boyfriend. He made a beeline for our table and stood directly behind the girlfriend who had no idea he was there. Steam and anger were blasting from both his ears, yet, before he could utter a single word, Shad turned around, looked directly at this dude and, thinking he was our waiter, said, "Hey buddy, bring me another scotch and soda."

Suddenly everyone was aware of exactly who this man was and that he certainly was not the waiter. The entire table, with the exception of Sonia's girlfriend, erupted in hysterical laughter. In a heartbeat, the entire situation was diffused. The girlfriend calmed her abuser; he exited embarrassed and she stayed for a most memorable dinner.

After three weeks of Dave and I destroying Jack's poker game, we were told the game could not handle the two of us winning so much money and one of us had to go. Since it was historically Dave's game, it was only fair that I stopped playing. Linda had just flown back to England and soon after, I returned to Lake Tahoe.

After living large in Hawaii for about four weeks, I still came home with about $15,000 above what I started with. Life was as good as it gets. We vacationed in one of the most beautiful places on the planet in the company of good friends while we played in an incredible poker game.

A week after I left, Jack ran out of money and the game was over. Dave flew home.

We looked forward to the next call.

CHAPTER 11

BOBBY & CARL
Two Texas Road Gamblers

Bobby & Carl
Two Texas Road Gamblers

The Horseshoe Club Casino that once was in the heart of Reno, Nevada is now barely a footnote in Reno's storied history. It was a throwback in time. A time when people who traveled west by car across America were exposed to an endless number of roadside billboards that read *Harold's Club or Bust*. A time when Harold's Club, The Mapes, Jessie Beck's Riverside were early destination resorts. All long gone now just like all the smaller gambling venues of *The Biggest Little City in the World*. Long gone like the long narrow Horseshoe Club Casino, a casino that had one Blackjack table at the club's open-air entrance on Virginia Street. The rest of the ground floor casino was filled with the sounds of bells and whistles and of coins dropping into metal trays. It was filled with colorful flashing lights seen through the haze of cigarette smoke that mixed with the smell of spilled drinks and human bodies. Bodies whom had sat way too long—mesmerized by the sea of old mechanical 'one armed bandits'.

There was however a basement in The Horseshoe Club Casino and in the mid-70's that basement had a poker room. There were no windows and the room was always dark except for the lights right above the three poker tables. It was like a poker room out of an old-time Hollywood film set. The place had a minimalist atmosphere; with an ancient overstuffed leather couch against one wall where many players and dealers had slept over the years.

I had become friendly with Dean Cooper, a poker dealer who had just finished his shift just as I cashed out. We began conversing about, of all things, poker! Dean was probably in his 60's. He said he had been both a player and a dealer for the last thirty years. In that time, he'd traveled all over the west looking for games or looking for jobs. He told me that the life he chose only lacked for one thing, a good partner that he could have trusted with his money and his life, a friend with whom he could have shared the road and shared all the good times, as well as the

bad times. "If you were lucky enough to have someone like that,"
he said, "it would make all the difference in the world." I am fortunate
that Missouri Dave became that person in my life.

Over my years as a player, I have run across only a few really
tight partnerships. Take Bobby Hoff and Carl McKelvey, now that was
a good one! It went way, way back to the 1960's. After a stint in the Air
Force, Carl had been part of a card-counting team working the Texas Blackjack games. That eventually ran its course and the gig ended.
Carl met Bobby in their hometown of Victoria, Texas, where Carl was
working a craps game and Bobby was a dealer. Victoria, a town with a
population of 59,000 at the time, had the highest per capita income in the
US for a place that size. Victoria, thus, had two thriving gambling clubs,
both illegal. In 1965, the Texas Rangers knocked down the doors of the
Aloha Club and gambling was halted. Bobby and Carl, now both out of
work, had become friends; they decided to seek their fame and fortune in
Las Vegas.

In their possession was a copy of Edward Thorpe's book, *Beat
the Dealer*, the bible for serious Blackjack players. They had studied it
from cover to cover. They loaded their meager belongings into a 1961
Chevy Corvair and set out on Highway 10 West. They made it as far as
Las Cruces, New Mexico, before breaking down and were forced to send
for money to carry on.

They arrived in Las Vegas broke. Needing to eat and to pay
for their motel, Bobby took a job dealing Blackjack at The Las Vegas
Club. Carl got a job as a break-in Craps dealer at the Mint, which paid
$8 a day. It was a trying time. They began taking shots at Blackjack,
but without an ample bankroll, they found it difficult. They met up
with Don Burleson, a fellow Texan from Corpus Christi. Don had
attained the indices needed to point count a four-deck Blackjack shoe.*
He formed a Blackjack team and Bobby and Carl were a part of it. At
this time, none of the Blackjack bosses believed it possible to count a
four-deck shoe. The team played around the Las Vegas Strip, playing
against the shoes.

There was a book called *Bringing Down the House*, written by Ben Mezrich, a true story about MIT students and ex-students who made a fortune by counting cards while playing Blackjack. Counting cards is not illegal; it's just that card counters are not allowed to play. Card counting involves making small bets when the deck is working against the player and making very large bets when the deck is favorable to the player. Counters are detected due to the large variation of the size of bets being somewhat easy to spot. In 1979, what the MIT team of counters was doing was having the expert counter at the table signal to his accomplice, the 'take off person.' When the deck was favorable, the accomplice would join the table and he would be the one to make the very large bet. The accomplice would play until the deck turned unfavorable and then leave with the counting undetected. That bunch made millions of dollars.

In 1967, long before the MIT team, the Don Burleson team, with Bobby Hoff and Carl McKelvey as team members, came up with the same idea. They put five counters at five tables with different 'take-off-persons' waiting nearby for the signal. This was, quite likely, the first time this concept was put into action and it went very well. At the end of each day they would meet at an apartment to cut up the spoils of the day's work. One day, unbeknownst to them, one of the counters was followed back to the apartment by a Griffin special detective agent who saw the rest of the team. He put it all together and the gig was up.

Bobby and Carl moved up to Reno, and then in the mid-70's they returned to Texas. Carl began booking sports with Treetop Jack Straus. Jack, who would go on to become the WSOP World Champion in 1982, took Carl under his wing and began mentoring him in the game of Texas Hold'em.

Bobby, on the other hand, hooked up with Sailor Roberts. It was the beginning of a lifelong friendship. Sailor, too, would go on to win the WSOP World championship in 1975. Sailor was quite the character in his own right. At one time he was living with the most stunningly beautiful younger woman. One day Sailor came home and told her he had lost all his money. She responded by saying, as the story goes, "Oh

Sailor, I'm so sorry. And I'm really going to miss you." Another time, Sailor moved to Alaska to play poker, though he did not fare well there. After returning to the lower forty-eight, he once stated that he lost so much money during that freezing winter in Alaska that, "Now every time it gets cold I go broke." Bobby prospered under Sailor's tutelage. Sailor also became Bobby's benefactor and when Bobby got broke, Sailor would put Bobby in action. By the late 70's both Bobby and Carl had become top poker professionals.

* * * * *

I first met Carl in 1979. We were introduced by a mutual friend in Las Vegas while playing in a Limit Hold'em tournament at the Golden Nugget Casino. With four players remaining at the final table, I drew out on Carl to bust him and to knock him just out of the money. I then went on to win the tournament. Later Carl and I adjourned to the bar and a couple of beers later, the seeds for a long friendship had been sown.

* * * * *

In 1979 an amateur poker player named Hal Fowler ended up in an epic ten-hour heads-up match with Bobby Hoff at the final table of the WSOP World Championship. Bobby was a massive favorite, though Hal Fowler kept getting lucky.

1) There was the hand when the board read: (**Q...J...7...8...K**). Bobby had a **pair of queens** when holding (**Q/6**). Hal had a **pair of Jacks** when holding (**K/J**). All Hal's money was in and the championship was on the line when a **King** on the river saved Hal.

2) Hal was all-in with **J/J** against Bobby's **Q/Q** when a third **Jack** on the river saved Hal again.

3) In another disastrous hand Hal had **A♦/8♦** and Bobby held **K♦/6♦**, both made a backdoor* diamond flush to double up Hal.

4) In the final hand Bobby made a big raise before the flop with **A/A**. Hal called with **7/6**. Hal then called half his money after a **J...5...3** flop, caught a **4** and made an inside straight that busted Bobby for the title.

First place money was $270,000 and Bobby received $108,000 for second. Hal Fowler famously became the first amateur to win the WSOP title. Bobby, needless to say, remained devastated for some time.

*　*　*　*　*

Bobby Hoff came into my awareness when Flyer pointed him out to me at the WSOP as one of the toughest players he ever competed against. In my early years, I never played much with Bobby, as we definitely played at different levels, but I was acutely aware of him. I was also cognizant of the relationship Bobby had with Carl McKelvey. I was once talking to Carl when Bobby joined us after just having a big cash-out in a tournament. When Carl asked how much dough he ended up with Bobby replied, "Well, not a dime. I just ran into the worst of all the ducks, that would be the dreaded de-duck." His benefactor had joined him for the payout, took the cash and deducted that amount from what Bobby owed him.

It's been said that Carl and Bobby were some of the last of the Texas Road Gamblers. Road Gamblers were players that went wherever they could find the biggest and best poker games. They would show up in towns, big and small, all over the states of Texas and Louisiana. When they found a game they really liked, they'd camp on it and then they became Road Ticks. They played under the condition of 'The Three Ifs.' First, if they could find a game. Second, if they could beat the game. Third, if they could get paid their winnings and make it out of town. They played a lot in Nevada, and when California legalized Texas Hold'em in 1987, Bobby and Carl began appearing in the Golden State.

Bobby was a drinker. I believe Bobby was called The Wizard because, when drinking, he could magically make a mountain of chips disappear.

Carl was a drinker. In the 1982 Super Bowl of Poker at the Sahara Tahoe, Carl found himself in a big heads up match with a fellow Texan from Dallas by the name of Everett Goolsby. They were playing for a considerable amount of money. Mr. Goolsby was also an accomplished drinker and had a big reputation for being a top player of two-handed poker.

In fact the year before, Everett Goolsby and Missouri Dave had a much talked about, alcohol-fueled heads up match, that did not end well for Dave. The two played for several hours with cocktails flowing and both players straddling the big blind (putting up twice the big blind). Then they began straddling the straddle (putting up twice the straddle) and it immediately became a drunken bravado-filled straddling contest of who could put up the last and biggest straddle until they both had all their money in the pot before the first card was even dealt. The pot held over $30,000. The dealer dealt each player two cards and then five cards were dealt in the center. Goolsby produced the winning hand and, just lickity-split-like, Missouri was broke having put in the pot an excess of $15,000 before seeing a single card. The game was over.

When I tuned into the game with Carl playing Mr. Goolsby heads-up, there was over $50,000 on the table as well as an ample number of empty cocktail glasses. Carl, who always had a smile on his face, was obviously having a good old time, as was Mr. Goolsby. Bobby, meanwhile, was driving up from Los Angeles and somehow had become aware of the two-handed game.

I don't know if Carl had been entrusted with all their combined cash or if Bobby was particularly worried about Carl playing Goolsby while he was drunk, but Bobby started calling the poker room from the road, just north of Fresno. This was before everyone had cell phones, so Bobby had to exit the freeway and use a public payphone from a service station. He was about four hours away when he talked to Missouri to get a report on Carl's status in the game. Carl had about $30,000 in front of him. Bobby asked Missouri to take Carl aside and ask him to cash out. During a bathroom break Missouri did just that and Carl simply laughed and ordered another drink. Further up the freeway in Manteca, Bobby called again. He was about three hours away. I spoke to him this time and told him Carl had all the money and Goolsby just bought in another $20,000. By Sacramento, just two hours away, Bobby was informed that Carl's stack had gone down to about $40,000. When Bobby was through Placerville and an hour from South Tahoe, he called again. Carl's stack was shrinking and a new player named Willie, who both Carl and Goolsby knew, had been allowed to join the game. There is a significant difference between playing two handed and three handed; adjustments needed to be made. The dynamics of the match had to have been affected when Willie joined the game. Besides, Willie was sober.

Finally Bobby arrived at The Sahara Tahoe. He dropped his car in valet parking and hurried into the casino. Now, Bobby was a slow moving man most of the time. This was the first and only time I saw him semi-jogging with a little hop in his step. Bobby arrived and there was no sign of Mr. Goolsby. What Bobby did see was the backside of Willie as he took all the chips and the bundles of cash to the cashier. All that remained of the poker game were several empty cocktail glasses, a crumpled-up pack of cigarettes and a dazed, but still smiling, Carl McKelvey, with not a single chip in front of him. Carl had beat Everette Goolsby out of $40,000 but it was Willie who ended up with all the money on the table.

In 1987, when Texas Hold'em could legally be played in California, I saw more and more of both Carl and Bobby. Bobby, though, was around more often than Carl, who still seemed to spend much of his time in Houston and San Antonio. One morning, leaving my hotel room in the San Francisco Bay Area, I ran into Bobby Hoff, who was staying in the same hotel and we had breakfast together. We were both in town to play in a good size No-Limit Hold'em game at Artichoke

Joe's. We spent a while catching up and sharing our thoughts about Texas Hold'em being played in California. Bobby headed off to Artichoke Joe's while I said I was forty-five minutes behind him with a few things to do.

When I eventually arrived at the game I did not see Bobby. I was told he was on his way back to Los Angeles. I was told this story: Bobby and Little Richie each bought in for $10,000. Little Richie is a good player and a friend of mine. Bobby is a world-class master of the game. It seems Richie won a big hand from Bobby right out of the chute and beat him out of his $10,000. Bobby bought in again for the same amount and again within a few hands Richie busted him. Bobby reloaded for $10,000 more and fifteen minutes later, Richie busted Bobby for the third time. Bobby disappeared out the door, grabbed a taxi and headed across the freeway for the San Francisco International Airport and caught a flight to Los Angeles. For me, the takeaway was this: regardless of the difference in the skill levels of two poker players, the deck can be the final arbitrator and the cards from said deck will deliver the verdict, at times, an upside-down one.

Over the years Carl would visit North Lake Tahoe to see Mike Weger, an old friend of his from his Craps dealing days. Missouri Dave, my wife Kate and myself would usually join them for a nice dinner and multiple bottles of good wine.

Carl would also show up now and again and wait for up to ten hours in order to get a seat at The Big Game in Reno, but that was a tough row to hoe. Other than that, I only ran into Carl occasionally.

On the other hand, I would see Bobby everytime I went to Los Angeles as he was a fixture at the Commerce Club. He was employed as a prop player in the biggest games in the joint. This meant he was paid a very decent daily wage for playing and he received company benefits, including health insurance. Bobby showed up to work five or six days a week, clocked in and put in his eight or more hours. This was a sweet arrangement for someone who absolutely tortured the biggest games at the Commerce Club.

In 2010 Bobby suffered a stroke. He passed in 2013. I believe that his daughter, his good friend Steve Lott and, of course, his old partner Carl McKelvey, were among those at his bedside in the end. One of poker's truly great players had departed and the legendary partnership of Bobby Hoff and Carl McKelvey, two men who lived every day like lions and not as lambs, had come to an end.

CHAPTER 12

HIGH COUNTRY POKER

High Country Poker

I was shocked when I looked over my shoulder and saw my old friend Derek Webb and his wife Hannah, standing behind me. Derek was a world-class poker player and our friendship began in Birmingham, England. Our paths usually crossed in either Great Britain or at The World Series of Poker, not at the Reno Peppermill; thus my total surprise.

It was many years ago and I was in Birmingham getting ready to make my first ever play at The Rainbow Casino. Before the game, when Derek realized I was over from America, he introduced himself to me and told me a little about what I might expect playing there. Over the ensuing years, I enjoyed playing in England and at The Rainbow.

When I saw Derek Webb that night in 1998, he told me he had created a casino game called Three Card Poker. This was a game he invented, patented and had licensed in the UK and in various states in America. He had placed it in numerous casinos wherever gambling was legal and he could get the necessary license. We spoke at length about his game and his business model, which was based on monthly leases of the game to casinos. Derek would provide the felt layout that would be placed on the table and a lighted sign on top of a pole that attached to the table. The casino would provide the dealers, who Derek would train, and the casino would bank the game and assume the profits and losses. His game's popularity was growing and his project was having incredible success.

At this stage of my career, I had a love/hate relationship with poker, which seemed to coincide with my win/loss cycle. I was always open to new possibilities, ways to make a living that did not involve the financial swings of playing for a living. Talking to Derek got the wheels turning. I went home that night and by early morning I had created the basic format for playing Texas Hold'em against the dealer. I was filled with hope for a new path forward.

My game begins with each player placing a bet in the Ante Square. The player places a second bet, twice the size of the ante, in the Bet Square. Then each player is dealt a two-card Hold'em hand. The dealer always holds the **Ace of Spades** as one of their two cards and is dealt a second card face down. The players view their hands and may raise by placing up to three times their ante in the Raise Square. Next, five community cards are dealt out. The players and the dealer each make their best five-card poker hand, using any combination of their two cards and the five community cards, exactly the way it is done in Texas Hold'em. The dealer determines winners and losers. If the player and the dealer tie, **the player wins all ties**. There are other aspects to the game, such as a deuce in the player's hand makes an instant winner; also, built into the game, there are progressive bonuses awarded for making specific high poker hands at no additional cost to the player.

Within a few weeks of my encounter with Derek Webb, I had hired a games consultant for his analysis and input. I contacted Keith Askoff, a friend and patent attorney from my Grateful Dead community, to help me with my patent. I presented my concept to my friend Scott Hotes, a brilliant mathematician. He agreed to conduct a mathematical analysis and to do all the calculations. He created a computer program that allowed us to change the house win percentage by simply adjusting the payouts for High Hands Bonuses. Everyone worked for a share in the project. We made the game viable for the casinos to make a profit and still keep the players interested. Finally, I got my old pal, Ron Allegrini, to join me as the person who could market the game and assist in the game's development and installations. Derek Webb continued to mentor me.

I quit playing poker altogether. I was consumed with the creation and marketing of my game. Through online poker and televised tournaments, Texas Hold'em was on the uptick. The beauty of High Country Poker was that it allowed non-poker playing people to play a form of the game on the casino floor.

After a year of intense work with the group I had assembled, I managed to get the game in two California Indian casinos. It was instantly popular. I then convinced Jim Roets, the Casino Manager of The Reno Hilton, to install the game and conduct the required beta testing for the Nevada State Gaming Commission. High Country Poker passed muster and we were granted the state license and began placing the game in Nevada – Reno, Sparks, North and South Lake Tahoe, Carson City and Las Vegas. At that point, I formed an LLC. I persuaded Rick Ketcher and Dan Giovanni to invest and along with some small original investors we were off to the races. I worked long and hard every day for about four years. Along with Ron Allegrini, we trained hundreds of dealers. We spent long days and nights working with the public, teaching folks to play the game. We attended gaming shows, we knocked on casino doors, and we contacted many people the two of us knew from our years in the poker business. It was a long, slow process but we were dedicated.

My confidence in High Country Poker rose to great heights. It began the first morning after I placed my initial game in a small Indian casino and was greeted by the dealer who congratulated me on the promise of becoming a new millionaire. It continued when the shift boss in a major Indian casino told me after the first time it was played, it had been jam packed and rocking the entire night. I saw a new future for my family; a future without the financial ups and downs of a poker player, a future with a big, fat bank account.

The Reno Hilton has a humongous electronic billboard in front of the hotel and casino. It sits next to the freeway so all the passing cars in both directions can view the sign. I recall the immense pride I felt when I saw the High Country Poker logo followed by *Only Place to Play in Nevada* in the bright and colorful marquee lights featured on that billboard. To say I was encouraged would be an understatement.

High Country Poker was poised to take off.

About a year after being granted a license in the state of Nevada, High Country Poker was being played in a dozen casinos. The revenue stream was modest and growing.

Then the whole thing hit a wall. And the wall began to crumble.

Casinos had become inundated with new games, and soon it became harder to get in the door.

Then we began to get dropped by casinos where we were already leasing High Country Poker. It started with the dealers. Ron Allegrini and I would train, depending on the casino, between thirty and eighty dealers. A trained dealer might not get to deal the game for a month or so after learning the game. By that time, they had forgotten most of what we taught them. They made mistakes and those mistakes generally cost the casino. Additionally, when they were running the game, because they lacked the expertise in it, players became bored watching the dealers fumble in confusion. They were inadequate in their explanations to customers who asked how to play, resulting in potential customers walking away, shaking their heads. Interest declined. The volume of business declined. One by one, the various casinos dropped us. After all our hard work and sky-high hopes, I had to return to each former client to retrieve our lighted sign and the felt layout. I walked from each with my heart broken. The game was finished.

I sold the patent and moved on. There are today one or two versions of casino games that allow the player to play a modified version of Texas Hold'em against the dealer. They may or may not be licensed under my original patent.

All in all, I gave High Country Poker everything I had to give. I put in about four years of my life; we spent over $100,000. I was mentored and helped by an incredible group of friends and associates. It was quite a ride while it lasted and when it was over I was really anxious and excited to return to playing poker for a living.

CHAPTER 13

THE BIG GAME

Old School Big Games

There have been many big games throughout the course of poker history. Of the Old School ones I know about, a few stand above others.

Back in 1956 a successful businessman, named Major Riddle, cashed in his chips in Chicago and moved to Las Vegas. He purchased a good size piece of the new Dunes Hotel and Casino. He did well, purchased other casinos and grew his fortune. He was a notoriously bad poker player but loved to play the game. The original Big Game in Las Vegas was built around Riddle. It has been said, "he was an awful stud player, but a far worse hold'em player" and the good hold'em players relieved him of many millions of dollars. It's been said, as the principal owner, he lost all of his huge stake in the Dunes Hotel and Casino in those poker games. In one game, with the board reading **K...K...9......9......J**, the story goes that Riddle instantly called Johnny Moss's $300,000 bet on the river holding two deuces and playing the board. Johnny held four nines.

*　　*　　*　　*　　*

In 1978 Larry Flynt, founder and publisher of *Hustler Magazine*, was shot by a Neo-Nazi serial killer in Georgia. Mr. Flynt was left paralyzed and in a wheelchair. Flynt was the founder of the Hustler Casino in the Los Angeles area and as an avid poker player had a fairly regular seven-card stud game in the casino's poker room. Some of the biggest names in poker were often in attendance along with the storied regulars. It was a huge $1,000 ante, $2,000/$4,000 limit game with a minimum $100,000 buy-in. Because Mr. Flynt was partially paralyzed and had trouble handling his cards different methods were utilized to prevent his opponents from seeing his hole cards. The games regulars made massive amounts of money as Larry Flynt was a consistent producer for years in his own game.

*   *   *   *   *

Missouri Dave and I once decided to take a road trip to the Pacific Northwest and pay a visit to our friend Dr. Kent Kramer and play some poker in Washington and Canada. For years we had heard of The Doctors Game in Seattle. Kent played in it and managed to get us seats in the game. It was called The Doctors Game not only because a number of Seattle doctors played but because the host was a doctor who had also lost a fair amount of money in it on a regular basis. It took place in this gentleman's incredible penthouse apartment in a Seattle high-rise building. The glass wall leading to the balcony provided a stunning panoramic view of Seattle and the Puget Sound. We both did well in the game. Some years later when playing in a Reno poker game, I asked a Seattle player I had just met if he ever played in The Doctors Game. The dealer interjected and said with both anger and passion it was her father's game in which he was blowing her inheritance. That conversation abruptly ended.

*   *   *   *   *

It was in the mid-eighties that The Big Game in Lake Tahoe began. Over the course of 27 years the game grew in size and prominence. Driven by a player called Cowboy Tom, the game was affectionately called The Tom Game by the regulars.

The History of the Big Game

The Board read **A...K...Q......J......10** and there was no possible flush. The game was Pot-Limit Hold'em. The pot weighed $1,000. Lonnie Mason had just bet $1,000, the size of the pot. His opponent, a gentleman called Tom, was quite obviously new to the game of Hold'em. Tom was a tall, ruggedly handsome, sturdy looking dude who hadn't said much all night. He wore a western cut blue denim jacket over a pearl-buttoned shirt, jeans, western boots and a brown Stetson. He looked like a cowboy, and that cowboy, at that moment, looked lost and confused. A small crowd had gathered. People were quietly scratching their heads wondering what the cowboy could be thinking. Everyone knew the Board played and that both men had the same Ace high straight, everyone, that is, except Tom. Finally, after a long time studying the board and his hand, Tom threw his hand away and Lonnie won the pot.

Genesis! It was the mid 80's and that might have been the exact moment when The Big Game in Lake Tahoe was born.

There was a core of us who had been playing $5/5 blind Pot-Limit Hold'em semi-regularly for a while: Missouri Dave, Flyer, Lonnie Mason, Stu Spears and myself. We would start the game and it would generally fill up quickly. That night Stu Spears had invited his friend Tom to play with us.

Tom and his family lived in South Lake Tahoe. Tom was a work-aholic, who ran a niche-business, founded by his father. The business was a major private employer in the state of Nevada. Besides the responsibil-ities of being a large-scale employer, Tom invested in real estate. He was a busy man indeed, but he began to set aside time to play Texas Hold'em. First it was every Friday night; however, the number of poker nights a month for Tom would expand and contract a great deal over the next couple decades.

There were several things about Tom that made for a good poker game: he was a gentleman and pleasant to play with, he really enjoyed playing poker, he really, really loved to gamble and Tom had boatloads of money. Because of Tom's dedication to family and work, he did not seem to have much of an outside social life. However, from what I could infer, the poker game offered him something he was missing. He liked us and he liked being one of the guys.

Almost as soon as The Big Game had begun, it got even bigger. The blinds went up to $5/10. The buy-in went from $300 up to $500.

As Tom became more familiar with the game he went from being a passive player to a more aggressive one. He quickly grew into this new persona of Cowboy Tom, and Cowboy Tom drove the action. He did not find many hands he could not play. That, combined with unlimited funds, made him both a great person to play with and a dangerous one. Several of us would lend Tom money when what he brought ran out. I recall a time, early on, when, after the game he wrote me a check for $10,000 and he asked me to wait until Wednesday to cash it. No problem. He approached me just before he made his exit and told me I could go ahead and cash it right away. He had forgotten that his secretary had transferred $50,000 into his account a few days ago! My first thought was, "Who forgets when $50,000 is deposited into your account?"

Shortly after the second year of playing together, Tom, who by this time pretty much called the shots, wanted to change from pot-limit to no-limit. Done. Not long after starting to play No-Limit Hold'em, the blinds went up to $10/25 and the buy-in was raised to $1,000. Two things about Tom that made the game really big: Tom just loved to play in big pots and Tom loved to bust other players even if it meant putting a lot of his money at risk. Along with the regulars, there was a constant flow of new blood in the game. It was 1987, the stock market was still going crazy and the game kept growing. We had a couple stockbrokers who joined us, as well as a recently divorced lady with a big settlement. Players came from Reno. Lots of tourists with pockets full of money stopped in. Quite a few players stepped up from smaller games and played until their money ran out. We had out-of-town pros drop in. We had the occasional celebrity and several retired major league baseball players join us for a night. Eventually, Tom wanted to get rid of the red ($5) chips so we started playing $25/50 blinds, and green chips ($25) were the smallest we used. The buy-in became $2,000.

At some point in the mid-90s we started having empty seats. Then finding players became difficult. By all means, we wanted to keep the game going, so we had to play a lot of short-handed poker. In fact, sometimes only three or four of us would play. Tom, who still played regularly, savagely pounded on us with his aggressive style and his unlimited bankroll. It could be scary, exhilarating and often stressful. It could be either most rewarding or financially disastrous. That small core of us managed to keep the game alive for a couple more years.

Then once again the game picked up steam and coasted through the millennium. Tom insisted on raising the blinds to $50/100 with a $10,000 buy-in. The amounts of money changing hands in The Big Game were jaw dropping. We still played every Friday and as the game matured and garnered a bigger reputation, getting a seat in the game proved quite difficult for outsiders. Around the time of the housing boom, sub-prime mortgages, an abundance of readily available cash and the expanding appeal of poker the game became larger and even more insane. The cream continued to rise to the top and Missouri, who had for quite a few years become the biggest winner, continued to dominate the game. However, for the other winning players, there was still loads of loose money to go around.

When the housing market contracted in 2008, The Big Game was affected. We ceased playing with regularity. By 2010 we were only playing about five or six weekends a year, mainly around national holidays. By then we had a regular group of players, most with substantial funds who showed up religiously. Four of us lived close to Reno and Tahoe, while the other five regulars traveled from as far away as southern California and the Bay Area. Seats in the game generally did not open up for ten or twelve hours and there was always a list of a few locals waiting. Consequently, it did not behoove out-of-town hustlers to show up to play. It was because of this difficulty in attaining a seat that the game remained semi-exclusive and strong for so many years. The game had become well known in the poker world. It was a great game, it was our game and we kept it going for twenty-seven years.

Although the game was first played at the Sahara Tahoe, it travelled from there to Caesar's Tahoe to Harvey's Lake Tahoe to The Reno Hilton to The Reno Peppermill to The Atlantis in Reno and finally back to The Peppermill, where we played for the last time.

By the time the game ended, we were playing $100/100 blinds with a minimum buy-in of $10,000. The game was huge. Often there was well over $400,000 in cash and chips on the table. The money was not for show; it was in action as cash moved around the table. Pots of over $100,000 were not uncommon. Cowboy Tom once won a pot that weighed about $176,000. The game would definitely get the heart pumping; sometimes, I wished I had a seatbelt.

In the end, the housing bubble burst and real estate tanked. For some this meant financial devastation. The Big Game was over. Those of us who still remained from the beginning, so many years back—Lonnie Mason, Missouri Dave, Cowboy Tom and I—played our last game together in 2014. It was an end of an era and the end of quite a storied poker game.

David Mamet

A seat opened and a stranger sat down.

It was late evening at Caesar's Tahoe as the Big Game was slowly starting to wind down. The buy-in back then was $1,000. The new guy was friendly and quite chatty. I got the feeling he was one of those guys who wanted everyone to know he knew what he was doing. The first time he got busted he made what I thought to be an obvious bad call. He spoke of how he had a tell* on the player he had just called, lost all the money he had in front of him, and couldn't believe he was not correct. I was never a big one for tells, like the guy touches his nose before he bluffs, which I assumed was the sort of thing he was referring to. On the second time around, the stranger bought in for $2,000.

I liked the guy, he was obviously intelligent and he was well spoken. As the game continued to thin out, I started to verbally engage with him more. The game got shorter until the last two players, aside from the stranger and me, racked up their chips and left. It was down to him and me. He had a fair amount of money in front of him and when I asked if he wanted to play two-handed, he said he did. I mentally committed myself to play until one of us was broke or he gave up.

Our conversation led to him telling me his name was David Mamet and he said he was staying at the Cal-Neva Lodge and Casino in Crystal Bay just across the state line from my home in Brockway. He told me he was a writer and a movie director and he was directing a film that was being shot mostly at the Cal-Neva. The more he told me about himself the more interested I became. He shared that he had written and directed the Broadway play *Glengarry Glen Ross*, for which he received a Tony nomination and a play I had just seen in London. He told me that he wrote and directed a film called *House of Games*, which was soon to be released. The plot was partially around a poker game, and the poker players in the film were the regulars in his weekly game on the east coast. The movie he was currently filming in North Tahoe was called *Things Change*, starring Don Ameche. He told me he was going to be on the North Shore for a couple more weeks. He asked if I could get a No-Limit Hold'em game together at the Cal-Neva. I assured him I could. He suggested I come by the Cal-Neva ten days from now on a Tuesday and he'd get me into the film. Perhaps bright lights and my name on the theater marquee were in my future. I was totally up for it.

Then the final hand came down.

Me   David Mamet

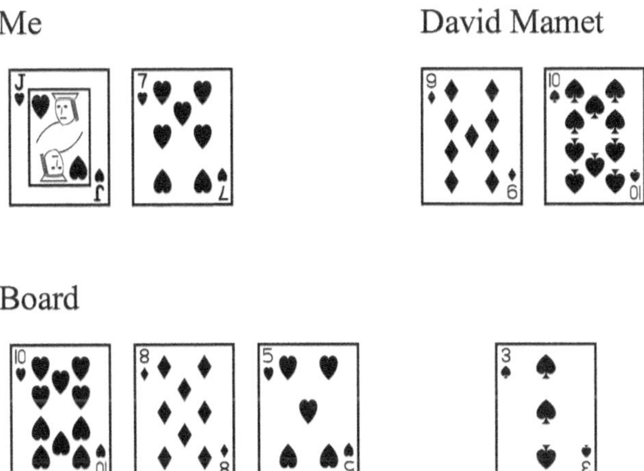

Board

With one card to come, Mr. Mamet checked and I moved all-in. It was going to cost all his chips to call. He must not have had a tell on me, as he thought longer than forever before he made a crying call. I needed a heart for a flush, a nine for a straight or a Jack for a pair higher than his pair of tens. There were fourteen cards out of forty-four in the deck that could deliver me the pot. And BOOM just like that, off popped a Jack on the river and the game was over.

David Mamet asked me to call him when I arranged a game at the Cal-Neva and said, "Goodnight."

The following week I assembled seven other players and we met at the Cal Neva poker room. There was an interesting vibe there with the lights, cameras and the action coming to day's end. David bought in and the game was about an hour old when I picked up two Aces and David, unfortunately, looked down and found two Kings. All the money went in the pot. Then, as he stood up to retire, he, with a bit of snide sarcasm and a mild touch of anger, declared me to be the world's greatest poker player and, once again, said, "Goodnight."

I did show up Tuesday, hoping to launch my film career, but I didn't have the heart to remind him of the invitation he once extended. And he didn't offer. I'm fairly certain Mr. Mamet had sizable poker ego and I think after having busted him twice, once by drawing out, he had seen quite enough of me. I said hello, stayed a half hour, put my dreams of stardom on hold and was on my way.

Big Hand in the Big Game #1:
Too Tight Tim

When one hangs out with poker players, one will hear countless poker stories based on the hand of the night. Most stories end in a horrible card on the River that cost one all their money, or, the terrible call an opponent made to only get lucky and win a pot they shouldn't have been in. Most poker players get tired of hearing these stories, the same plot over and over, but we listen to them knowing they are generally a form of therapy for the storyteller.

Over twenty-seven years of playing the Big Game, there were a huge number of Big Hands played. For a variety of reasons, the ones I have chosen to write about stand above the others.

*   *   *   *   *

This hand was included because it was a tricky hand and I was in it. We were playing at Harvey's in South Lake Tahoe. The blinds were $25/50. There was a player called Too Tight Tim playing that night. He was an accountant from San Diego who knew the game quite well but never ever gave away a dime. When he put any large amount of money in the pot you needed, as they say, to check your hole cards because he had the hand.

Player A opened for $50. Too Tight Tim raised and made it $200. Player B called next to the button and I called on the button with **A/2 suited**. Player A called the raise as well. I put Too Tight on either a big pair or A/K. Period.

The Flop: **9...2...2**   The pot held: **$875**

Everyone checked to me and I, certain that I had the best hand, checked with the hopes of getting a big play on the next betting round. On 4th street an Ace came. The board read: **9...2...2.......A**.

Player A bet $500. Next, Too Tight flat called. That call got my absolute total attention. He, to my way of thinking, could only have one of two hands: Ace/King or two Aces. One I could beat and the other I could not. I was now playing the hand on full alert. Then Player B also called. I wondered: *How many Aces are there in this deck?* The action had come around to me. I was thinking that unless Too Tight had two Aces, I had the best hand; certainly not many cards on the River could hurt me except another Ace, but it was very unlikely there could be another Ace left in the deck. I figured I could still get a big play on the River. So, rather than raising, I also called.

On the river came a **5**. The pot sat at **$2,875**.

Me

The Board

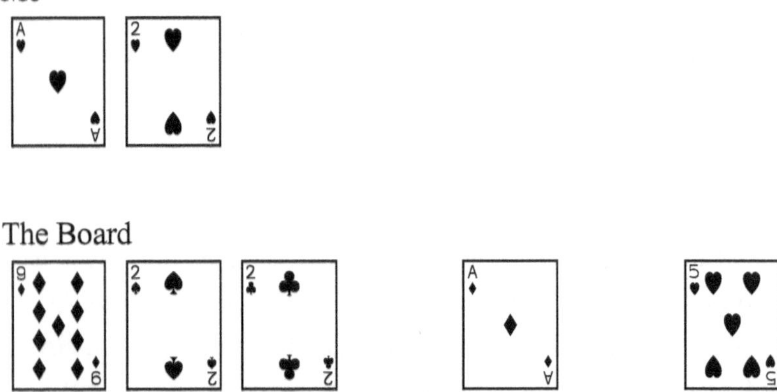

Player A took a long time to check. Too Tight also checked. Finally Player B checked. Now I was convinced Too Tight had Ace/King. I bet $1,600 expecting at least one caller. Player A contemplated calling before folding. Too Tight took his time then raised $3,000 more.

When playing poker for substantial sums of cash, like we were doing then, sometimes something happens that tells you all is not what you thought it was – that your hand you were so certain was the best, is not the best. It is totally shocking and somewhat debilitating. At that moment, in that hand, I had just been totally shocked. Every dollar of that pot had been mentally stacked and placed in front of me. With Too Tight's $3,000 raise, the rug was abruptly pulled out from under me. I had wanted a call. I certainly did not want a raise. Knowing my opponent the way I did, I assumed I was beat; but before throwing away my full house I needed to figure out if and how that was even possible.

It was obvious to me that Player B was also thinking of calling, and then he very reluctantly folded. Through their body language, I read the desire of both Player A and Player B to call; I felt both had to have an Ace or the last deuce. There simply were not enough Aces in the deck for Too Tight to have two Aces (**A/A**). I knew, beyond doubt, that Too Tight would not have raised me $3,000 with **Ace/King** (**A/K,**), with that hand he would only have called. I also knew he would not have put in $500 on 4th Street without a very big hand; therefore, this was definitely not a bluff. Yet, he would only raise in this spot if he thought he had the best hand. He would not have called $500 with two fives in hopes of catching another five. He did not raise before the flop with 5/2. Then it came to me. And I knew. I knew Too Tight could only possibly have one hand: he had to have two nines (**9/9**) in the pocket, giving him nines full of deuces, a full house better than mine.

Including my last bet, Too Tight's call and $3,000 raise, the pot stood a smidgen over $9,000. If I made the $3,000 call and my opponent had any other hand I deemed possible, other than pocket nines, that $9,000 would be shoved to me. But calling $3,000, when it goes against all the available information and my strong conviction about my opponent's behavior, is not good poker playing. Paying $3,000 on a hope I was wrong or to satisfy my curiosity about the correctness of my thinking would be out of the question.

I do not like to throw away full houses; not many poker players do, but I managed to find the one and only hand my opponent could have and play the way he did, and, so, I threw my full house away.

A couple of years later I ran into Too Tight Tim in a game in Los Angeles. I told him what I threw away and he told me I made a good lay down, as he did indeed have two nines.

But I was certain of that already.

Big Hand in the Big Game #2:
The Call

There was a key hand that was to have a lasting effect on the Big Game for its duration. It was no surprise it came down to Missouri Dave and Cowboy Tom.

Tom was not an outstanding player. He was, though a hyper-aggressive one. His grasp of the game and all its nuances, although improving, was not that high for a person playing in a game as big as ours. Tom, however, was an extremely dangerous player and he totally grasped the use of brute force. Tom's personal wealth, his desire to gamble and his absolute fearlessness was what made him so dangerous. At this point in the evolution of The Big Game, Tom had been pounding on us so badly with his massive cash advantage it was hard for some of us to stand the heat or muster the heart to call when Tom threw $10,000 bundles of cash in the pots like they were nothing. We mortal players found it difficult to take the chance of going broke with a lot of money in front of us with a marginal hand. Consequently, Tom leveraged our fear to his benefit. He made a habit of constantly robbing us when all the cards were out. And just when you'd had enough and decided to call Tom down, quite often you found yourself with no chips left in front of you.

We had been playing $25/50 blinds and the buy-in had been raised to $5,000. Missouri had gotten busted several weeks back and Mark Peterson had staked him for half his action. Dave bounced back, made some money for Mark and they split out prior to the game on this particular night. Dave sat down with $10,000 of his own money in his pocket; he bought in for $5,000 and was on his second buy-in and was then playing with empty pockets.

It was late that night and Dave had built his money up to about $13,000. The cards were all out. No flush was possible.
The Board: **5...6...K......10.......J** The pot: about **$2,500.**

Dave bet $1,500. Tom reached down and grabbed several $1,000 chips and a $10,000 bundle of one hundred dollar bills, slapped it down in the pot and said, "All-in."

Many years before that night, Flyer described to me the sound that a $10,000 bundle makes when it hits the pot. He said it was sort of a *thwump*. I know that sound. I also know the other sound that only I hear that comes after the *thwump* when I hold only one pair; it's the sound of that sinking feeling I feel way deep in my belly.

And Dave that night in that hand held only one pair. Dave's hand was **King/Queen**, a **pair of Kings** with a **Queen kicker.**

Missouri Dave

Board

I have played more poker with Dave than any other human.

I know there are two distinct Missouri Daves. There is the drinking and gambling and having a rip-roaring good time Dave, who can run his chips up and down, like a high-speed elevator. When that Dave is at the table, the party is on. Sometimes it goes well for him and other times it can be very costly. He has a short memory and processes losses quite quickly. Dave knows he plays better poker than most and will recover his potential losses tomorrow or next month. The other Missouri Dave is a laser-focused assassin to whom most of his weaker opponents appear mentally naked and defenseless. Bolstered by a lifetime of playing, he has total command of every aspect of the game. His intuitive abilities are finely tuned. It would be fairly accurate to say Missouri Dave plays poker on a higher plane than most. Cowboy Tom played on others' fear. Missouri Dave played with absolutely no fear. He never heard the *thwump* of $10,000 bundles of cash. Tom, one more time, was up against one of the toughest, most focused poker players I had ever known.

Dave's hand that night couldn't beat much. I don't know what all went into Dave's thought process. I would bet big money he did not think that if he lost this hand he might not be able to play again for a long time. I think like that; Dave does not. I'm guessing he did not bow his neck and say to himself, "Fuck it! I'm sick and tired of Tom pounding on me." No, I believe he looked at Tom and drew from a lifetime's immersion in the game, combined with an intimate knowledge of Tom's mind, and said with a calm confidence, "I call."

All went quiet until Tom's cards were propelled into the muck.

Dave placed that now silent, *thwump-less* $10,000 bundle behind the mountain of chips he had just stacked.

It wasn't the size of the pot that made this hand so significant; for in the ensuing years there would be countless pots that would dwarf this one. No, from my lens, the $26,000 then sitting in front of Dave afforded him an important cushion, which would allow him to maneuver and take control of the game like only a focused, non-drinking Missouri Dave could. Furthermore, he had momentum, a momentum that from the moment Tom's hand hit the muck, Missouri Dave rode to become an unstoppable force in the future of The Big Game, a game that was destined to become much, much bigger.

Big Hand in the Big Game #3:
The Biggest Pot

Harvey's Resort Hotel and Casino in South Lake Tahoe was the home of the Big Game probably for the longest stretch of time.

Harvey's was also the first place I worked at Lake Tahoe. In the summer of 1968 I had a job as a dishwasher for two weeks. I washed dishes on the dish line and I scrubbed pots and pans in the big stainless steel sinks. While I've never owned a wristwatch, I've always known the time. From my first job on the dish-line in Harvey's, in a kitchen without windows, I learned you could pretty much tell the time by potatoes. The potatoes, that is, that arrived on dirty plates. First came hash browns then French fries. At 10:45am the number of plates with each would be about equal. By noon it was all fries. Then came mashed and finally baked. It was imperfect, but accurate enough for a hard-working, yet somewhat bored dishwasher. The kitchen was on the same floor as the poker room. I had come such a long ways from washing off yolks from other folk's plates. I had come from washing big pots to trying to win big pots on the same floor of that very same building.

This is the story of a big pot, a really big pot.

The Big Game had its origin in South Lake Tahoe. Many of the players had roots from there as well. Our old friend Ron Allegrini was the poker-room manager. Many of the dealers were from the old Sahara Tahoe back in the day. It was a familiar and welcoming place to play poker. It was at Harvey's that the biggest pot in the history of The Big Game was played.

The blinds were $25/50.

Mohammed, known as Mo to the others, was in the midst of a successful career in the tech industry, lived in the San Francisco Bay Area, and had a seat in the Big Game for a good number of years. His mood was always upbeat, after all he was playing poker and poker was a game he loved. He was an intense competitor and when in stroke and was making hands he became wildly creative and very dangerous as his stacks of chips started going up and down like they were on 'Mr. Toads Wild Ride.' Mo opened the pot for $50, with the **Queen and eight of spades (Q♠/8♠)**.

After making some big scores on the east coast, a bright, young hotshot player named JJ was sitting at that moment with about $70,000 in front him. JJ and his girlfriend had rented a house in South Lake Tahoe for the summer and they had been playing in the biggest games around the lake. JJ was a very knowledgeable, aggressive player with a good size bankroll and no fear of putting his money in the pot. With the **Ace and Jack of spades (A♠/J♠)**, JJ entered the pot for $50.

Cowboy Tom called the $50 with the **six and eight of different suits (6/8)**. Tom sat with about $80,000 in cash and chips.

Chris Hansen had also become a regular in the game some years ago. Chris was a highly disciplined, rock-solid player with little or no waste in his game. Besides being a winning poker player, Chris was one of those 'jackpot wizards' who made an impressive living playing slot machines and video poker machines. In the short version, these wizards played machines with progressive jackpots; that is, jackpots that increase in size each time a coin is dropped down the chute. For those who understand the mathematics of the machines, the jackpot eventually may become large enough that, playing optimally (video poker) and trying to hit the big prize, becomes a profitable play. It is a long term proposition. Sometimes you hit and make a bucket full of money as jackpots can run into the tens and even hundreds of thousand dollars. Conversely, sometimes you whiff and lose a bunch. In the long run a player will make a sizable hourly wage. The play requires a good size bankroll and the balls to risk it. Chris that evening sat next to the button with over $35,000 in play. He raised the pot to $300 with **two nines (9/9)**. Both blind hands folded and Mohammed, JJ and Tom called the raise.

Mohammed: **Q♠/8♠** JJ: **A♠/J♠** Tom: **6/8** Chris: **9/9**
The Flop: **10♠...9...7♠**. Pot: **$1,275**.

Mohammed bet $2,000 with a Queen high flush draw and an open ended straight draw. JJ called with the nut flush draw and an inside straight draw. Tom, with the bottom end of the straight, raised $10,000 more. Chris, with a set of nines, moved all in for a total of $35,000. Mohammed folded. JJ with the Ace high flush draw and an inside straight draw tanked for what seemed like eternity before he finally called the additional $33,000. Tom then moved all-in and JJ immediately called Tom's raise with his remaining $34,000.

Chris was in for the main pot of about $108,000; the side pot between JJ and Tom weighed $68,000. In all, there was approximately $176,000 wagered and riding on the last two cards. On Fourth Street came the 4 of clubs. The River brought the 6 of clubs.
Main Pot: **$108,000**. Side Pot: **$68,000**. Total: **$176,000**.

Mohammed (folded on flop)   JJ

Cowboy Tom   Chris

Board

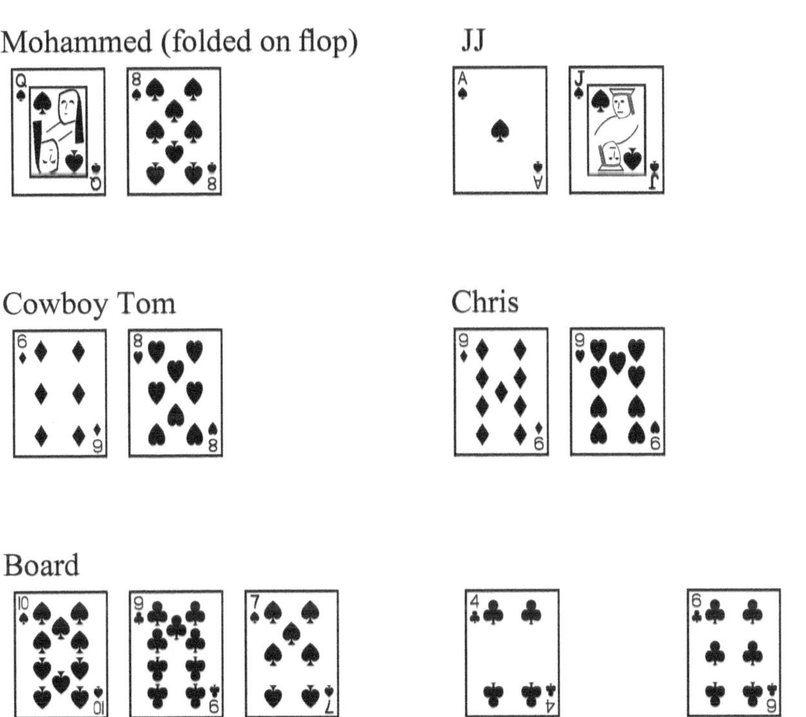

Because the fourth nine failed to materialize and the board failed to pair and give Chris a full house, and neither a spade nor an eight appeared to make a flush or a higher straight for JJ, Tom won a pot worth

$176,000, the biggest pot ever in the many years of playing The Big Game. Tom, who flopped a ten high straight with a **six and eight off-suit**, had to sweat out the final two cards. He only stacked up that monstrous pot when those final two cards failed to help his opponents.

In the Big Game, I naturally rooted for myself, and, of course, I rooted for Missouri as he was my closest friend, my long-time partner on the road, the best man at my wedding and the guy I could always borrow money from. I liked all the other players, but I didn't make a habit of wishing one would win over the other. That is with the exception of Cowboy Tom. Tom was also a pal, but Tom lost so much money overall that I could not help but root for him to win big pots. Besides, it was really good for the overall health of the game. Tom was absolutely giddy in his excitement from winning such a monstrous pot. Dave said it was as if losing all the money he had lost in the past did not matter, only that pot at that moment was what counted. And good on Tom.

Big Hand in the Big Game #4:
Two Kings

In some circles in Texas a **King /Jack of diamonds** is known as a Red Roper.

My friend Denny Dahlgren was playing a tournament at the same table as Doyle Brunson when Doyle saw a player turn over the hand he called a Red Roper. Doyle then related this story about a Texas poker player named Red Roper. Once, a longtime ago, Doyle ran into his friend, Red, who was experiencing a run of bad luck and was dead broke. Doyle, knowing Red had a wife and kids, handed him $200. "It's not a loan," said Doyle, "It's just some walking around money to keep you all in groceries."

A week later, Doyle walked into a poker room and there sat Red Roper in a No-Limit Hold'em game with at least $15,000 in front of him. Before Doyle even took a seat in a larger game, a crowd started to form around Red's table. A wealthy Texan, who had just joined the table after buying in for $20,000, had raised the pot a couple hundred dollars. Red re-raised some four hundred more and the new fella moved all in for all Red's money. Red sat in silence as he stared at his hand and stared at his opponent and stared at that massive raise for all his money. After an inordinate amount of time Red finally said, as he turned up his two Aces, "If I can't play this hand for all my money, I have no business playing in this game." With that, Red threw his Aces in the muck, grabbed his money and chips and left the building.

The moral of this story is: playing poker with money you can't afford to lose will compromise your ability to play good poker.

* * * * *

It was late. Nine of us had sat down at the Reno Hilton fifteen hours ago, at ten o'clock on Saturday morning, and before we realized it, it had gone past midnight and was about one o'clock on Sunday morning. Most of the players had called it a night. We were down to a four-handed game: Cowboy, Missouri, Boyd Fricke and me.

Boyd had been one of the mainstays of Reno poker for many years. He was a good player who made his money at the card table and he played in The Big Game off and on for years.

I was about a $5,000 winner and I was making plans to quit. For the last three sessions playing in The Big game, I had been on a bad run. Whenever I was on a bad run, I made a point of tightening up my game and, above all else, booking a win. In other words, I would go to great lengths to stop the bleeding and change the downward momentum.

Just before I stood up to leave, the next hand was dealt. We were playing $25/50 blinds; I was on the button, Tom was first to act. He opened the pot with a raise to $300. I looked down to find my two cards were both Kings (**K/K**). I raised Tom $700 more, making it $1,000 to enter the pot. Missouri Dave had the small blind. When he called the $1,000, bells and alarms went off in my head. Dave always gave me a ton of respect and my raises a lot of credibility. To call the $1,000, I knew he must have held two Aces or two Queens, no chance he had Ace/King and really not much else. Boyd had the big blind and he also called. Boyd had a big hand but I was certain he did not hold two Aces. It got back to Tom and he raised $2,000 more.

I found myself in a conundrum. I knew I had Boyd beat. I thought I had Tom beat but I wasn't positive. I was scared to death of Dave's hand. So many times, I would get pissed off at myself for taking a hand when I knew I was done with the game. It could be particularly upsetting if I had a desperately needed win sitting in front of me and I blew it. However, this time, although I felt that the correct play was to go all-in, my heart was weak from weeks of being battered. I knew that if I went all-in Dave would be done with the hand if he did not have two Aces. If he did, I was most likely busted. Boyd would fold. Tom would call no matter what and even if my hand were the best, I would need for my hand to hold up until all the cards were dealt. Winning a pot as big as this one was destined to be would pull me out of my rut and put me back in the comfort zone. I desperately needed this win, yet I was taking too long to act. Weakness was emanating off of me. I needed that win. *What to do? What to do?* I took the coward's way out and folded my two Kings.

Dave re-raised another $10,000. Boyd folded. Tom called. The flop was something like **9...6...2 rainbow***. Dave went all-in with a bet of approximately $20,000. Tom called. The next two cards were inconsequential. Dave turned over the one hand I had not considered: **two Kings**. Tom threw his hand in the muck. I was stunned.

After the game, Dave and I met at the bar and we talked about the hand. He told me if I would have just called Tom's raise he would have assumed his two Kings were the best hand and he would have made a huge re-raise; I would have then put him on two Aces and folded. If I would have moved all-in after Tom's raise, he would have, most likely, put me on two Aces and folded and I would have been buying the drinks instead of Dave. I remained in mild shock as I listened to Dave recount the hand from his point of view.

Even though I lost $1,000 on that frustrating last hand, I still booked a much-needed win for the night of about $4,000. Although if I had played with a little more heart, perhaps I would have had a better story to tell. That night I was reminded once again of Jack Straus and lions and lambs. And after writing this story, I thought about Red Roper.

Big Hand in the Big Game #5:
A Psychic Hit

Over many years I had played a lot of hands, a lot of very big hands, with Cowboy Tom. He always had tons of money in front of him and he wanted to play big pots, the bigger-the-better-pots. Tom, obviously, was the guy, the guy everyone wanted to play with, the one spot at the table where a small fortune could be won or lost on any given hand.

When a hand was played, Tom usually had the worst of it, but always having so much money and a total disregard for that money made him incredibly dangerous to play with. There were so many times over the years that Tom would put all his money in a pot with me before the flop just on the chance he would bust me. When all the money went in the pot before the flop, I almost always had two Aces, occasionally two kings. Nothing else. Period. Tom did not care. The money meant nothing to him. The action and the chance to bust me was what he craved. And bust me he did, an inordinate number of times. He'd call my all-in bets before the flop for many thousands of dollars, sometimes as much as ten or twelve thousand dollars, with hands like five/six suited or eight/five suited or nine/ten off-suit or who remembers what else.

So often, when the cards were dealt out, he'd say something like, "All I have is two pair," and, of course, all I would have was a lonely pair of aces. He would say, "I missed my straight…but I made my flush." I'd say, "Take it Tom," and then I'd go outside, take deep breaths and nearly scream. In the big picture, I did extremely well playing against Tom, so I had no complaints; it was just those moments when that awful stuff happened that I suffered it hard.

We played so often together over the many years that I made it a habit to completely focus on Tom when he played a hand. I studied Tom. I knew his face, its tics and its grimaces. I knew how he bet, how he moved his chips. For years, I listened to what he said and how he said it. I felt him and I absorbed all that I could. With Tom at times, I would strongly intuit the texture of his hands or what he'd do with a hand prior to him doing it. On a few rare instances, I would be struck with some sort of a psychic jolt about a hand with Tom. It was like I knew, absolutely knew, when something shocking and out of the ordinary had happened or what cards Tom held.

On the day of this particular game I was short on money and only had one $10,000 buy-in. I needed to play it close to the vest. It was early evening, about midway through the session when a hand I will always remember came down. We were playing $50/100 blinds.

Missouri opened the pot with a raise to $300. I looked down and found **two Aces**. I did not want to re-raise and win a small pot right there; rather, I wanted Tom in the pot and I knew there was a very good chance Tom would re-raise on the button and I could then make a big play on the pot. I had about $13,000 in front of me. Of course, this was a risky strategy, but it was an ironclad rule of mine not to go broke with two Aces if I did not get a big raise in the pot before the flop. Without me making a big pre-flop raise I was prepared to throw away the hand anytime the pot was destined to get really large. No one else entered the pot and Tom, on the button and to my disappointment, only called. The flop came **10...9...7** rainbow, and a bolt of lightening hit me directly between my eyes.

No doubt about it, **That Flop Was All Tom**. I was so positive that right at that point, I was totally done with that hand. Tom could have sneezed and I would have thrown away my two Aces. But Dave checked, I checked and Tom, with his allergies inactive, neither sneezed nor bet. He too checked. The area right between my eyes was still vibrating from that bolt of lightening. I was still positive that the flop had Tom written all over it.

Then something crazy happened. Fourth Street brought an Ace giving me three Aces. I lost my focus on Tom and switched my attention to that great glorious Ace just added to the board. Dave checked and I bet $1,000 and Tom took a moment to think about it. His hands, he did something with his hands, something distinctly different. His two hands started to move ever so slightly towards his money, then his hands stopped like maybe he rethought what he wanted to do. They waved almost mysteriously over his cards, not actually touching them, just waving very slowly back and forth. Was he going to raise? Was he perhaps going to throw his cards away? I learn a lot by watching people's hands. Sometimes when I play a person heads-up I only watch their hands. In ring games (full games) when cards are dealt, I usually pay more attention to my opponent's hands than I do to their eyes. The hands can say a lot. But in that instance on that day, I was unclear. He did that thing with his hands, something different, something out of Tom's ordinary signals from his hands, something that grabbed my attention. And because I remained both excited and distracted by the addition of that beautiful glowing Ace to the community cards we shared, I didn't know what I was being told. Tom thought longer; he shrugged and made what seemed a reluctant call. Dave folded. On the river came a four. Pot: **$3,050**.

Me

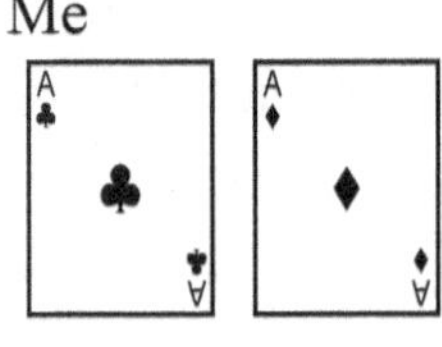

Board

I bet $2,000. Tom thought maybe all of thirty seconds. I was praying he would call. He reached down in front of him, picked up two $10,000 bundles of $100 bills and tossed them into the pot. I was stunned. At that moment I was somewhere other than right there in that poker game. It was like I was up against a wall, alone and dazed. I was unable to focus. The absolute certainty I initially had about the flop was a thing of the past. I had become absolutely distracted by the Ace on Fourth

Street. I had become lost thinking about my top set.* I could only see the three Aces. Though his fingers once seemed to have had a message for me, I had been unable to decipher it. Tom's two hands were no longer talking. There were only two combinations of cards Tom could have that could beat mine: the **J/8** and the **8/6**. I could certainly beat numerous hands that Tom might raise me with. It wasn't often I did not know what to do, but this was one of those times. All my money was at stake and I sat lost in my indecisiveness. The poker game had come to a full stop. I needed to do something. I needed to act on my hand. I was mentally dysfunctional; then my eyes watched as my hands, on their own volition, pushed my remaining chips into the pot.

* * * * *

I seemed to be floating. My mind registered the irritating sounds of slot machines somewhere in the background and then I felt the relief rendered from that first blast of fresh air. I was no longer playing in a poker game. My car found me, somehow it started and it was driving me away from where I'd been. It's a fifteen-minute journey from seat number four in the poker game to Interstate 80. Just before I entered onto the freeway to head west over the Sierra, I returned to my body and became cognizant of where I was and why I was there.

It was then, driving up the mountain that I was able to begin processing what had happened to me back in that poker game that was still going on, but now, without me. As I drove, taking those mountain turns, I looked back at that hand and, with just the sound of my Honda Del Sol's engine humming in the background, it became all too obvious what had transpired. From years of camping out in Tom's head and circumnavigating his being, I was gifted some sort of psychic hit on the flop. My intuitive senses were sending signals loud and clear. I had allowed the Ace on Fourth Street to distract me. Tom's hands tried to tell me what he was thinking, but I was unable to interpret the message from those hands. That Ace was just way too big of an obstruction. I

239

had disregarded my personal rule of never going broke with two pocket Aces without getting in a big raise before the flop. I became confused, disoriented. In the final hand I played that day, Tom's Jack/eight (**J/8**) completed a hand that remains etched deep in my memory.

Big Hand in the Big Game #6:
Jumpy Jim

All those years that we played in The Big Game there was an abundance of extraordinary hands that came down. Clearly in each session there were a couple of hands that stood out and the stories of those hands would circulate through the local poker community and sometimes beyond. This is one of those stories, one I will never forget. We were playing in the Reno Peppermill. To this day, I still find the way the cards stacked up, the people involved and the way the hand played out was absolutely amazing.

It was more or less the usual line-up of players. Everyone bought in for at least the minimum $10,000. A few bought in for $20,000 or $30,000 and Cowboy Tom and Missouri Dave each put $50,000 in chips and cash in front of themselves.

Playing with us that day was a guy called Jumpy Jim. There was a reason he was called that. Jumpy Jim was a man in constant motion. He kept jumping up and down between hands, he literally could not hold still. He was always talking on the phone or just talking. At times he would randomly pop up from his chair and drop a few dollar tokens in a nearby slot machine. In this game and because they put up the most cash, Missouri Dave and Cowboy Tom made the rules by which we conducted the game and they had the final say as to who was invited. I organized the games but usually with input from Tom and Dave. Now Tom did not like to play with Jumpy as his mannerisms annoyed him. Tom preferred order to chaos. I liked Jumpy in the game. I liked his action, I loved his good sense of humor and he made me laugh. Tom agreed to let Jumpy play but first Tom laid down the law: "Turn off your phone, keep the noise down and stay in your friggin' seat." Jumpy was left with no choice other than leaving and so he agreed to Tom's conditions.

Here's how the hand came down. The blinds were $50 and $100. Missouri in first position entered the pot for $100. He held a pair of Aces (**A/A**). Jumpy was the next to enter the pot and called $100, holding a pair of fives (**5/5**). Everyone else folded to Tom, who, on the button, raised $400 more with a Jack/ten (**J/10**). Missouri called Tom's raise. Now a solid player in Jumpy's spot calls the $400 and sees the flop. Period. The others seated at the table that day had many years of experience playing No-Limit Texas Hold'em at a very high level. Jumpy was relatively new to the game and he must have wanted to be in on the raising as well so he said, "Well let me raise, too," and made it an additional $400. Tom called Jumpy's raise and now it was back to Dave to act and the door was open for Dave to make a big raise with his two Aces. Dave called Jumpy's $400 raise and mounted the pot with a $4,000 raise. Jumpy, who had only about $12,000 left in front of him had no choice but to fold his two fives; he simply could not risk one third of his remaining chips when he would obviously need to improve on his lowly pair of fives. Tom, with a huge stack of chips and $10,000 bundles of bills in front of him, easily made the call of $4,000 more.

The dealer delivered the flop of: **J...10...5**

Dave: **A/A**   Tom: **J/10**   The Flop: **J...10...5** Pot: **$10,850.**

(Jumpy who no longer was in the hand had thrown away: (**5/5**).

I looked over at Jumpy, who would have flopped a set of fives, and I could see he had gone completely pale; his body began to tremble slightly. Dave bet $6,000. Tom called and raised $10,000 more. Dave called. With the massive action, Jumpy, though not having left his chair, began silently to convulse, his eyes started to dart about.

There were only three cards in the deck at this point that would allow Dave's one pair (Aces) to overcome Tom's two pair (Jacks and tens). Dave could catch one of the two Aces left in the deck or the one remaining five to make a bigger two pair (Aces and fives). On 4th Street, that last remaining five slid right off the deck. This card did give Dave two pair, Aces and fives, a higher two pair than Tom's Jacks and tens. It would have given Jumpy four fives. In the pot was **$42,850.**

Missouri Dave   Jumpy (folded pre-flop)   Cowboy Tom

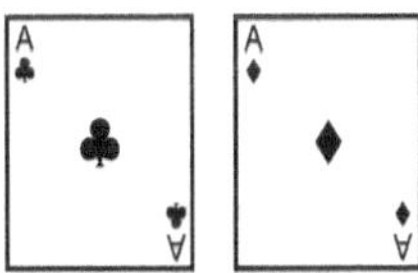    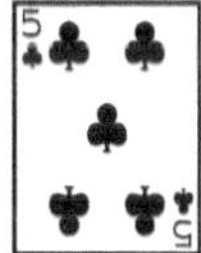    

Board

Dave checked. Tom went all-in. Dave with very little hesitation called. Jumpy had now wrapped his leg over his shoulder and around his head; he looked like Jumpy 'the human pretzel.' His mouth was opening and closing but no words were coming forth. There was this high-pitched sonic noise emanating from somewhere deep in his being and his eyes were weirdly spinning in their sockets. At this point, the pot weighed **over $100,000.** The last card was a blank (a card of no significance) and Missouri Dave stacked the chips.

Then, pulsating on the chair that once held Jumpy in a human form was an orb of energy, spinning, vibrating, casting off neurons and protons and sweat and sparks, with strange utterances emanating of which the only discernible words were "fives" and "four." Then said orb fell to the floor and with one mighty spring-loaded bounce, Jumpy was launched up into the poker cosmos, through the universe of *'Oh shit, oh dear, oh shit, shit, if only!'*

The fact of the matter is that if Jumpy had not made his ill-advised raise of $400 he would have seen the flop, caught a five to make a set of fives, made four fives on 4th Street and tripled his stack to about $39,000.

Even though he was able to put his bodily pieces back together, Jumpy Jim was never the same after that. In fact, he never spoke another word and sadly only left his chair when he departed from the game broke.

Big Hand in the Big Game #7:
The Biggest Pot I Ever Won

When I reflect back on a lifetime of playing poker, it's easy to see I have traveled a long way from playing with the Guamanians back in high school or running a poker game in my college fraternity.

Poker has been good to me. I've made a decent living; we own a home; I've always paid my taxes; and I helped raise our three children. I have lived in the mountains for most of my adult life, and I have traveled cross country and overseas. I never spent a lot of money on clothes; I've always driven old used cars; and I never bought expensive toys. In fact, since I gave away my skis, my toys have consisted of a retired softball glove and my racquetball gear. I've heard a lot of live music and before Jerry Garcia died, I hung with The Grateful Dead. I exercised like a madman and I ate healthy food. Following a short story about his family, my favorite Canadian musician, Fred Eaglesmith, said as he stood before a large audience, "I'm as wealthy as anyone in this room." He paused in the silence of that hall for five or eight seconds and then finished his statement, "because I have enough." Slowly the large audience 'got it' as a wave of acknowledgement swept over the crowd. And I too pause because I too have enough. Money or possessions have never been my driving force.

However, finishing a session in a poker game as a winner always felt good. And there's no greater feeling to a poker player than winning a big pot. When a big pile of chips, with loads of one hundred dollar bills is pushed to you just after the $10,000 bundles of cash are separated and tossed your way, there is no feeling quite like that. The joy of stacking those chips and reorganizing your newly acquired wealth is pure poker pleasure. Even without the bundles and all the one hundred dollar bills, winning pots in a poker game got the juices going.

On a night in 2012 at the Reno Peppermill, those juices were really flowing when I won my biggest pot ever. It happened over forty years after hopelessly trying to play $2/4 Limit Six-card Stud for a living at the Sahara Tahoe way back in 1971.

Although I had bought in the game for the minimum $10,000, I had won a few decent pots and I managed to run my money up to over $32,000 before the hand was dealt. Having that amount of money in front of me, combined with a fortunate turn of the cards and the perfect opponent, made winning my biggest pot ever possible.

We were playing $100/100 blinds. I was dealt the **A/10 of dia-monds (A♦/10♦)** next to the button. Tom opened the pot and made it $400 to go and I called along with two others.

Me: **A♦/10♦**   The Flop: **10...5♦...2♦.**   Pot: **$1,700.**

I had the top pair with an Ace kicker and the nut flush draw. Tom bet $2,000. I raised $4,000 to $6,000 total. Everyone else folded and Tom called. Fourth Street was a second ten, giving me three tens with an Ace kicker and the nut flush draw. Tom bet $10,000. I moved all in for almost $16,000 more. Tom called. The River brought an **Ace,** giving me a **Full House, tens full of Aces.**

Me   Cowboy Tom

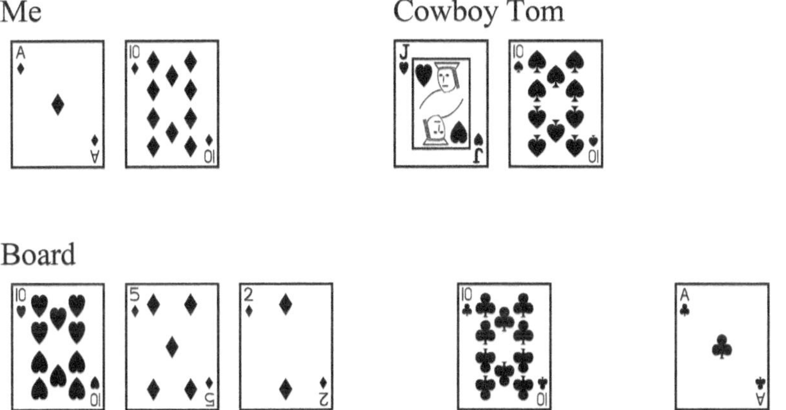

Board

The dealer pushed to me one of those pots with chips and bills and bundles of cash. I tipped the dealer a black chip ($100), and I said, "Thank you." Then I quietly went about sorting those bills and stacking those chips. When I was through, I counted what I had in front of me and it was a little over **$65,000**. Very silently, I was ecstatic.

An Odd Hand in the Big Game

It was in the morning after a full day and a full night of another action-packed hurricane-like whirlwind of cash circling around the poker table. The winds had calmed, cash was secured and all had gone, that is, all except Jeff Borris and me, the last two men still sitting at The Reno Peppermill that day. This is a story not about a big pot or some masterful play. No, the pot never grew to its potential and in fact, the hand was played rather poorly. What was unique was the totally odd nature of the hands.

Jeff was a good dude. I liked him a lot. We were very similar in many aspects of our lives and miles apart in others. How were we similar?

#1. Baseball and the Giants. Jeff was a big-time sports agent. He owned his own agency. His clients, I believe, were exclusively baseball professionals. He counted Barry Bonds and Tim Lincecum among his stable of players, as well as quite a few others from the San Francisco Giants.

As for me, I loved baseball; it was my favorite sport and I was a rabid Giants fan. I had 25% of Giants season tickets for several years and was fortunate to be in the stands when Barry Bonds achieved several milestones. I was in the stands the night Tim Lincecum pitched a two-hitter and struck out fourteen Atlanta Braves in a division playoff 1-0 win. I bet Jeff was there too.

#2. Jeff and I both loved to play poker.

#3. Jeff and I were both family men.

#4. Jeff had a summer home on the water in the Tahoe Keys. I had a key to Missouri Dave's rental home on the Tahoe Keys just a stone's throw from Jeff's.

#5. Jeff was a racquetball player and he played well. I played racquetball three days a week, and I loved the game. Jeff and I played each other once and we played fairly even.

In those ways we were similar.

How we differed is best put forth in two ways. First is the manner in which we each arrived at The Big Game the night before. Jeff flew into Reno on his private chartered executive jet. I drove to Reno in my 1997 Honda Del Sol with over two hundred thousand miles on the odometer. Second, Jeff maintained worries that he would die young from all the stress in his life. Me, I had very little stress and I was already too old to die young.

We were playing two-handed when Jeff declared he needed to get to the airport to meet his plane. He suggested we play ten and only ten more hands. I agreed. Jeff had about $50,000 in front of him, while I had about $20,000. We had a $200 big blind and $100 on the button. The played hands ticked off: one, two, three, up to nine played hands, with almost zero chips exchanged. It was time for the final hand, hand number ten, and then Jeff would be off to the airport and I would be headed back to Nevada City.

Jeff was ready to bounce. He was standing with his chips racked up. The cards were dealt. Jeff called the $100 on the button. I looked down and found the **J/6** off suit. I told the dealer to put the flop out. BOOM! The flop was: **J... 6...6**. I had flopped a full house. I didn't want to lose Jeff so I checked. Jeff checked behind me. A **nine** came on the turn. The board read: **J...6...6......9**. I needed to try to get some money in this $400 pot, so I bet $400. Jeff called. The river brought a **5**. Me: **J/6**   Jeff: **?/?**   The Board: **J...6...6......9.....5.** The pot: **$1,200.**

I bet $1,000. Jeff raised me $2,000 more. I was fairly positive I had the best hand. I put Jeff on holding **6/5** or, more likely, a 6 with a random card. There were only two possible hands I could not beat, both of which would make a higher Full House. The first was two Jacks, which I felt was unlikely because he did not raise before the flop. The second was two nines. Even though Jeff obviously had a huge hand, I absolutely loved my chances. I was hesitant to raise in case Jeff then moved all-in and I would be put to a decision. The possible hand that concerned me was Jeff holding two nines. If I raised and Jeff went all in, I could not live with myself if I called off all my money after letting a nine beat me, a nine that would have come off the deck for free on 4th street. Basically, more than any other thing though, is the fact that I had mentally checked out of the game nine hands earlier and I was only playing as a courtesy to Jeff. Thus, at this point, I did not want to play with the possibility of involving an additional $16,000 in a hand I had not been mentally prepared to play. It was the very last hand of a long night and I decided to wimp out and play like a lamb. I flat called.

In hand number ten, the absolute final hand of the night, we found another way we were similar as we ended up splitting the $7,200 pot. We each had our own **J/6** off suit. That was a fairly odd way to end the game indeed.

Board

Me

Jeff

CHAPTER 14
CALIFORNIA

In 1987 it became legal to play Texas Hold'em in California. I began traveling between California and Nevada to play poker. In 1990 Kate Winningham and I began our lifelong partnership in which I fully embraced Zak, Jake and Maia (her three children) as my own. In 1994 we moved to Nevada City, a historic old gold mining town in the lush California foothills. In 1996 we threw an epic party for my 50th birthday in which Kate and I had a surprise wedding between sets when the band took a break.

Besides my travels, I eventually found a hometown game.

The Gold Rush Casino and Gaming Parlor

The Gold Rush Casino was a totally derelict poker room in Grass Valley. It was a bar with no customers and without a bartender. In the adjoining back room there was only an occasional poker game. When I inquired, I had no interest in the small Limit-Hold'em game. Then one night a few years later in 2001, I wandered in again only to discover a full Pot-Limit Dealer's Choice game in progress. At that moment, I became a brand new regular.

In 2002, Sue Barrows purchased the business. She did a major remodel of the place and opened what was to be a lively poker-room fronted by a lavishly decorated, intimate little bar. The poker room was accessed from the back parking lot or by passing through the bar, which was separated by a partial glass wall. There were three poker tables, a single Blackjack table and a cashier's cage in the back. I started playing there whenever there was a bigger game. The 21st century gold rush was on and the new Gold Rush Casino and Gaming Parlor was about to become my own personal gold mine.

There were two games I played there. The first was a $2/5 No-Limit Hold'em game and the second was a $2/5 Pot-Limit Dealers Choice game. I played those games several pegs better than the rapidly growing local clientele. I had the run of the place. A few of the dealers often played after their shifts; a lot of that money found its way to me.

Sue, the owner, loved to play and she was an action player. In California, the house is not allowed to bank the Blackjack games; thus Sue contracted a corporation to do the banking. The gentleman who managed the corporation-banked Blackjack money had an arrangement that allowed him to play the corporation money in the poker games. This guy had an exaggerated sense of his abilities and he literally brought handfuls of corporate green chips from the Blackjack table into our poker games. So, in a way, a great deal of the money from the local players, from the employees, from the owner and from the Blackjack game, was ending up in my pockets. The Gold Rush was good to me and it was only ten minutes from home. Life was good!

I was about to become friends with several very colorful characters who regularly patronized The Gold Rush. First and foremost was a gentle giant named Clayton McNealy. Clayton was a burly tattooed poker player, a mountain of a man with a magnetic personality. He grew up in the historic mining community on the nearby San Juan Ridge. He was part of a large extended family that went back generations. The first night I met Clayton I inquired, "What do you do?"

He responded, "I mine."

"What do you mine? I asked.

"I mine my own business."

As we became friends, Clayton and I would fill our ice chests with Heinekens and would take regular beer breaks behind the club after the bar closed. There we bonded over many late-night/early-morning Heinekens.

Clayton was a major slot machine player in Nevada. Because he was such a high roller, he was extended V.I.P. treatment in most of the casinos in Reno. There is a great story of Clayton driving home from Reno one night in the company of another rather flamboyant local called Blackjack John. John was a hippie/Deadhead and he and Clayton ran together. On one particular night when John and Clayton were coming home from Reno, Clayton wanted to stop at the Boomtown Casino to play slots. John was really tired and just wanted to get home. Clayton made John a proposition that if John agreed to stop, Clayton would split with him any slot machine Jackpot he might hit. Fate would have it that Clayton hit a slot machine for $100,000 Jackpot that night. Immediately upon getting paid for his big score, Clayton cheerfully handed a then wide-awake Blackjack John $50,000 in cash.

Another local character was Global Mike. Mike looked like a bookkeeper and stood out as totally straight amongst the congregation of pot growers, renegades, gamblers, night crawlers and derelicts that passed through the card room. Mike was an excellent poker player. He was totally versed in the mathematics of poker, had a nice disposition and fit right in amongst the chaos of the Gold Rush.

The Gold Rush became a late-night hub in Grass Valley. The poker games occasionally went all night. Locals would come and go; you would never know who would sit down and drop a bunch of dough. Everyone was friendly and the place would take on a party atmosphere more often than not. In every respect, it was an exceptional place for me to play poker. Eventually it was sold and the room was reborn a couple blocks away as Towers Casino.

Michael Ondaatje

It started one morning with a phone call. Unlike some of those previous morning calls before, I wasn't broke and it wasn't a call to tell me about a poker game.

It was my old friend Janis Arch calling to ask if I would like to meet with the brilliant and highly acclaimed writer, Michael Ondaatje. Mr. Ondaatje was writing a new novel in which two of the main characters were poker players. Janis is a master massage therapist and the ex-girlfriend of Missouri Dave. She had been living in San Francisco the past few years and had recently been doing bodywork on Michael Ondaatje. During one of her sessions, while discussing his latest literary project, the subject of poker players came up. Janis told him of her history with Dave and myself. Michael felt that if a meeting could be arranged, he would love to use us for a character study and part of his research into the world of poker.

It was a late March morning and I sat waiting in the second floor lobby of The National Hotel, an old Victorian hotel in Nevada City. I looked forward to meeting Michael. I was a big fan of his book, *The English Patient*. Since I was the only person in the large lobby it was easy to connect when Michael came up the stairs. He had a medium build, looked fairly fit, sported a gray beard and had unruly gray hair. We introduced ourselves and began a conversation that would last into the late evening. He had spent the previous day in Lake Tahoe with Missouri Dave and had a good sense of who we were and how we arrived at our chosen profession. Michael and I talked poker, politics, personal history, the impending Iraq war, more poker, family and travel. I offered lots of stories from my life as a poker player.

Kate joined us for lunch at Ike's Quarter Cafe, an organic Cajun themed diner, and the best eatery in the county. We walked around Nevada City and I introduced Michael to quite a few folks I knew who were out and about. The air was full of tension as the American invasion of Iraq was imminent and on the mind of everyone we met. Nevada City is a small progressive enclave in a fairly conservative county. Nevada City has been referred to as being the Berkeley in the middle of Utah. Our little town was predominantly anti-war in what appeared to be nationally a well-supported endeavor. The prior weekend with our 15-year-old daughter, Maia and her best friend Alina, Kate and I had boarded one of five buses chartered by the *Nevada County Peace Coalition* that traveled to San Francisco, where we joined several hundred thousand people in a huge anti-war march. I took Michael to KVMR, our local community radio station, gave him the tour and introduced him around. We drove to Grass Valley to The Gold Rush Casino and there he met the owner, Sue Barrows, and he was given the tour of the small three-table poker-room. Michael would reference most of these places in the book he was writing at the time.

Both Dave and I shared many poker stories with Michael, as well as what we knew about card mechanics and thieves. Later in the year Michael and I corresponded by mail and I helped write the poker scene that took place in Las Vegas involving Texas Hold'em. I felt honored to tell Michael my story and to be used as a source by such a universally respected writer. Michael Ondaatje's book was called *Divisadero*. It took place mostly in San Francisco, Sonoma County, Nevada City, Lake Tahoe, Las Vegas and southern France. The character called Edward Dorn, described as a Deadhead, hippie poker player, was loosely based on me. The freewheeling, pool shooting, poker player called Coop had some characteristics similar to those of Missouri Dave.

Dave and I both looked forward to the publication of *Divisadero*. We read the book and saw characters whose personal traits mirrored ours in some ways. The big exception was his fictional characters could and would cheat at cards. Nothing could be further from our true natures. Admittedly, it did feel good to see many aspects of each of us weaved into these characters playing out on the pages of this famous novelist's work.

Freddie Deeb

In my early years of poker, while playing in Reno, I took a strong liking to a player for his distinct personality and his high degree of integrity.

Freddie Deeb was a young Lebanese man, small in stature but with a huge heart. He was a good dude and we forged a friendly connection. Often I would see Freddie in the early afternoons trying to get a buy-in. He had an open line of credit with me for one buy-in any time he needed it, as long as I had it. Freddie could do magic with a single buy-in. Most days he'd run it up in small poker games and he'd be able to buy into the biggest games by the evening. He would almost always repay the loan the next time our paths crossed. When the civil war was raging in Lebanon, Freddie provided not only for his wife and daughter here, but also for family back home. The point is Freddie was both a responsible man and 100% consistent in paying back what he borrowed.

As poker took off like a rocket in the early 2000's, televised poker tournaments entered people's living rooms and the sports bars and the hotel lobbies across the country and around the world. Winning players became recognizable. They were turned into instant poker celebrities. It had been a while and I had lost track of Freddie. But suddenly there he was playing on the screen in the world's biggest poker tournaments and treated like one of those celebrities. I felt good for Freddie.

It was nearly a half dozen years after I began to watch Freddie's star rise that I found myself occasionally traveling to Los Angeles to play at the Commerce Casino. One of the things I loved about the Commerce was their spa. I'm a sucker for a steam-room and a massage. One afternoon, I was sitting alone in the steam-room and in saunters this guy with a towel wrapped around him and I, with my vision partially obscured from the rising steam and without my glasses, said, "Good afternoon." When the gentleman responded in kind, I recognized the voice. "Freddie, is that you?" I said. And, indeed, it was my old friend from Reno, Freddie Deeb. We hadn't seen each other for over fifteen years.

We did some catching up, which led to talk of Freddie's rapid ascent in the poker world and his playing successfully in major tournaments. He had won some really big numbers. Then he shared with me that upon his rise in the poker world, he fell victim to a rather severe infatuation with casino games; Freddie became a serious player of Blackjack, Baccarat and Craps. It was that infatuation that had gotten him broke and in debt a few years prior.

Poker has a certain addictive quality. After all, even though it is a game of skill, there is an element of gambling involved. A few good examples of advantages achieved by skilled players in the very short version of playing poker says that the good players put themselves in the position to be a favorite to win a hand more often than the lesser skilled player, and then they trust the odds of winning in the long-run. The good player understands the price of a hand winning and then accounts for the money involved, relative to the size of the pot, to dictate whether to fold, call or raise. The good player knows how to take charge of a hand and control the action. The game is exciting; the adrenalin courses through the body, and, as the human condition dictates, both are contributing elements of addiction, to which anyone spending a considerable amount of time in a casino may become vulnerable. Such excitement and adrenalin occur, of course, not only at the poker table. In fact, it is no secret that in gambling games like Blackjack or Craps, anyone is subject to getting too caught up in the rush. The huge difference between these games is that good poker players have a big edge in their favor. The player of casino games, in contrast, has no such edge and is, in the long run, destined to succumb to the odds and lose.

Freddie told me when he was lost in his temporary addiction to those casino games, he had gone through the bulk of his poker winnings, maxed out his credit cards and had borrowed from close friends to the tune of over a million dollars. He recounted when the bank's manager called, saying the problem had gotten out of hand, that he was behind in payments and the bank needed Freddie to address his debt. Freddie shared with me that he told the banker he would have the whole debt repaid within the year but insisted the bank not call him and badger him about the money again. He said the banker agreed and that they both kept to the bargain. Within a year the credit card balance was back to zero and all his friends had been repaid.

That to me was amazing. I've been around a lot of excellent poker players at their zenith, who, through various addictions to activities, such as sports betting, Blackjack, the consumption of alcohol, drugs, sex or whatever, fall to their nadir and never recover. Freddie's belief in his own self discipline and his confidence in his own abilities allowed him to not only make a huge promise to the bank, but also to make good on that promise and square up his debts with his friends. It was just like the totally reliable repayment of the loans I would extend to him on Reno afternoons, back in the day. Only this time, the numbers were massively larger.

A Pair to Draw to:
Mackey & Dave Olson

This is the story of how two of my very close friends first met.

Buried deep in my memory is a picture of a really young poker dealer from The Sahara Tahoe in the early 1970's, off work but still in uniform, drink in hand, his nose running, his eyes glazed, a big smile on his face, as he constantly yelled, "Raise the pot!"

I've known James 'Mackey' MacLaren since that time. I was a recreational player just learning my way around the card room, at The Sahara Tahoe. Mackey was a dealer who would get off work, go to the bar to tune up and then return to the poker room and liven-up a poker game. He kept one arm for drinking and the other for raising. Mackey partied hard, he loved life and he made you laugh. Moreover, he proved again and again to be a man of integrity. He once spent an extended period of time living with Missouri Dave in Hawaii, playing poker and getting into good trouble.

After years of dealing poker and at times playing for a living, he landed a responsible and financially rewarding job. He moved to Southern California when an old friend in the casino business offered Mackey the position of Shift Manager of the Asian Games section of the Commerce Casino. Mackey went to work each day in a tuxedo and oversaw a booming operation where the Asian money just kept pouring into the club. His job paid well and the tips were huge.

I met Dave Olson through Missouri Dave. He was one of the better poker players from the Pacific Northwest. Dave Olson was big in stature, not only physically, but also with his presence and his heart. He was a soft-spoken gentle human until the whiskey kicked in, at which point, he occasionally lost the soft-spoken thing. He was anything but your nine-to-five modern-day man. He was a professional poker player, but at times he worked in casino management as a floor-man and a card room manager. At one point in his life of unconventional jobs, Dave took a daily drive around Los Angeles with over $100,000 cash in the trunk of his car as he paid and collected on sports bets for some L.A. bookies. Dave had his fingers in a lot of pies.

When I was told the story of how these two dear pals of mine first met, I could not stop laughing. It happened late one night at the Commerce Casino. Dave Olson had been playing in a big No-Limit Hold'em game and one of the other players kept calling him a big pussy. Over and over again this dude would call him a big pussy. Dave had been drinking heavily.

It was quite late on a slow night and there were not a lot of poker games going. Mackey had just finished his shift and wearing his tuxedo, was walking towards the High-Limit section of the card room when he was suddenly stopped dead in his tracks. There in the midst of a full poker game, right smack-dab in the center and on top of the poker table, stood some crazy fucker with his pants undone and his big old schlong hanging out. It was Dave Olsen with his penis in the other dude's face shouting, "Does this look like a fucking pussy to you?"

When I was told this story, in the presence of both Dave Olson and Mackey, my first inclination was to wonder if Mackey, being in management, had inserted himself into this wild and extraordinary situation. Did Mackey have Dave thrown out? No, according to Mackey, he said to himself, "Now, that's someone I really need to know."

Mackey and Dave Olson are still close to this day.

Tristan

Somehow the conversation had just turned to arm wrestling. Tristan had the physique of a bodybuilder, the mouth of a sailor and the ego of a rock-star high on himself. Rather than acting on his hand in the poker game, he was preoccupied with the challenge involving upper body strength he had just issued to any one of us who sat at the table for any amount of cash.

It had been a few weeks since I first met Tristan. That day, when I walked in early for one of the weekly $10/20 No-Limit Hold'em games at the Deuces Wild, I was told of the new player who made his debut the previous week when I had missed a game, a very rare occurrence. I was told the guy was loud and brash, full of bluster, a wild gambler with tons of dough, who tended to be a bully in the poker game. I was soon to realize that that was a sugarcoated description of a very different sort of an individual. Within minutes Tristan sat down at the table directly to my right. We were introduced. The very first words out of his mouth came in the form of an off-color joke that, besides being hugely disgusting and politically incorrect, it was not even slightly humorous. I knew, straight away, he would not be coming to my house for dinner.

Meanwhile, back to the night when Tristan was busy badgering the table about arm wrestling, I looked up and saw my friend Jimy Manley coming in the door. Jimy was a Grass Valley painting contractor, a local poker player, and in contrast to Tristan, a humble, soft-spoken, human being. Moreover, Jimy had competed and won several statewide arm wrestling competitions. I hurried on up to Jimy and quietly told him I'd back him if he felt like arm wresting. He said, "Yeah, let's go." In a heartbeat I was back at the poker table.

"OK, Tristan," I said. "I'll pick any old 'yay-hoo' in this card room and I'll put up $100 against you in an arm wresting match."

"You're on, sucker."

"Right, I'll take Ralph the skinny bartender over there." I paused. "No! No wait, he's maybe a bit too skinny. I'll just take that dude up at the desk buying chips."

"Sure, whoever you want," Tristan replied.

"Hey buddy, yeah you at the desk, excuse me, how would you like to arm wrestle this guy for $100 of my money?"

"Me? Yeah, OK, why not?" answered Jimy.

Tristan was about six foot one, had long arms, a big chest and was about 220 pounds of muscle and unfiltered bullshit. Jimy, on the other hand, was about five ten, weighed about 200 pounds, had short arms and was built like a fire hydrant.

All three of the poker games came to an immediate halt. Everyone in the room gathered, three deep around the two combatants. Tristan stretched his arms, his legs, his shoulders; the deep breaths he inhaled and exhaled sounded like those of a horse gasping for air. Jimy stood silent and stoic like the Buddha. They faced up. Tristan was wildly intense. Jimy smiled. I put my hand on top of their locked grips. I counted down from five, lifted my hand and started them. Tristan let out a loud grunt. His muscles bulged, his body trembled, his legs vibrated like a dog trying to poop a peach seed. Neither of their arms moved a millimeter in either direction. Jimy continued to smile. Then, Jimy, holding steady, straight up and down, calmly asked Tristan, "Are you ready?" and in one swift motion of overwhelming power, he took Tristan down as if there was absolutely no resistance.

I winked at Jimy as I handed him a $100 bill.

The more I played poker with Tristan, the more I warmed to him, but we had a huge way to go to overcome his loud and arrogant ways. I found he had a troubled past and deep down there was certainly some decency within him.

* * * * *

It was late on a Tuesday about a year after the contest of stern wills and strong arms, that Eric Ram, a new face, walked into Deuces Wild. He bought a thousand dollars in chips and sat down in our poker game as it was winding down. Within thirty minutes the game was down to him and me. He did not flinch. Because he bought in for $1,000 rather than the $500 minimum, it told me he had confidence in his abilities and his demeanor suggested the same.

As we played I soon came to realize he overrated his own abilities. I liked Eric straight away; he was personable, had a friendly smile and we conversed back and forth about a few things. It was when I learned he was a racquetball player that I took a much greater interest in him. When he shared with me that he went to Sacramento State University on a racquetball scholarship I was duly impressed. When he told me he'd played a lot with Ron Freeman, the very best player in Nevada County, his pedigree was confirmed. As for poker, Eric was a decent player.

A week later, I was at Deuces waiting for the game to get underway when Lynn Johnson, the area racquetball pro and E-Force equipment rep, walked into the poker room. He went up to Tristan, seated across from me, and handed him two new racquets. Lynn and I were both surprised to see each other away from the gym and we shared a couple quick giggles. When Lynn departed, I told Tristan that I too played racquetball. I asked where he played and how well he played. There was no hesitation on his part to tell me he played in Roseville and he flat out destroys everyone in the club.

Lynn Johnson was a top racquetball player before years of injuring nearly every one of his body parts slowed him down. Even with his physical limitations, he could still play at an exceptional level. His passion for the sport was so great that I imagined him still playing even if he was down to hopping on one leg and holding the racquet between his teeth. The next time I saw Lynn, I asked him how well Tristan played. He told me he was a decent player. With that statement I pretty much knew all I needed to know.

Eric Ram's path crossed mine again in another poker game. I mentioned to him that Tristan played racquetball. Eric told me he had heard of him but they had never met.

Some more time passed and again Eric and I ended up in the same poker game. This time he told me he had heard more about Tristan; moreover, he had heard the story of the now infamous arm wrestling match at Deuces. The wheels had been turning in his head and he asked if I might be interested in arranging a racquetball match between him and Tristan for some cash. He said I could have a piece of the action. I said if the opportunity ever presented itself, perhaps I'd try to make it happen.

So one day, there we were, Tristan and myself in the usual No-limit Hold'em game at Deuces when Eric walked up to the table, sat down, said hello and got dealt in. Now I was thinking just how in the world am I going to finesse this conversation so it leads to a match for cash? I didn't want to be too obvious and I wanted it to come about absolutely organically.

"Have you met Eric, he's a racquetball player?" I said to Tristan.

Tristan instantly responded. "Oh, yeah? Do you want to play three games for $10,000 a game?"

There was a pause. Finesse was totally obliterated. Eric was taken aback but he told Tristan, truthfully, he hadn't played in over a year and that if he lost he might have a hard time covering $30,000. But he might be interested in playing for $1,000 a game if he had a few days to tune up. The match was set for three days later.

I took one third of the action and I arranged for Eric to come to Grass Valley beforehand and play a couple games of doubles, with me as his partner, against Ron Freeman and his partner called Bud. We split two hard fought games and I knew that no 'only a decent player' would stand a chance against Eric.

The match was set for Roseville, a suburb of Sacramento. Several poker players, as well as myself, showed up for the match. Eric won the first two games 15-3 and 15-4. When Tristan said he wasn't feeling well, he asked to put off the third game for two days. Before I left, Eric handed me $1,000 and confidently said, "I'll pay you now. He has absolutely no chance of beating me."

As the years went by, I continued to play a fair amount of poker with both Eric and Tristan. Eric and I, naturally, remained friends. As for Tristan, it was said he was the director of a company founded by his father-in-law. I was once invited to a couple of home games at Tristan's place. He lived in a big upscale house with a large swimming pool in a gated community. His wife seemed pleasant and welcoming and together they were raising a very bright, personable, young son. For that reason alone, Tristan went way up in my estimation. Furthermore, to his credit, when Tristan lost a bet, he paid up without hesitation.

It was right before the Pandemic officially began when I last saw Tristan; he was having dinner with a friend at the restaurant in The Stones Gambling Hall near Sacramento. We said hello, shook hands, chatted a minute. I remember saying to him as I was leaving, "It was nice to see you." I opened the door, stepped out into the evening heat, paused for a second and then it struck me so very clearly, I really meant what I said.

CHAPTER 15

ON THE RIVER

An Evolution of Poker

I come from a time when the poker community was a small society, populated with some of the best people, people honor-bound, who would lend and borrow thousands of dollars solely on a person's word. Conversely some of the worst people who would cheat the unsuspecting out of their last dime. It was a community connected through yearly tournaments that were not yet overpopulated; a community connected by road gamblers who passed through America's card rooms spreading the stories that became embedded in poker mythology. I am from the old school. I recall as a young man, being star-struck the first time I saw Amarillo Slim walk into the poker room at The Dunes in Las Vegas. I remember drawing the same tournament table as Johnny Moss, then a living legend fondly known as *'The Grand Old Man of Poker."* I sat across from poker royalty as we waited for the game to begin. Mr. Moss asked to see my antique pocket watch I had set on the table and as he admired my watch he shared the story of the pocket watch his father bequeathed him long before I was born. I remember being impressed with the first poker game I saw where $10,000 bundles of one hundred dollar bills were bound together like bricks sitting in front of players. Little did I know then that I would one day sit with bricks of my own. And little did I know then that the old school poker I would become a part of would one day change immensely.

* * * * *

I had grown up in Southern California and was home from University to celebrate my twenty-first birthday. It was the afternoon following my big day when I first walked through the doors of El Dorado Card Room in Gardena, California. I entered to a mass of green felt tables, to the cricket-like clatter of poker chips, the hum of hundreds of gamblers gambling. I recall with absolute clarity the incredible excitement I felt so long ago. Gardena was the home to a host of large casino-size poker rooms in the Golden State. The sight of so many players, both men and women, young and old, of all ethnicities, as well as the sound of poker chips being bet, stacked, shuffled, and shoved into pots would, one day, become second nature to me. To this day, however, whenever I enter a poker room, I still feel that same special thrill.

As far back as my memory goes, playing poker in California has always been legal. The problem was the only legal games were draw poker and lowball draw. That was a problem because, when compared to Texas Hold'em, those games were far less complex and incredibly boring.

In 1987, the laws regarding poker in California changed. The state legislature legalized the playing of stud poker, flop games such as Omaha and Texas Hold'em, as well as various house games, such as Pai Gow poker and some forms of Blackjack.

By that time I had become a top player in Northern Nevada and I first thought this was bad news for me. Players, who used to come to places like Lake Tahoe and Reno, could now find a game in Sacramento and the San Francisco Bay Area. I was immediately impacted. It effectively slowed down the local action. Many players and dealers left Lake Tahoe and resettled in different parts of California. Those of us who stayed in the Reno/Tahoe area had to either travel more for poker games or organize our own games. We telephoned players to set up games for particular days at particular times. The good news was there was a whole crop of new players whose skills were yet to be developed. Nonetheless, I did begin to travel to games in California because the action was good and, most significant to me because my lungs needed relief, California state law prohibited cigarette smoking in public places, which included card rooms. By playing more in the Golden State, I almost entirely eliminated trips to Las Vegas. My first priority was The Big Game. After that, I played a lot in Lake Tahoe and I traveled extensively around California.

Then there were two transformational occurrences that were to significantly alter the arc of poker.

The first was the advent of online poker. In 1998 people began playing poker at home on their computers. This created a whole new sub-culture of poker players. As for me, I chose not to play poker on a computer screen. I reiterate, I am most definitely old school. To me, poker is not a computer game played between avatars. I believe poker is a game best played in person, between people, face-to-face. I want to talk to my opponents, observe them, listen to them, feel their hearts beat, and trade stories. At times I want to have a beer with them and I want to interact with them in ways only humans can. Poker to me has always been part of our western heritage. I found it difficult to embrace it as being part of our technological future.

The second impactful event occurred the day poker became widely televised. In 2002, both tournaments and live games were picked up by network television. For years ABC's *Wide World of Sports* had aired The Main Event of the World Series of Poker on television, but it did not have a large audience. What made televised poker an overnight success was the development of the technology that allowed a player's hole cards to be shown, with a delay long enough to prevent cheating, as each hand was dealt and played out.

Worldwide interest in the game began to increase. From these two phenomena, many new players were born and poker's popularity skyrocketed. Then there was the *Moneymaker Effect*. In 2003, an amateur player named Chris Moneymaker parlayed an $86 buy-in in an online event into a seat in the Main Event at the WSOP. When Chris was the last person standing, he collected $2.5 million dollars for winning the World Series of Poker Championship event. Moneymaker served as an inspiration to both amateurs and online players and has been credited with the tremendous increase in new players. The global explosion of poker was in part due to the *Moneymaker Effect*. In 1985 I played in the $10,000 buy-in Main Event at The World Series of Poker along with 139 other entrants. In 2006 the number of entrants had rather miraculously reached 8,773. Poker had become popular amongst players and spectators alike. Top players, featured on TV, had gained rock star-like status. For better or for worse, the game had undergone seismic changes.

Added to this mix was the American real estate boom, fueled by the onslaught of subprime loans around 2007. Home values had been going steadily up and people were making lots of money as the value of homes increased. Subprime mortgage loans became readily available. Almost anybody, regardless of traditional credit status, could easily get a loan to buy a home. The mortgage industry was flourishing. People were flipping houses and buying second homes. Business was booming. The stock market was on fire. People were going into debt mortgaging their homes not only to buy second homes but also to buy stock, to pay for vacations, to purchase new cars, and for recreational purposes, such as playing poker. Cash was abundant and everywhere. Folks were smoking big fat cigars, even though many future balloon payments loomed large. From all of this, there was a period of wild, action-packed poker games that made my life fun, exciting and profitable.

In 2005, a player who had become a regular in The Big Game invited me to play in a game he was hosting in his business office in Sacramento. It consisted of mostly Sacramento players, some of whom I knew. There were two poker tables, a couple of very accomplished dealers; there were drinks, good food and armed security. At this Sacramento game, we were playing $10/20 blind No-Limit Hold'em. I did great. Unfortunately my friends who were hosting the game bought their poker chips in a boxed set from a Costco. It so happened that some lowlifes playing in the game also visited Costco, purchased their own chips and filtered about $6,000 in black $100 chips into the game over two weeks. The hosts made good on their loss; however, the game then moved to Auburn to the Deuces Wild Card Room, owned and operated by Phil Hawkens. Auburn was better for me, as it was much closer to home. We played $10/20 blind No-Limit Hold'em every Tuesday and Thursday.

The Auburn game was on fire. Money continued to flow as the economy was barreling ahead at full throttle. We had a steady line of mediocre players with pockets full of cash filing in regularly. We had beginning players hoping they could, as we say, 'earn while they learned.' Among us, there were a few strong players. Almost all of the players were pretty good guys and were enjoyable to play with. Everyone was friendly and there were always lots of laughs. Often it was a big party and lots of alcohol was consumed. Consequently, the games at times lost all sense of decorum, making it difficult to concentrate. All in all, though, there were not many games like these. Seats were locked up ahead of time, and I always had a seat. Entering the card room before each game and seeing which players had seats reserved, inspired the excitement similar to Christmas mornings. I still played in The Big Game, when we had it, but the games at Deuces were more than enough to earn a very good living.

It took me years of playing poker to learn the nuances of playing No-Limit Texas Hold'em at a very high level. There were aspects of the game that required years of study, thought and experience to perfect. I always held what I knew close to the vest, providing me an edge. I would not give away my knowledge, and I did decline many offers to tutor players. I would discuss poker only with Missouri Dave, Joe B and my close circle of friends.

With the arrival of televised poker and online poker, I became really upset that so many experienced players began educating the new players. There were lots of new books written. Poker commentators would analyze plays on televised tournaments. Some smart guys held poker boot camps for weekends of learning. Others had subscriptions for online lessons. There were paid seminars. Poker calculators could be easily accessed online and therefore in games on smartphones. Everything that could be explained was explained and everything that could be exploited for profit was. People just plain talked too much about the way a hand should have been played, just to prove how smart they were. The bottom line for me was what took me a lifetime to learn was now given away or sold on the poker marketplace. I found it all disgusting.

Next came two more events that significantly altered the arc of the modern game of poker.

The first was the crash of the subprime mortgage/housing market and the ensuing Recession in 2008. The money began drying up, and the guys with envelopes full of cash stopped coming to the poker rooms. Games went from having all the seats reserved, long waiting lists and having feeder games to needing to phone around and invite players in order to fill a game. The poker economy was contracting right along with the national economy.

Second, in 2011, the government shut down online poker. The biggest sites, *Poker Stars* and *Full Tilt Poker* along with *Absolute Poker*, were no longer in operation. Overnight, the make-up of poker games changed. Instead of the regular players in games there was a sudden influx of new, ex-online players sitting in live games. These guys looked like college students, accountants or young tech nerds. They played differently. They studied game theory, they analyzed, they calculated and they had been educated by those who sold knowledge. Online, a player with one computer screen will probably play three times as many hands in an hour as in a live game. Sometimes these guys were playing on two or more screens at once. In terms of the sheer number of hands played they were getting three, four or maybe six years of experience in one year. Because the less skilled online players had been weeded out when the economy contracted, these new guys were the cream of the online crop. They approached the game differently. Many played awfully damn well.

With less money in circulation, poker's economic pie shrank. With an influx of those new, bright, young players, that pie had to be divided into ever smaller pieces. Marginal poker players began dropping by the wayside. Making a living playing poker had just gotten tougher and that would continue.

For better or for worse, it seemed the very essence of the game of poker had profoundly morphed into a distant version of the game I once knew.

From my vantage point, it seemed like the days of the old ways were gone. Gone was the loose, yet close-knit, fraternity of poker players.

Many old-timers succumbed to age; others retired or went broke. The presence of old school players became diluted in the mass of their new age counterparts. It seemed gone were those distinctive old characters; players who played and drank whiskey, who spit chew into coke bottles, who sported Stetsons, wore their best western apparel, Tony Lama boots, bolo ties, colorful vests, fedoras and Panama hats. Players that once populated tables everywhere had been replaced by bright young students of the game, many in designer jeans, shirts with button-down collars, headphones and sunglasses. Many would drink bottled water often requested, believe it or not, at room temperature. A few even played as they watched movies on their smartphones or iPads. Some spent more time staring at each other and wasting everyone's time looking for tics and tells that most likely didn't exist.

As for the future, the poker talent is bountiful, undoubtedly there are plenty of unique characters and there are already many incredible stories. In 2007, for example, a young Norwegian lady named Annette Obrestad was the youngest player ever to win a WSOP bracelet, when at the age of 17, she won the Main Event at the WSOP Europe with prize money over $2 million dollars. As an online sensation, Annette amazed the poker world when she won an online tournament with a field of 180 players almost entirely without looking at her hole cards.

Although the game of poker has become so much larger in scale and has undergone such a significant evolution, I'm hopeful that the new breed of talented young players will themselves be both the keepers of the old tales and traditions as well as writing the next chapters in the good book of poker.

A Post Game Gathering of Old-Timers

It was a late Saturday night in 2014, after an all-day session of The Big Game in the Reno Peppermill. Like everyone who put in twelve or thirteen hours of intense competition, I was mentally exhausted and ready to decompress. A bunch of the old guard planned to meet at the bar next to the poker room. I showed up to find Lonnie Mason sitting at the bar.

At that time, Lonnie lived in Oceanside, along the beautiful sand beaches of sunny Southern California. In 1968 Lonnie first moved to Lake Tahoe, the same year as myself, and started dealing poker at Harvey's Lake Tahoe Hotel and Casino. That particular poker-room came to be known as a snatch joint, meaning it was a poker-room where the dealers would rake (or snatch) from the pot as much as they could get away with. The unsuspecting customers were usually tourists, as the locals knew better than to play there. The joke amongst Harvey's dealers was, "They would rake the entire pot and shove the winner his own stack of chips." Lonnie dealt there until he was able to launch a career in real estate. From there he bought a local motel and created The Fantasy Inn. This was an adult themed motel where each room was outfitted with a round bed in the center, mirrors on the ceiling above it, a red heart-shaped Jacuzzi, room service champagne and porn on the TV. The Fantasy Inn caught on quickly. Lonnie prospered and he built a couple more Fantasy Inns, one in North Tahoe and another Reno.

Along with his motel venture, Lonnie had also become an exceptional poker player. Lonnie sat in the game that long ago night when Cowboy Tom first played poker with us. Tom and Lonnie had a friendship that went back a few years through the Tahoe real estate community. Lonnie became one of the bedrock players of The Big Game from the night it started until that last time we all played together.

I will always remember the first time I sat in a poker game with Lonnie Mason. Like so many of my poker friends our relationship has a defining poker hand. It was a $10/20 Limit Hold'em game in 1976. I held **K/Q** and when the dust settled the board read **K...Q...Q......3......2.**

Lonnie turned over **K/K** and I was both stunned and broke. We would go on to play a lot of poker together over the next forty-five years.

Me   Lonnie

Board

Joe Barbario strolled into the bar of the Reno Peppermill after me. Joe had been an all-around hustler for as long as I knew him. He was a rock solid poker player as well as a talented sports-better and he had a keen eye for making a buck. Joe and I moved in the same circles over the years and the years had been many. The very first time I played No-Limit Hold'em, it was long ago in the basement of the Horseshoe Club Casino in downtown Reno. Jim Monaco and Ron Bowman, a couple of authentic old-school gentlemen, ran a good room. The place was dark, though the tables were well lit; as poker rooms go, the room felt like the real deal. I learned a valuable lesson that night playing No-Limit Hold'em for the first time: **Q/J suited** is a good starting hand in limit poker but not a hand to call an all-in bet in no-limit. I was up against **two Aces** and that was when I first became acquainted with Joe Barbario.

Next to join us at the bar was Missouri Dave. Since the poker room was picking up the tab for all our drinks, Dave ordered another round of drinks and tipped the bartender $100.

Golfer Mike had just finished a shift dealing poker and was walking through the casino. He stopped to say hello and have a drink. Mike was from North Tahoe and we had known each other for at least thirty-five years. Besides being a terrific golfer, Mike was the short-stop and I was the second baseman on nine or ten competitive softball teams in North Tahoe. There was a time when softball was a huge part of both our lives. We always had beers after the games, and he and I would often end up playing poker or making the rounds at the local bars, chasing the ladies into the following morning.

A couple of others dropped by the bar as well, and, as the gathering of old friends grew, the conversation turned to drugs. Age-wise we were mostly all in our mid to late 60's. We were a bunch of guys who had lived through and participated in the white powder wave that swept across America and saturated the poker community. Partly because of the culture of where we all grew up, pot had been in every-one's life at some time. Most of us had consumed different amounts of Quaaludes. Some may have tried speed. Missouri and I once came across some opium, smoked it all one night in South Tahoe and woke up in Las Vegas.

While at university I discovered the music of the Grateful Dead. I went to my first show in 1968. Over the years and until the death of Jerry Garcia I went to about 60 or 70 shows. I met Kate at a Dead show in Oakland, California. Grateful Dead shows were a gath-ering of like-minded people. They were a big party. People would trip about and shake their bones to the music with thousands of their best friends, most of whom they'd never met. Each show was a joyful cel-ebration and various psychedelic drugs were, for many or most, a big part of that celebration; my friend Frodo and I were eager partakers. He and I often traveled to shows together and Frodo had just joined us at the bar.

The history of drug-aided memories amongst that group that night at that bar in the Peppermill was sordid and extensive.

Lonnie said, "The only drugs I do these days Is Triazolam. It really helps me sleep."

I responded, "I take a third of a Zanax after poker games to take the edge off. It allows me to drift off."

Missouri chimed in with, "Sleeping pills don't work for me; my go-to is old black and white re-runs of Perry Mason. Those put me right out."

"Did that guy ever lose a case in court?"

"Just one," said Dave. "But, oh man, I do get slammed with the Gout and Indocin pills have been a lifesaver."

"I take Lipitor for my Cholesterol."

"Yeah, me too."

"Crestor works best for me."

"I tried that but it made me jittery so I switched back to Simvastatin."

"The only pharmaceutical I take is Thiazide diuretics for my blood pressure, and, oh yeah, my daily dose of Prilosec for the GERD."

"Me too on the Prilosec."

"And me."

"Norco has saved my life with all the back pain I've suffered."

"Joe B had to take up to ten of those a day when he sat dealing poker in Oceanside."

"I learned a combination of Norco and Soma worked best for my pain but Soma has gotten difficult to get."

The absolute irony of that conversation about drug use was not at all lost on any of us and in an instant the hysterical laughter became contagious.

That was the last time many of us would see each other; certainly, the final time we would all be in the same place together. We were people bonded by our history and our mutual experiences. Bonded through the playing of poker together for over four decades, in a particular time around Lake Tahoe. That unique culture at the Lake will never be the same. It was an extraordinary time. But times do change, as do we. And time had aged us all.

Poker, Easy Money and Getting Old

"Playing poker's a hard way to make an easy living." That is an old saying amongst professional poker players.

As a teenager, I became infatuated with the game of poker. Perhaps the dream began that far back, most likely it began later. But the dream of playing poker for a living had at some point entered my being. My first attempt at fulfilling my dream did not end well. It was discouraging but the dream never died. I paused. And in 1975 I opened the card room at The Fanny Bridge Inn. I moved from there to playing in Nevada. I started to gain more confidence and some positive momentum.

I was twenty-nine years old, I had a solid and creative approach to the dealer's choice games and I was one of the most consistent winners. I became a student of Texas Hold'em. A friend covertly gave me David Sklansky's book called *Hold'em Poker*. I read it and read it again; I studied it until I totally understood all the concepts presented in the book. I guarded the book and its valuable information. I knew my knowledge was a big edge and I knew that such knowledge was best kept to myself and perhaps my closest confidantes, so we actually smuggled the book around. My play improved; I began to move up the ladder of those reputed to be winning players.

With success came money and money started coming easier each month I played. I recall my first big-at-the-time win. It was 1976 and the first time I played in the weekly Sunday night $10/20 limit Dealer's Choice game at the North Shore Club in Crystal Bay, Nevada. The casino was just over the Nevada state line, only a quarter mile from my house. I won $2,500 that night and I was feeling on top of the world.

I started playing in bigger Hold'em games, and the higher I played the bigger the wins. A medium-size win in a big game went so much further towards paying the bills and building a playing bankroll than a medium-size win did playing $2/4 Six Card Stud. After the first couple years, when games were mostly limit poker, I was playing in the biggest games in the Reno/Tahoe area.

In 1977, I began making the occasional weeklong trip to Las Vegas. The Golden Nugget had a seven-day tournament once a month. Whoever won the most money playing $10/20 Limit Hold'em in those seven days would get $1,000 plus a trophy. I found I could play with the best medium limit players in Las Vegas, and I took home the trophy a couple times. I played every Sunday in the Dealer's Choice game at the North Shore Club. I played all over Reno. In 1978, The MGM Grand opened with a big, new, shiny poker room. There I became a regular in the $15/30 and $30/60 games. There were a whole lot of tourists and hometown champions coming through Reno with pockets full of dough and I was amongst a sprinkling of sharp players who relieved many of them of their cash. Money started coming easier. I beamed with confidence and at times I got cocky.

I had begun connecting with other players. Flyer, Missouri Dave, Joe B, Ian Markman, Mark Porter and Rick Ketcher had all come into my life. We were part of a small local poker fraternity where money was borrowed and loaned. Because somebody always had money, I knew I could go broke and be back in action the next day. Knowing that refinancing was only a handshake away gave me the confidence to play fearlessly. Amongst our bunch, debts were a matter of honor. With others, lending could be a shaky proposition. I always carried a list with me detailing who owed me and how much. I recall a time when Missouri looked at my list of debtors and was doubled over with laughter at the number of deadbeats that owed me money. I dare say I was almost always paid what I was owed. Dave, on the other hand, kept his list in his head and forgot who owed him more than a few times. He lent money willy-nilly. In one game, Dave lent $1,000 to a player he did not know; in fact, Dave didn't even know the guy's name. When the dude didn't show up the next day to pay him as agreed, Dave laughed it off as the cost of doing business.

In 1979, we started playing Pot-Limit Hold'em on Tahoe's south shore. Again, I became a student. Pot-Limit and No-Limit Hold'em were to Limit Hold'em as chess was to checkers. With strong mentoring from

Missouri Dave and Flyer, I easily made the jump from limit poker to pot-limit and no-limit. Dedicated study began to be reflected in my earnings; the size of my winnings became exponentially greater. Eventually I became one of the bigger winners in the No-Limit Hold'em games in Northern Nevada.

A year after I had split up with Karen, Dave and I moved back into my house on the North Shore. We had become partners, which must be a notch or two above great friends. We often shared the road together: Las Vegas, Canada, Montana, Colorado, Hawaii, Kansas City, Seattle, Los Angeles, and the San Francisco Bay Area. We enjoyed our freedom. Often we lived large and at times we lived small. It was extraordinary that when it came to money, we were two heterosexual men living like a platonic married couple. Whoever had money bought the groceries and picked up the tab. If one needed money you could just take what you needed from the other's bankroll and sort it out later; it was all about honor and trust. It was a unique and special bond we shared, one that I would always cherish. For nearly ten years, we spent a month every year as guests of the Binion family at The World Series of Poker. At times we had pockets full of cash and other times we scrambled to pay the bills. Through it all we tried to live our lives to the fullest.

When Texas Hold'em became legal in California, the games in Reno and, especially, Lake Tahoe dried up. California players started to stay in California to play, while a lot of Tahoe players left for the Golden State. We who were left had to start organizing games, coordinating players in order to make games happen. It was then Dave and I traveled more.

Missouri, Lonnie Mason, Cowboy Tom, Flyer, Stu Spears and I had started The Big Game around 1987. We ran the game; we promoted the game; we made the rules. For years some of us had to play shorthanded even when grossly underfunded and playing against a very aggressive Cowboy Tom with all the money in the world. We did it and kept the game going year after year. The game kept getting bigger; the blinds first started at $5/5, and by the last three or four years that we played they had increased to \$100/100. The buy-in went from \$300 to \$10,000. In the end, some people were buying in for upwards to \$50,000.

For nearly fifteen years of my poker career, I traveled back and forth to England. I played a lot of poker there. In the early 90's I left Tahoe and moved to Nevada City. During the great poker renaissance, ignited by televised poker, the Internet and the sub-prime real estate boom, poker was incredible and money came easier than ever before. During this time, I began playing at the Gold Rush Casino in Grass Valley, only a couple of miles from home, and I made a lot of money there. I also played twice a week in a monstrous \$10/20 No-Limit Hold'em game at The Deuces Wild in Auburn, California. When that game shut down, a pal and I hosted games in Sacramento. In Grass Valley, The Gold Rush Casino became Towers Casino and I did well there, too.

And then things began to go south.

The games at Towers Casino lost steam and bigger games became less frequent. Still it was okay, because I always had The Big Game. I had it until I didn't. In 2014, Cowboy Tom, whose fortunes were tied to real estate, quit playing and the game ended after a run of about twenty-seven years. Another large game at the Peppermill Casino in Reno was good for a while but it got overrun by tough out-of-town players who sucked the life out of it. Eventually, the final straw made me have to re-evaluate how I approached my game of poker; I had gotten old.

There I was one day realizing that I was over seventy years old; the games were tougher, the money scarcer, and my mind was not nearly as sharp as it was in my youth. Critically, all the support I once could count on was no longer. My old poker-playing network was gone. People quit playing, some got hopelessly broke, Joe B passed away, Missouri moved abroad and stopped playing. I looked around and realized I could no longer afford to go broke because I could no longer refinance with a phone call or a handshake. If I were to go broke I would be flat outta luck. Thus, I needed to make a huge decision. With age, my cognitive skills were ever so slowly eroding and my vibrant young opponents were sharp as tacks; I could keep playing in the biggest games around and run the risk of going broke, or I could start playing in smaller games and try to grind out enough to pay the bills and keep my shrinking bankroll intact. After a lot of deep soul-searching and intense contemplation, I decided, as painful as it was, to set aside my ego and play in small games a couple of days a week and try to cover the bills.

I decided to play now and then locally at Towers but I would do most of my playing at Stones Gambling Hall in Sacramento. Stones had a good size poker room with about twenty-five tables and a large adjacent area for casino games, like Blackjack and Pai Gao. Stones would spread $1/2 and $1/3 No-Limit Hold'em games daily and they ran a $3/5 game when there were enough players. That was a huge drop-off in the size of games for me. I remembered some years back when I said, "I would not play in a game as small as $5/10, but now I found myself driving two hours to play in one." Fast forward a few years and I now found myself driving an hour to play $1/3. Oh my! How my poker world had changed! And I was not alone. One day at Stones I looked across the table and there was Flyer. I had not seen him for about ten years. Flyer, who was then hovering around eighty years old, evidently had come to the same decision as me and he too was playing $1/3 No-Limit Hold'em a couple times a week.

My thoughts went back to 1980, to the second Annual Amarillo Slim's Super Bowl of Poker at the Sahara Reno. It was the first night of live play. I was sitting in a $5/10 No-Limit Hold'em game when there was a stampede past my chair. I looked up and a growing crowd appeared around the $25/50 game a couple of tables away. The quick forming crowd always signaled a giant pot was brewing and one was. I tuned into the hand after the flop and all the money amongst three players was in the pot and my friend, Flyer, wearing a flowing kaftan, was one of the participants. The hand looked like this:

Flyer

Johnny Moss

 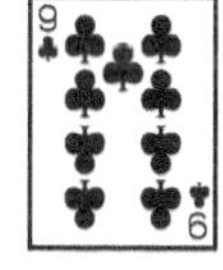

Oklahoma Pat

Board

The pot was approximately **$120,000** in 1980 dollars, plus a small side pot. The hands were turned face up and the players were discussing *doing some business*. Flyer had three Jacks, Johnny had the nut straight and Pat had a flush draw. Bobby Baldwin, a former World Champion, when asked, was giving his analysis of the chances of each player winning the hand. The crowd had gotten bigger than any previously ever seen around a poker game in Reno. In that crowd were most of the best players in the country who were drawn to play in the second most prestigious tournament in the world. So, there in Reno that night, Flyer, Oklahoma Pat, along with Johnny Moss, a former World Champion who was affectionately known as *The Grand Old Man of Poker*, were for about fifteen minutes in the spotlight, smack dab at the dead center of the poker universe. And then at Stones Gambling Hall, some forty years later, Flyer and I sat in relative obscurity playing at a level we never dreamed we would be playing.

One afternoon at Stones, Flyer said to me that he had a hard time dealing with the high level of arrogance amongst the Stone's top players as they played in a $3/5 No-Limit game. He looked at me and said, "You know, those guys really have no idea!" I so thoroughly understood what he meant. Oh, and the hand at Slim's tournament so many years ago in 1980, the players decided not to do any business and the hand was dealt out. The final two cards brought a **9♠** and **10♥** making a straight on the board and a three-way split.

* * * * *

As for me, my decision to lower my sights and settle into playing small, in the final analysis, seemed to be the correct one. My bills were paid. I kept my bankroll intact. My stress level was lowered. My poker ego was put on the shelf. Although money no longer came easy, life was still good.

And then the Novel corona virus pandemic marched across the planet. Card rooms were shut down and poker, as I knew it, was over. That's when I picked up my pen.

* * * * *

Writing, an endeavor I had never before embraced, became both a passion during the days of social isolation, as well as a means to get my poker juices flowing. Poker can be a powerful drug. It produces the adrenalin associated with gambling and competition, the excitement of winning or losing money on the turn of a card and the social interaction that takes place from the hours of sitting with adversaries, friends and strangers alike. I always needed that in my life; I looked forward to every poker game with varying degrees of enthusiasm and sometimes, with The Big Game for example, eagerness that bordered on elation. With writing, I was able to visit old memories and put them to paper, speak to old cronies and get their takes on events and their stories as well. I was getting what I needed without suffering the inevitable disappointments and losses that come with playing the game. Writing this book has been the perfect substitute for my passion for playing poker.

As I looked back at my body of work, it felt appropriate that I honor the relationship that has meant so much to me over my years of playing poker with one final story about Missouri Dave.

* * * * *

Dave was part of my family. I will never forget when my son, Jake, was five years old and he asked me, "Papa, did Uncle Missouri Dave's mama name him after that country?"

In 2004, Dave moved to Thailand where he has lived seven months a year with his sweetheart of the last fifteen years, spending the balance of each year in Lake Tahoe. As he closes in on becoming an octogenarian, he continues to seize each day, to grab it, embrace it, ride it and squeeze every minute of joy out of it. Dave still lives his life on his own terms.

Our friend Denny Dahlgren told me this story. It's a story of being in Las Vegas during a big tournament and having dinner with seven other well-established poker professionals when one of them made a disparaging comment about Dave. Another chimed in, saying, "If he was all that great of a player why doesn't he always have tons of money?"

That was when The Razor spoke up and offered a most eloquent defense of Missouri Dave. "Let me tell you," he said, "the day Missouri Dave dies, everyone at this table will most likely, but not necessarily, have more money than him; however, I guarantee you, and without any doubt, Missouri Dave will have had more fun in his life than all eight of us combined."

Missouri Dave should be remembered as a good human being, a totally unique one-of-a-kind person, as a great poker player with unquestioned integrity, one whose generosity required he share what he had with his friends, one who lent money to strangers. Truth be told, Missouri Dave has never lived a day as a lamb, but has lived a lifetime as a lion. It has been my honor to run with a lion.

The End

285

Missouri and Me with icy cold long neck Buds
in North Lake Tahoe circa 1990.

Author Glen Garrod in 1996

On the way to winning Harvey's Lake Tahoe's "Final Four of Poker"
for the second consecutive year.

From a section of the 1985 WSOP Main Event group photo
of participants taken prior to the event.
Back row, top left: Hans 'Tuna' Lund, Art Jungblut,
Glen Garrod in straw Stetson, Missouri Dave, Austin Squatty.
2nd row: 1975 WSOP Champion Sailor Roberts, 'Top Hat' Ken Smith

At Best-ball Golf Tournament in Incline Village, Nevada.
From left: Flyer, Missouri Dave, Jacque Steward, Dale Steward,
a friend, Glen Garrod.

The group photo from the Heads Up Match Play Tournament
at the Cal-Neva Lodge in Crystal Bay, Nevada circa 1990.

Glen Garrod, center, in straw Stetson, his arm over the shoulder
of Mike 'the Wig,' then the Peach next to him. In front laying on the floor
is Flyer, who later won the tournament.

Appendix

Rank of Poker Hands

High Card

One Pair

Two Pair

Three of a Kind

Straight

Flush

Full House

Four of a Kind

Straight Flush

Royal Flush

Glossary of Poker Terms

Backdoor

A hand made when only one card from the flop plus the two cards from Fourth Street and the River define the hand. For example, only one diamond is flopped but the next two cards are diamonds to make a **backdoor flush**.

Bad Beat

A hand that is beat when either very few cards remain in the deck that can beat you, a hand that is beaten with huge ramifications or a big hand beaten by a bigger one in which the player is destined to play (also called a cold deck).

Blackjack Shoe

Four, or possibly more, decks are combined, shuffled together and placed in a plastic holder or box called a shoe. It's done because counting a single deck is far easier and more accurate than counting multiple decks.

Blinds

Blinds are used in lieu of an ante. Blinds are money posted to the left of the rotating dealer button. The player to the immediate left of the dealer button puts up the small blind. The big blind is usually twice the amount of the small blind and is put up by the player to the left of the small blind. Sometimes games are structured so the two blinds are equal amounts. The amount of the big blind determines the amount required to enter the pot. The larger the blinds, the bigger is the game.

Board

The face-up, community cards in front of the dealer shared by players in Texas Hold'em, Omaha and Crazy Pineapple.

Button

Because poker rooms have a center-dealer, there is a dealer button that rotates one position after each hand is played. The next deal starts with the player to the left of the dealer button. Each player puts up both blinds each round and therefore each player has the chance to be the last person to act each round.

Buy-in

The minimum amount of money a player is required to put up in order to enter into a poker game; also the amount of money required for entry into a tournament.

Case Card

The fourth and final card of that rank; for example, if three Queens are known to be out of the deck, the fourth Queen is called the case Queen.

Cold Deck

A deck that gives two players big hands that results in one player losing a large amount of cash. A cold deck may be on the square or it may be stacked before hand for the purposes of cheating.

Crab

A three or often called a trey in a deck of cards.

Dealer Button

The same as the Button.

Flop

The first three community cards dealt on the Board.

Fourth Street

The fourth card on the Board.

Heads Up

A game between just two players

Live Game

This is a poker game with real live players playing for cash (also called a cash games), as opposed to tournament games or online games.

Muck

The accumulated/pile of dead or discarded cards in front of dealer.

Nut Flush (Nut Straight)

The highest possible flush (or straight).

Nuts

The best possible hand.

Over-pair

A pair higher than the highest card on the Board.

Pocket

In Hold'em, the player's two-card hand is his cards in the pocket. Pocket Aces, for example, are two Aces the player holds in his two-card hand.

Position

To act on one's hand **after** another player is to have position on that player. To have position on your opponent is an advantage. At the beginning of every hand the player with the button has position on all other players.

Pot-Limit

The amount of money in the pot is the maximum size bet allowed at each player's turn to act. For example, when the total amount of money in the pot is $50, Player A may bet $50. Next Player B may wish to call and raise the size of the pot. The pot now holds the original $50 plus Player A's $50 bet plus Player B's call of $50 (a total of $150) so Player B then raises $150. Pots can grow exponentially fast; therefore, though strategies differ, pot-limit is closer to no-limit than it is to limit poker.

Producers

Losing players with lots of money. Also referred to as whales.

Rail

A barrier, either real or imaginary, around the poker table. When a player asks for the rail to be backed up, he is asking that the players watching the game be moved further back from the table.

Rainbow

A flop with three different suits.

Rake

The money taken out of the pot or the hourly charge that goes to the operator of the poker game.

Ring Game

A full game as opposed to a short-handed game.

River (card)

The fifth and final card on the Board.

Set

When a player holds a pair and the dealer deals another of that pair onto the board to make three of a kind.

Straddle (the Blinds)

A straddle of the blinds is a **voluntary blind**, twice the amount of the biggest blind put up in the position on the immediate left of the biggest blind.

Suited

When both cards in a players two card hand are the same suit.

Tank

To take a lot of time considering what to do when it is a player's turn to act on their hand.

Tell

A clue to the size or nature of a player's hand detected through the body language or betting pattern of one's opponent.

Tight Player

A conservative player, one who takes few chances and gives little action.

Top Pair with an Ace Kicker

The top pair is a pair of the highest card shown on the Board. The Ace kicker is the highest kicker possible should it come into play.

Top Set

A set (see Set above) of the highest card on the board.

Turn Card

The same as Fourth Street.

Window Card

The first card one sees when a dealer turns over the flop or when a player turns over their hand.

Texas Hold'em

In the game of Texas Hold'em each player is dealt two cards face down. There is an initial betting round based upon a player's two cards. For players remaining in the hand, three cards are dealt face up in the center of the table. These cards are called the Flop and are cards common to all players. There is a second betting round. For the remaining players there is a fourth card dealt face up. This is called Fourth Street or the Turn Card. There is then a third betting round. For the players remaining there is a fifth and final card dealt face up. This card is called The River. There is then a final betting round. For the remaining players there is a *showdown*, where each player exposes their Hole Cards. The winner is the player with the **best five-card poker hand**, with each player using the combined cards of his hole cards and the five community cards on The Board.

Example of Texas Hold'em Hands

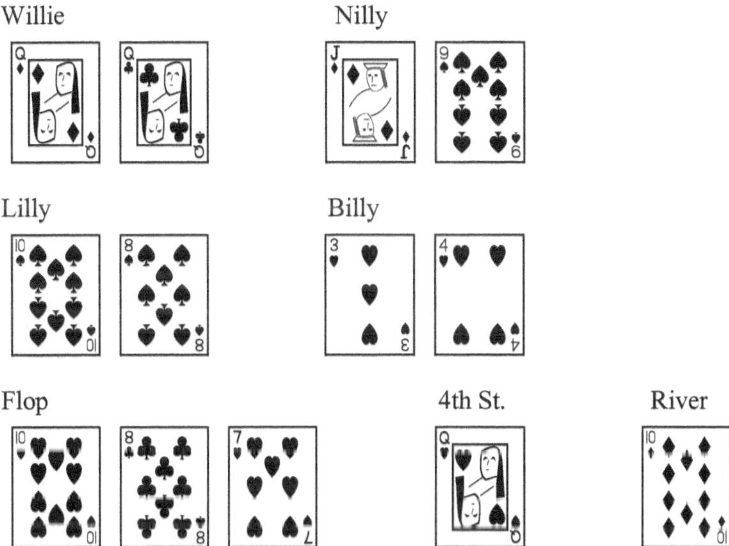

On the flop, Nilly has the best hand with a Jack high straight.

On Fourth Street, Billy has the best hand with a heart flush.

On the River, although Lilly has a Full House with Tens full of eights, Willie has a higher Full House with Queens full of tens.

High-Low Games

In High-Low games, players make their best High poker hand and/or their best Low-ball hand and they split the pot between them, unless one player makes BOTH the best high hand and the best low hand, in which case that player wins the entire pot.

High-Low Declare Games

In High–Low declare games, with all the cards out and the betting over, players have to declare whether they are going for **the high hand, the low hand, or both ways**. Players put three poker chips in their right hand, put their hand under the table and come up with their right hand closed around the chips, palms up and, when all are ready, they open their hands in unison. One chip is for low, two chips are for high and three chips are for both ways. If you go both ways you have to win both ways. When going both ways, if you lose or tie one of the ways, you have lost the entire pot. This is called declaring. If after declaring, all players declare going the same way the best hand wins the entire pot.

Addendum

Limit Hold'em games usually seat a maximum of nine or ten players. Pot-limit and No-limit Hold'em traditionally seat nine. In Dealer's Choice games, however, seven or eight players are seated, as, at times, the dealer runs out of cards in a hand. When that happens, the cards in the muck are usually shuffled and re-used. Each poker game has house-rules to deal with all situations and contingencies.

Thank you for reading *Missouri & Me, A Poker Odyssey*.
If you found it to be a good read, please spread the word
and recommend it to a friend or three.
Glen Garrod

For additional copies of
Missouri & Me, A Poker Odyssey,
or the Kindle E-book
go to the website: missouriandme.com

Acknowledgements

I owe so much to so many for helping me tell my stories.

Certainly without my special relationship with Missouri Dave, this book would not have been possible. Mentor, partner in so many adventures and dear friend. Thanks for sharing the road.

Credit and appreciation goes to Flyer, my other significant mentor; for allowing me to be privy to your unique outlook on life, for your humor and for all the belly laughs you provided over the years.

I am forever indebted to the amazing Eve Imagine for her editing, for being my writing coach, for her constant encouragement and for believing in my stories. Thirty-five years ago I met this sixteen year old, tie-dyed hippie girl hanging out at the baseball diamond all starry-eyed over our rightfielder. Without Eve this book would not have been possible.

To all the highly respected poker players that I faced so often across the green felt who shared from their lives and offered their stories, I say thank you. Rick Ketcher, one of my oldest friends in the poker world, whose good heart and kind soul always steered me in the right direction whenever I wavered. Dave Olson who critiqued my writing, insisted I publish my work and contributed his tales from his many years as a player from the great northwest to the card rooms of Southern California. Carl McKelvey for sharing with me his stories about his life as a Texas road gambler and his lifelong partnership with the great Bobby Hoff. My old friend Freddie Deeb, from a young man in Reno to a bona fide poker superstar, he always stayed true to his roots. Freddie kindly allowed me to share one of his many stories. To Roger Rodd, Karl Fox, Denny Dahlgren, Lonnie Mason, Chris Hansen, and with apologies, to any poker players I missed.

Thank you my old friend Kathy Dotson; graphic artist, cover designer, formatter (one who formats), physical trainer, wife, mother, Deadhead and the person who came along when I needed her the most.

Special appreciation goes to Deke Castleman, the editor for Huntington Press in Las Vegas, Nevada, for his guidance, insights, kindness and advocacy; thank you Deke, you are such a good man.

To my son Zak Sequoia, I offer my heartfelt appreciation for lifting me over all the hurdles posed by computers and modern technology. Living in Australia, Zak was only a phone call or an email away. Thank you Zak for explaining how all that digital stuff works.

A big shout out to Paule "Wanna Cracker" Castro for lending his remarkable tech expertise in building my website. Thank you Paule.

Another big shout-out to my friend the world-renowned novelist Michael Ondaatje. And thanks to Michael's literary agent, Ellen Levine, for her valuable suggestions.

For all the family and friends that assisted me in one way or another I am humbled by your kindness: my daughter Maia Lipkin, our Suzi Sequoia, Norm and Jenny, Eric Tomb for his editing assistance, Mike Berlin for his opinions and photography, Dick Cooper, Ben Cooper, Brion Dunbar, Lucas Turner, Jamey and my old friend from Oxford, Julian Peto.

I offer a special recognition to the indomitable force that she is, Lisa Lilly, for her help and inspiration. You rock mama!

I am totally grateful to the exceptionally brilliant Syd Brown for her generous late inning proof reading and who conducted a master class on when not to use a semi-colon. I had no idea how much work was still to be done.

Finally, I can't thank enough my partner in life, the beautiful Kate Winningham whose constant support, never-ending patience, invaluable encouragement, proofreading and everlasting love were essential to this entire endeavor. Everyone should be so lucky.